HAND-WOVEN CARPETS
ORIENTAL & EUROPEAN
BY A. F. KENDRICK

KEEPER OF THE DEPARTMENT OF TEXTILES
AT THE VICTORIA AND ALBERT MUSEUM

AND C. E. C. TATTERSALL

WITH 205 PLATES, OF WHICH 19 ARE IN COLOUR

DOVER PUBLICATIONS, INC.
NEW YORK

Published in Canada by General Publishing Company, Ltd., 30 Lesmill Road, Don Mills, Toronto, Ontario.

Published in the United Kingdom by Constable and Company, Ltd., 10 Orange Street, London WC 2.

This Dover edition, first published in 1973, is an unabridged republication of the work originally published by Benn Brothers, Limited, London, 1922, in a two-volume edition limited to 1000 sets. The present edition is published by special arrangement with Ernest Benn Limited, London.

International Standard Book Number: 0-486-20385-9
Library of Congress Catalog Card Number: 73-77381

Manufactured in the United States of America
Dover Publications, Inc.
180 Varick Street
New York, N. Y. 10014

PREFACE

A brief explanation of the nature of the link between this volume and Neugebauer and Orendi's excellent *Handbuch der Orientalischen Teppichkunde*, published in 1909, is due to the reader. By arrangement with Messrs. Hiersemann of Leipzig many of the illustrations in that volume have been made use of, and these have been supplemented by a large number of new ones in colour and half-tone. The scope of that handbook did not render the text easily adaptable as a basis for the text of the present volume. The necessary amplification and revision would have entirely destroyed its character, and to undertake the task would have hindered rather than furthered the end in view. These considerations explain why the text of the present volume is entirely new. Responsibility must in no case be laid, therefore, at the door of the earlier writers, except in regard to a few statements, of no vital import, which could have only been verified by reference to the original carpets illustrated but not now accessible. The great value of Neugebauer and Orendi's work lay in the varied and admirable series of illustrations of carpets woven within the last hundred years and in the descriptive notes appended. When it first appeared, there was no other book of so modest compass and price which aimed at classifying the bewildering variety of types of Oriental carpet obtainable by those who had the money to buy, and no other book has since taken its place.

The literature on the subject of the older carpets was already fairly voluminous. Of all such works, that published under the auspices of the Austrian Government after the great exhibition of carpets at Vienna in 1891 remains the chief. The truly magnificent series of coloured illustrations to that work places it beyond all chance of rivalry for many years to come. But they also render it unobtainable, except occasionally at a price which would represent more than a year's income of many a serious student. The text was naturally subject to the limitations of the time. The day had not then come when a sound historical survey, covering as wide a range as the exhibition itself, could be written.

A supplementary volume, with descriptive text by Dr. Friedrich Sarre, was published in 1907.

Next followed Dr. F. R. Martin's book, *Oriental Carpets Made Before*

v

PREFACE

1800. This eminent Swedish traveller and writer took a fearless and original line, and although the lapse of time has not since tended to confirm some of his theories, a great deal was added to the common stock of knowledge. Martin's work was published in 1908.

Two years later the exhibition of Muhammadan art was held at Munich. A remarkable collection of carpets was brought together on that occasion, and they received due attention in the fine publication, *Meisterwerke Muhammedanischer Kunst*, produced at the close of the exhibition as a record of the principal works of art shown.

All the books so far mentioned are costly and scarce. The frequent references made to them in the following pages are called for by the impossibility of adequately illustrating, especially in colours, a subject of so wide a range in any volume of moderate size and cost. The books are accessible in our national libraries, and the student of the subject cannot afford to miss any available assistance in consulting them.

The number of smaller and less ambitious volumes on the subject of carpets is gradually growing. Few of them claim to embody much original research, although in their discursive way they are not without value, and they do a useful service in contributing to the available stock of illustrations. They have a place in the list of useful works at the end of this volume.

Dr. W. von Bode's book, *Vorderasiatische Knüpfteppiche*, published in 1902, should be particularly mentioned, as being, within the modest limits set by its author, a scholarly and indispensable book.

Work still remains to be done in clearing up obscure points, especially, though not entirely, in regard to the early history of the subject.

A number of the carpets illustrated in this volume are already well known to students, but they are such as cannot be ignored without disadvantage in a volume dealing, however briefly, with the subject as a whole.

The Council of the Royal Society of Arts have kindly accorded permission to adapt a paper on English carpets read before them and published in the *Journal* of the Society (Vol. LXVII, 1919, p. 136) for the purposes of this work.

My collaborator and colleague, Mr. Tattersall, is responsible for the classification of the modern carpets and the technical notes throughout. Such value as the book may have is largely due to him.

My thanks are due to the following for their courtesy in allowing the reproduction of carpets in their possession :—The Duke of Buccleuch, The Duke of Northumberland, Lady Cunliffe, The Hon. Lady Hulse, Lord Verulam, The Hon. H. McLaren, M.P., The Earl of Ilchester, The Mobilier National (Paris), The Louvre, The Gobelins Museum (Paris), The Museum of Decorative Arts (Paris), The Vienna Museums, The Berlin Museums, The Leipzig Museum, The Victoria and Albert Museum (London), Mr. George Mounsey, Mr. Lionel Harris, The Girdlers' Company, Dr. W. von Bode, Dr. Friedrich Sarre ; and to M. Albert Lévy, of the Librairie Centrale des Beaux-Arts, Paris, for permission to reproduce Plate 26 from his *Exposition des Arts Musulmans*.

It is an agreeable task to record my indebtedness to Mr. Victor Gollancz for dispositions which have lightened the labour and added to the pleasure of writing the following pages.

A. F. KENDRICK.

September, 1922.

CONTENTS

PART I.—HISTORICAL

PART II.—TECHNICAL

PLATES

LIST OF PLATES

The plates appear after page 194. Those with numbers followed by an asterisk will be found in the color-plate section.

LIST OF PLATES

LIST OF PLATES

xiii

LIST OF PLATES

LIST OF PLATES

LIST OF PLATES

LIST OF PLATES

PART I

HISTORICAL

CHAPTER I

INTRODUCTORY

The pile-carpet, though long ago naturalized in Europe, is an alien in the Western world. Its origin, in the East, is the outcome of conditions very different from those which control its use in Europe, and if pile-carpets are now made to serve similar purposes in their native home, the reason must be sought in the spread of western habits of life. With us carpets serve as an agreeable background for chairs and tables; they help to cure draughts and give the room a cheerful tone; they soften the impact of the shoe on the floor, and deaden noise. Their use is warranted by these services, which the pile-carpet renders better than any other floor-covering; but they are not indispensable. The mind must be disencumbered of such associations before the genesis of this toilsome and ingenious type of weaving can be made clear. To produce a pattern by interlacing continuous threads of different colours is natural enough, and there is general agreement that the simple process of weaving is to be reckoned among the earliest artistic efforts of prehistoric mankind. But to set the threads in a vast number of short lengths up on end, and to pack them so tight together that they keep that position, entails so much toil, and uses up so much material, that the contrivance can only be regarded as a response to conditions not common to all men. There can be little doubt that a wandering shepherd-life, which involved the need and at the same time provided the means of supplying it, gives the right explanation. We think of some nomad tribe of shepherds, following their flocks from one pasture to another, with no roof or floor but such as they could carry with them from place to place. They needed a tent over their heads, and at times they needed even more a dry and warm covering for the ground of their temporary abode.

The wool of the flocks—whether sheep or goats—or even of the camel and yak—offered an ideal material for weaving into a compact and durable texture. The invention did not merely provide an agreeable addition to the household effects; it met an elementary need and became indispensable.

From these nomad surroundings the carpet found its way into the dwellings of agricultural neighbours, and its adoption by all classes of people came about in due course.

In the West, it is now completely domesticated, and consequently we find it hard to realize that the pile-carpet was practically unknown among us before the fourteenth century, very rarely seen before the fifteenth, and not in general use before the eighteenth. The date of its advent may be approximately traced. Its strange patterns and bright colours excited wonder and interest, and painters everywhere made use of its decorative qualities.[1] Centuries were yet to pass before it superseded the layer of rushes or the plaited rush matting in general use, and still common in great houses in England as late as the days of the Stuarts.

As the Oriental carpet became known and used over a wide area, the obvious simplicity of the knotting process caused attempts to be made here and there to meet demands by local production, and at last in this way a craft evolved by nomad shepherds in the heart of Asia spread thence over the civilized world. The machine-made " Axminster " of modern times, with a daily output amounting to thousands of square yards in Great Britain alone, is a direct successor in one line of descent.

It is only in general terms that the origin of carpet-knotting can be discussed. The clue to the actual locality, and even to the approximate date, of the invention is lost beyond prospect of recovery. It has been suggested that pile-carpets were made as early as five thousand years before Christ.[2]

Carpets of some sort must have been used in very primitive times. Homer refers to them by a name which they still retain over a large part of Europe ; but the unchanged name must not be taken to signify that the nature of the fabric to which it is applied has not changed. While it is just possible that pile-carpets were known to the Asiatic Greeks of Homeric days, it would be rash to base any argument on such an assumption.

The designs most favoured by the ancient Greeks for the textile ornamentation of their houses were hunting scenes and subjects from mythology and history. The carpet-knotting method would be tedious and cumbersome for such representations. It is true that such subjects

---

[1] Dante achieves an effect no less vivid by similar means. In describing the bright markings on the back of the monster Geryon he says, "Never did Tartars or Turks make cloth with more colours in ground or pattern " (*Inf.* xvii).

[2] The late Sir G. Birdwood, in *Oriental Carpets*, Vienna, 1892.

are to be found in the days of the highest development of the industry in Persia, but they tax the utmost skill of the carpet-knotter, and they would not have been deliberately chosen under the primitive conditions of Homeric life. As records of the Mesopotamian civilizations we have the marble slabs from Nineveh. Those showing floor-coverings have patterns of lotus-flowers, rosettes and diapers. Nothing is left to show how they were made, but the tapestry method is more likely to have been used than any other.[1]

The skins of beasts, or some kind of pileless woven stuff, would serve in a primitive community as a floor-covering for special occasions, and those who could not come by such luxuries, or whose habits of life did not admit of their use, found a sprinkling of rushes or leaves a passable substitute.

It is indubitable, though surprising, that somehow the Oriental method of pile-knotting in wool became known in Europe by the end of the twelfth century of our era. A happy chance has preserved to the present day some portions of a panel made then at Quedlinburg, in the Harz-Mountain region, by this method, and now preserved in the Schlosskirche there. This work, which measured about 24 ft. high by 20 ft. wide, represents rows of scenes illustrating Martianus Cappella's " Marriage of Mercury and Philology." It is obvious that it was not intended to be spread on the floor, although it was found in use on the floor of the Abbess' Stall in the church early in the last century. The nuns by whom the work was done must have had access to a piece of carpet-knotting, probably without realizing that it was made for a floor-covering. The method of knotting is that used in Turkey carpets, but the need of fine lines for the figures was met by devising a single-warp knot, unknown in the East, for those parts.[2]

The possibility that the nuns of Quedlinburg made an independent discovery of this knotting process is so very slight as to be negligible. The hanging is known to have been made in the time of the Abbess Agnes (1186–1203) and it affords a unique piece of evidence of the actual importation of pile-carpets into Europe before the end of the twelfth

---

[1] See A. H. Layard, Second Series of *The Monuments of Nineveh*, London, 1853, Plate 56.

[2] J. Lessing and M. Creutz, *Wandteppiche und Decken des Mittelalters in Deutschland*, Berlin, Pls. 1–7. The process continued to be used for wall-hangings in Germany until the sixteenth century, although for such a purpose it is wasteful both of time and material. Its use for small details to relieve tapestry-work, as seen sometimes in mediæval German hangings, is effective.

century. There is nothing else to show that they were brought in earlier than the fifteenth century, except representations in paintings; and even those are not conclusive. Carpets seen in pictures of the fourteenth century might equally well have been woven by the more primitive tapestry process. A strange obscurity hangs over the origins of carpet-knotting everywhere.

In considering the traces left in the East itself we are much in the dark. There are no pile-carpets existing which are demonstrably earlier than the Quedlinburg hanging, except the fragments lately found in the desert sites of Central Asia. Those regions must be very much nearer the original home of carpet-knotting than Quedlinburg, and anything of the kind discovered there has a peculiar interest. Nothing but small fragments have been found up to the present. Von le Coq's expedition brought to light at Qyzil a red piece with portion of a pattern in yellow outlined in brownish black, but there is not enough to reveal the nature of the pattern.[1] Sir Aurel Stein's excavations afford no better clue.[2] These fragments are obviously worthy of the closest examination, as presumably they were all made well within the limits of the first millennium; their significance cannot properly be measured until further investigation and research are made possible. Leaving them out of account, the oldest existing Oriental carpets appear to be those in the mosque of Ala-ed-Dîn at Konia, first brought to notice by Dr. F. R. Martin,[3] and attributed by that eminent authority to the early years of the thirteenth century. Towards the end of that century, the Venetian traveller, Marco Polo, wrote that " the finest and handsomest carpets in the world " were made in Turkomania (i.e. Asia Minor[4]).

The conditions under which pile-carpets may have been first devised have already been touched upon. Where the invention took place is still an open question. Sir George Birdwood[5] is inclined to favour Egypt as the home of a very early civilization. But it is a real question whether civilization had much to do with the discovery. Moreover, there are serious objections to the claim of Egypt. The soil and climate of the country render carpets a luxury rather than a necessity; wool, the natural

---

[1] F. Sarre and T. Falkenberg in Berliner Museen, *Berichte*, XLII, 1921, p. 110.

[2] Sir M. A. Stein, *Desert Cathay*, London, 1912, Fig. 116, 4 ; *Serindia*, 1922, Vol. IV, Pl. 37.

[3] *Oriental Carpets*, 1908, Pl. 30. See *post*, p. 45.

[4] *The Book of Ser Marco Polo*, translated and edited by Colonel Sir Henry Yule, 3rd ed., London, 1903, Vol. I, p. 43.

[5] Vienna, *O.C.*, 1892.

material for making them, was not used by the ancient Egyptians; and the wealth of textile material hitherto turned up by excavators in the burying-grounds, varied as it is, includes no example of carpet-knotting. Arguments of a similar nature apply to India. China has no better case. The native textile materials of these three countries are, respectively, linen, cotton, and silk. We shall do better to look for the ideal home of woollen pile-carpets in uplands where the cold is sharp at times, where a nomad people require a portable floor and keep flocks for the provision of the wool. On these grounds, the great plateau of Persia, the highlands of Anatolia or the plains of Central Asia have the best claim. Carpet-weaving reached its highest limits of attainment, and is known to have been practised from early times, both in Persia and Anatolia. The task of balancing the claims of these two regions to priority might be endlessly pursued without getting any nearer to a solution. There is more hope of further developments in regard to Central Asia, where so much research is going on, and the near future may throw a flood of light on this question, as well as on others equally obscure.

CHAPTER II

PERSIA

In any systematic record of pile-carpet weaving it is advisable to begin with Persia. To do so is convenient, and almost inevitable. It is true that the Persian carpets were not the first to become known in Europe. All available evidence seems to show that they were not known at all for some centuries after pile-carpets were first brought in from the East. Of all the carpets represented in European pictures of the fourteenth, fifteenth and sixteenth centuries, not a single one is Persian. The configuration of Persia and its place on the map were obstacles to the transport of bulky wares which long continued to be almost completely effective. A few carpets from Persia found their way to Europe in past centuries. Here and there a Persian carpet in a church or palace in Italy may have been imported straight from the loom, just like the Anatolian. The carpet shown in Plate 5A belonged formerly to Signor Stefano Bardini of Florence. Others also from the same collection had probably been long in Italy[1] ; but had there been many of them in that country before the end of the sixteenth century they would assuredly have been copied by the painters. A woollen carpet with inscriptions and arabesques in silver was in a Spanish cathedral until a few years ago.[2] A very remarkable Persian carpet from Mantes Church was acquired for the Louvre in 1912, where it is exhibited in the large Oriental gallery.[3] It has a pattern of Chinese dragons, phœnixes and " unicorns " amid cypresses and fruit trees, on a blue middle ground and a red border. This carpet was probably made in the last years of the sixteenth century. A fragment of the border of another fine Persian carpet of about the same date, with a pattern of interlaced arabesques, formerly in the Cathedral of Troyes, is now in the Victoria and Albert Museum.[4] A carpet in the Cathedral of Cracow will be referred to later. The famous hunting-carpet in the Austrian imperial collections (Plate 10)

[1] See (e.g.) Martin, O.C., Figs. 61, 109, 127.
[2] Illustrated in colours, Ancient Oriental Carpets (supplement to the great book published at Vienna), Pl. II ; see also Martin, O.C., Fig. 131.
[3] Illustrated in colours in G. Migeon, L'Orient Musulman, Paris, 1922, Pl. 36.
[4] Illustrated in colours, Martin, O.C., Fig. 108.

is supposed to have belonged at one time to the Czars of Russia. The neighbourhood of Russia to the north-western provinces of Persia accounts for the number of fine Persian textiles in that country. Probably it was in North-West Persia that these carpets which have long been in Europe were made. They would have been conveyed to the nearest port on the Black Sea, and thence by water to Constantinople (whither multitudes of Persian carpets have since been carried); or perhaps in some instance by direct passage in trading ships of the countries concerned. The carpet in the Salting Collection (Plate 14) with an ode by the Persian poet Hâfiz worked into the border in silver thread is supposed to have been sent from the loom to the Turkish sultan's palace at Constantinople; from thence it passed into Mr. Salting's possession not many years ago. The celebrated silk and gold carpets were exceptional, as they were borne by special embassies from the Shah to the European Courts (see p. 31).

The British Muscovy Company of Merchant Adventurers found their way through Russia to Persia before the end of Queen Elizabeth's reign, but it was a troublesome and interminable land journey from Persia to the White Sea or the Baltic, and in the meanwhile the harbours of Asia Minor afforded easy access to the carpet-producing districts of Anatolia.

The consequence was that most of the carpets imported were from Anatolia, and the term " Turkey-carpet " bid fair to make good its claim to be applied to all pile-carpets.[1] The subsequent fame of Persian carpets brought about a reaction, and to-day the appellation as often as not is inexcusable, unless it be conceded that the name of the country whence the best pile-carpets have come may be legitimately applied to any carpets of the kind. How far back the making of pile-carpets goes in Persia we do not know, and probably we never shall. The oldest existing carpets to which dates can be assigned with confidence are not Persian; but that is probably due to accidental circumstances. It is safe to assume that carpet-knotting was either invented in Persia or came in with nomad tribes from the North at an early date in the history of the craft. Whether that happened two thousand years ago, two thousand five hundred years ago, or even fifteen hundred years ago we cannot say.

A description of a sumptuous carpet of very early date has long

---

[1] The French traveller Jean Chardin, who visited Persia in the second half of the seventeenth century, explains that Persian carpets were still included in this general term in his day, because they came by way of Turkey before the ocean route was explored (J. Chardin, *Voyage en Perse*).

survived the carpet itself, as well as all others of its time, in the annals of the Arabian writers who recorded the conquest of Persia.

When Ctesiphon, the Sassanian capital near the site of the later city of Baghdad, fell into the hands of the Arabs in A.D. 637, the carpet was found in the famous White Palace.

The late Dr. v. Karabacek, of the Vienna Royal Library, extracted from the Arabian manuscript the following account of the carpet.[1] It was originally made for Chosroes I (A.D. 531–579) and his successors used it ever after until the last Sassanian king Jazdegerd, but only during the stormy and rough winter seasons when it was impossible to stay in the garden. On these occasions the drinking feasts which usually took place outside were transferred to the carpet, for its pattern represented a garden in the bloom of spring. The carpet was called " The Winter Carpet " or " The Spring of Chosroes." The materials of this carpet were notable and rich : silk, gold, silver, and semi-precious and precious stones. The middle space of the carpet represented a pleasure-garden planted with trees and spring flowers, and intersected by brooks and pathways. The broad surrounding border represented magnificent flower-beds, and the blossoms were shown by blue, red, yellow, white and green stones. The yellow colour of the earth was represented in the background of the carpet with gold ; the banks of the streams were rendered by stripes, between which stones clear as crystal made the representation of the water so perfect as to deceive the eye. The pathways were indicated by stones as large as pearls, stems and branches were made out of gold and silver, the leaves of the trees and flowers as well as all the plants were made out of silk, and the fruit out of coloured stones.

Though it would be expecting too much of us to ask that we should accept this description as a bare statement of facts, especially in view of the lively fancies of the Oriental imagination, it would nevertheless be a mistake to treat the description of this carpet as being a pure fable. To judge from the nature of the materials and the size (it was said to be 60 ells square), it cannot have been of knotted pile. Rather must it be classed with the elaborate embroidered carpets such as have been made elsewhere in the East down to modern times. For all that, account should be taken of it, since the description of the pattern is one that might be used with little modification for carpets made in Persia more than a thousand years later. No such carpet is shown in any of the Sassanian

[1] *Pers. Nadelmalerei Susandschird*, Leipzig, 1881.

reliefs or silver-ware now existing, but the veracity of the story is attested by several existing carpets of far later date.[1] Some years ago a carpet made a thousand years after the one described by Karabacek was discovered in a Styrian hostelry ; it has since passed into the possession of Dr. A. Figdor in Vienna. The design obviously represents the flower-beds of a garden through which runs a maze of water-channels opening into small lakes, much in the manner of Chosroes' carpet. The water is represented in silver thread, and fish are seen, with water-fowl swallowing them. There are flower-beds, and the streams are bordered by trees with birds in the branches. The carpet is knotted in wool, with gold and silver threads for many details.

The variations, which bear the character of a much later epoch, cannot efface the impression that here is a striking confirmation of the old description ; in fact, one may almost suppose these later carpets to be conscious imitations. The design is peculiarly suitable for a carpet, and it is one which would naturally be evolved in a country where flower-gardens have always been so intimately associated with daily life. Consequently there is no occasion to assume that the theme of Chosroes' carpet was singular in Persia at the time. A few more such carpets are known, but there is nothing to bridge the gap of more than a thousand years between the time of the Sassanian ruler Chosroes, when the first was made, and that of Shah Abbas the Great, in whose reign Dr. Figdor's carpet was most probably woven.

Two garden-carpets are in the possession of the Hon. H. D. McLaren. One of them, made perhaps a little later than the carpet just described, is the largest existing of its kind. It measures 31 ft. by 12 ft. 6 in., and it seems to have been even larger originally. The water is rendered by a clever arrangement of zigzag lines producing a shimmering effect when seen foreshortened. This is the usual convention where metal threads are not employed. There is a square pond in the middle with a central island and four swimming birds. A broad water-channel runs off from this in four directions as far as the borders of the carpet. Minor channels, interrupted at intervals by circular mounds, divide up the rest of the space. The water is everywhere edged with a strip of soil represented in dark blue, upon which trees and flowering plants grow, with birds in the branches. Square and star-shaped beds with blossoming

---

[1] A Sassanian silver dish in the Stroganov Collection shows a king seated on a mat of some kind with a free floral pattern and a wavy stem border (A. Riegl, *Ein Or. Teppich*, p. 16).

trees and plants fill the intervening spaces. The narrow floral border all round is on a white ground.[1] Mr. McLaren's smaller carpet is of the same type, but less complete (Plate 2). Another carpet of the kind, but more diversified, with ducks and fish in the water, and hunting-animals and birds on the land, is here illustrated (Plate 3). This fine carpet passed some years ago from Constantinople to America by way of Berlin, but it has since been brought back to Europe. Mr. Carl Robert Lamm of Naesby House, near Stockholm, the possessor of some fine carpets (several of which will be mentioned later), has two woollen carpets of the " garden " type. Both are relatively late examples—perhaps not made before the eighteenth century. The finer of the two, measuring about 10 ft. by 6 ft., has a large pond in the middle from which branch four broad water-channels, all showing fishes and water-plants. At the sides are four square ponds. The zigzag lines for the water are in red, green, blue and white, giving a rippling effect of colour. Broad deep blue borders, varied with flowering plants, edge the water. More formal arrangements of flowers, on a red ground, fill the remaining space. Mr. Lamm's other carpet is not complete ; it shows a stream running throughout the length, while the ground on either side is divided into squares with formal floral patterns in fairly light colours.[2] It draws near in design to the carpet reproduced in Plate 4, but the latter shows a further modification of the earlier motives. The large rectangular space in the middle with the flowering plant replaces the pond, unless indeed the plain dark background is meant for water. The small squares covering the rest of the space, each with its plant, shows that a garden is depicted, though without the almost indispensable water-channels.

This carpet brings us to the point where the traditional " garden " design dies away into the general stock of decorative motives. But in order to grasp the basic idea of Persian carpet designs it must be borne in mind that most of them have some relation, more or less direct, to a garden or park. Inevitable modifications, brought about by centuries of repetition, may have reduced the scheme to a formula, but even under its disguises the origin is often unmistakable.

The designer of Chosroes' carpet aimed at bringing indoors for the winter-time the outdoor setting of a Persian garden in spring. Let this conception be widened to bring within its compass the sports in

---

[1] Reproduced in colours in W. A. Hawley, *Oriental Rugs*, New York, 1913, Colour-plate VI.

[2] These two carpets are reproduced by Martin, *O.C.*, Pl. 24 (in colours) ; Fig. 104.

the open country, with the huntsmen and animals, the trees, birds and flowers, and let allowance be made for the conventional perspective proper to Eastern art, and the majority of Persian carpet patterns are made clear.

Brief reference to the varied guises these designs assume will be made later. Some other features foreign to the soil of Persia, but appearing there at an early time, must first be accounted for. In the art of Western Asia, and even of Europe, during the last thousand years there is abundant evidence of the subtle and penetrating influence of Chinese design. The outward forms in which the singular art of the ancient and exclusive civilization of China found expression—the dragons, phœnixes, conventional clouds and waves, symbolic objects, and the peculiar types of architecture and costume—seem to have acted like a spell on the craftsmen who met with them, although there is nothing to show that a moment's thought was given to the complex philosophy which called them into being. It is natural that Manchurians, Mongolians, Coreans, Tibetans and people of more or less kindred stock to the Chinese, though of ruder civilization, should make use of Chinese wares and copy their ornamentation so far as they were able. But the effect of Chinese art upon a people of totally different race, like the Persians, with a great artistic tradition of their own, is not so easy to understand. Yet it is there. No more potent external influence is to be found in the carpet designs of Persia and Western Asia than the Chinese. The question when it first made its appearance is involved in another, that of the date of the earliest existing Oriental carpets. Two examples reproduced in this volume may be instanced. The first (Plate 37A), a carpet of Asia Minor, has a design obviously representing the Chinese dragon and phœnix. The carpet will be discussed in a later chapter (p. 46); it need only be pointed out at the moment that, whatever the actual date of this carpet may be, the motives represented on it had certainly found their way to Asia Minor before the fifteenth century, the period to which the carpet has been assigned. The other carpet (Plate 5A) is Persian. It belongs to a group to which an even earlier origin has been ascribed. The intention of the craftsman to represent the Chinese dragon is again beyond dispute. The archaistic rendering has led an eminent authority, Dr. F. R. Martin, to attribute the carpets belonging to this group to the thirteenth century, a period when Chinese motives are already quite frequently seen on the lustred pottery of Persia. Even this is not the first appearance of such motives in Western Asia; it is rather due to the fresh impetus given by the irruption of Hulagu the Mongol, who caused Chinese craftsmen to follow the track of his conquering armies. He is said to have transferred a hundred families of Chinese craftsmen to Persia about the year 1256. It is perfectly safe to assume that Chinese motives were to be found on the Persian carpets at that time, but it may be questioned whether any existing carpet is so old. The complexity of the subject requires a cautious student to be on his guard, for such motives persisted for at least four centuries after, and the relatively coarse texture of such a carpet as that reproduced in Plate 5A might account for the angular rendering, and in some degree for the archaic appearance. A very similar carpet with the same motives on a brilliant red ground, belonging to Mr. Lamm at Naesby House in Sweden, is attributed by Dr. Martin to the middle of the thirteenth century. Another carpet, with leopards attacking various animals among trees, rendered in the same primitive angular manner, he assigns to the end of the century. A third, with large angular palmettes and floral patterns, is ascribed to about the year 1320 ; and a carpet in the Kaiser-Friedrich Museum at Berlin, with floral ornament within formal compartments, to the middle of the fourteenth century.[1] Thus several distinct Persian types are traced back to a remote period, the evidence adduced being that of lustred pottery and dated Persian miniature paintings. The eminent Swedish authority has done a great service to students by investigating and recording these parallels, which are perfectly just. But the example of the garden-carpet of Chosroes is a warning of the length of time that pattern motives linger in the East with little essential change. The risk of error is particularly to be guarded against in the case of pile-carpets. Wherever the fineness of the texture is reduced, and this may take place at any period, and at any place, an angular treatment is inevitable, bringing about a deceptive appearance of archaism.

Similar problems have faced those who have attempted to assign dates to the carpets of Asia Minor by comparison with representations in European pictures, and the consequences have been the same, although each line of inquiry is in the right direction, and most valuable in its results.[2]

As an illustration of the difficulties met with, the carpets reproduced in Plates 5 and 6 may be compared. The first belongs to the group attributed to the thirteenth century. It came from an Italian church,

---

[1] *Oriental Carpets*, Pl. 28, Figs. 58, 59 and 64.
[2] See Dr. von Bode's important essay on Decorative Animal Figures in old Oriental Carpets in the great publication *Oriental Carpets*, Vienna, 1892–4, p. 1. Also J. Lessing, *Alt Orientalische Teppichmuster*, Berlin, 1877.

whither it probably went as a new carpet; but that circumstance affords little help in dating it. The other (Plate 6) is similar to a carpet exhibited in 1910 at the Munich Exhibition, and attributed there, no doubt rightly, to the sixteenth or seventeenth century.[1] In each, the field is broken up into irregular lozenge shaped spaces by means of broad multi-coloured bands, intended at least in part, and perhaps entirely, for long leaves overlapping one another, and relieved with slender floral stems super-imposed.[2] The enclosed spaces are filled with dragons or palmettes, and other palmettes are placed at some of the points where the bands join. There is a narrow border of angular floral forms on a white ground. This description serves equally well for both carpets, and it is almost a question which is the older of the two. A greater multiplicity of detail, with a certain waywardness of treatment in Plate 5A, singles that out as the earlier, although there is little likelihood that it was made much before the sixteenth century.[3]

These carpets were probably made in N.W. Persia or Armenia. The Armenians, of kindred stock to the Persians, were skilful carpet-weavers. One argument in favour of this attribution is the existence of such examples in Italy.[4] The Armenian region was conveniently situated for the transit, having access to the Black Sea, while the difficulties of transport from the heart of Persia excluded bulky goods of that country almost entirely from the Mediterranean trade. Another point to be ob-served is that the prominence of Chinese motives excludes the south of Persia, where such motives hardly penetrated at all. Greater help still in placing these carpets is afforded by a remarkable example which found its way to London in 1899 (Plate 7). This carpet resembles in texture and colour, and to some extent in pattern, that illustrated in Plate 6. The chief difference is that there are no dragons. The spaces are larger, and the middle palmette is replaced by a radiating floral device. Its special significance lies in the Armenian inscription knotted in at the upper end. It reads thus: " I, Gohar, full of sin and feeble in soul, have knotted this with my own hands. May he who reads pray for my soul." Then follows the Armenian date 1129, corresponding to A.D. 1679.

---

[1] Munich, *Meisterwerke*, Pl. 65.

[2] The use of leaves or leaf-shaped panels as a background to hold floral forms is a common feature of Persian textile design in the seventeenth century.

[3] Dr. F. Sarre (*Ancient Oriental Carpets*, Leipzig, 1906–8, p. 1) considers the fifteenth century the earliest possible date.

[4] Besides the example already mentioned Dr. von Bode obtained one from a church near Venice (W. Bode, *Vorderasiatische Knüpfteppiche*, Leipzig, 1st ed., p. 110).

The route this carpet took to the West late in the nineteenth century may be that by which such carpets in Italy came long before. It was taken by Turks from an Armenian church and was carried through the province of Batum to the Black Sea, whence it found its way to London.[1]

The first carpet of this class to attract general attention was shown at the great exhibition of Oriental carpets held at Vienna in 1891.[2] It had been obtained from a mosque in Damascus, and was then the property of Herr Theodor Graf, but it has since been acquired by the Kaiser-Friedrich Museum at Berlin. Both Chinese dragons and " unicorns " (ch'i-lin) are represented ; an effect of considerable age is given to this carpet by the unusually subdued colouring. A few years ago the Victoria and Albert Museum acquired the example (already mentioned), with dragons and " unicorns," remarkable for its black ground which gives full salience to the archaic forms. The dividing bands are in pale blue and yellow, and the narrow formal border is white (Plate 8). Another example in the same collection, less archaic in design, has dragons on a red ground (Plate 5B). This carpet is rather later in date, and obviously not earlier than the seventeenth century. Agreement is more universal in regard to the early origin of another type of design. There is generally a large central panel extending practically across the whole width of the carpet, and broken up by different-coloured grounds ; smaller panels extend to the right and left. The ornament throughout consists of slender floral stems, running into spirals, interlaced with arabesques. The restraint and severity of the design point to a date before that of the Ardabil carpet, and probably within the limits of the fifteenth century, though features of the type are retained in later carpets. There is an example in the Victoria and Albert Museum (Plate 9).[3]

Before reverting to the carpets with the simpler patterns of trees and flowers, some other more complex types may be mentioned. One is the " hunting " carpet, which first appears in the sixteenth century. The best example, and one of the most celebrated of all carpets, is in the Imperial Austrian collections at Schönbrunn (Plate 10). It is woven in silk and gold and silver thread. The huntsmen, mounted and armed with spears, swords and arrows, attack lions, leopards, wolves, boars, deer, antelopes, wild asses, jackals and hares. The ground of the carpet

[1] The Victoria and Albert Museum was not able to do more than take a photograph of this carpet before it left the country again.

[2] Vienna, O.C., 1892–4, Pl. 36.

[3] Others are reproduced, in colours in Martin, O.C., Pl. 2, and in *Ancient Oriental Carpets*, Leipzig, 1906–8, Pl. 4.

is salmon-pink. A large eight-lobed green compartment in the middle has great gold dragons and phœnixes, following Chinese models more closely than those on the carpets hitherto described. The deep crimson border has a succession of winged figures repeating a scene in which a kneeling figure offers a bowl of fruit to another, who is seated and wears a crown. Such winged personages, often engaged in the ordinary occupations of humanity, will be met with again. Each of the corners of the carpet shows a fourth part of the central design. The heads of men in the palmettes of the outer green border, and of lions in those of the inner white border, will be noticed. The miscellaneous nature of the quarry and the confused haste of the riders galloping pell-mell in all directions give a pantomimic air to the scene, but the picture is true to the traditional way of hunting in Persia, as well as in India and Central Asia,[1] still followed, at the time this carpet was woven. All the animals in the neighbourhood were driven into a prepared enclosure, which the hunting-party entered afterwards, to engage in an indiscriminate massacre.

The elaborate dress of the figures on the Schönbrunn carpet suggests a royal hunting-party. The carpet was probably woven in the time of Shah Tahmasp (1524–1576).[2] There is an old tradition that it was received by the Austrian Emperor as a present from Peter the Great of Russia. Another carpet no less celebrated, though of a different type, is dated within the period of Tahmasp's reign. This is the great carpet from the mosque at Ardabil, a small town of the province of Azerbaijan, in the north-west of Persia (Plate 11). The reason why such a work of art should have come from a town of so little note is made clear by the circumstances of the time. Tahmasp was the second king of the Sefavi or Safidian dynasty—the first line of native rulers since the overthow of the Sassanian dynasty by the Arabs more than eight centuries before. The eponymous ancestor of the new dynasty was Sheikh Safi-ed-Dîn who, dying in 1334, was buried at Ardabil. There also Shah Ismail, father of Tahmasp, was buried. The veneration in which the tombs were held, and the association with the ruling house, raised Ardabil to

---

[1] The cheetah or hunting leopard is not seen in this example, though it is found in others. The animal was employed in Persia from an early date, and was still used when these hunting-carpets were woven.

[2] Dr. F. R. Martin suggests that Tahmasp's Court painter, Sultan Muhammad, may have designed the carpet (F. R. Martin, *Miniature Painting*, p. 117). It is illustrated in colours in Vienna, *Oriental Carpets*, Pls. 81, 86–89. See also Munich, *Meisterwerke*, Pls. 42, 43. A carpet of somewhat similar design, in the collection of Baron Maurice Rothschild, is illustrated by Bode (*Vorderasiatische Knüpfteppiche*, 2nd ed., Fig. 3). It was obtained from the Marchese Torrigiani in Italy.

the dignity of the religious and national capital of Persia ; its prestige lasted until Shah Abbas rebuilt Ispahan. A carpet of this size and importance can only have been made to the order of Tahmasp himself for the mosque where his ancestors were buried. The date upon it (A.H. 946 = A.D. 1540) is sixteen years after the death of his father, and most of that time would have been taken up in making it and its fellow. A cartouche at one end of the carpet contains a woven inscription which has been translated as follows :

> "I have no refuge in the world other than thy threshold.
> There is no place of protection for my head other than this door.
> The work of the slave of the threshold, Maqsûd of Kashân, in the year 946."

The first two lines are the beginning of an ode by the Persian poet Hâfiz (d. 1389). It is most likely that the carpet was made at Ardabil ; the Court would naturally wish to watch its progress, and it would have been as easy for the weaver to go there to make it, as for a carpet of this size (34 ft. 6 in. by 17 ft. 6 in.) to be transported from Kashan when made. It remained in the mosque until shortly before its acquisition by the Victoria and Albert Museum in 1893. Fifty years earlier it was seen by an English traveller, W. R. Holmes, who visited Ardabil in 1843. He wrote of it as follows : " On the floor (of the long lofty ante-chamber to the principal tombs) were the faded remains of what was once a very splendid carpet, the manufacture of which very much surpassed that of the present day. At one extremity was woven the date of its make, some three hundred years ago." [1] The disparaging note of its condition, if ever warranted, is no longer applicable. The carpet has been skilfully repaired, parts of another carpet of similar design, removed from the mosque at the same time, having been sacrificed for the purpose. [2]

Some idea of the design of the carpet will be gained from the illustration. The pulsating blue ground is covered with thousands of flowers. The great circular panel of lobed outline in the middle is yellow, with sixteen pointed compartments radiating from it in yellow, green or red. All are filled with cloud bands, arabesques and floral stems in colours. Two hanging lamps are represented, to the right and left of this central device. A fourth part of the same device is repeated at each corner. The panels in the border are red and yellow, on a ground of deep purple tone.

---

[1] W. R. Holmes, *Sketches on the Shores of the Caspian*, 1845.

[2] What remained of the second carpet passed into the Yerkes Collection ; it has since been sold again, but it remains in America.

It will be observed that human and animal forms, both prevalent in Persian carpets of the time, are not included. Such representations would not have been suitable for a mosque. The design is of a double character. The central ornament, with its sixteen radiating ogival panels, belongs, not to the ground like the floral stems, but to the dome overhead. Such embellishments may be found on Persian domed ceilings. There is an example in the vestibule of the college of the Shah Hussein at Ispahan, where the ceiling has in the middle a circular panel with sixteen pointed projections and sixteen ogival panels radiating from them, very similar to the device on the carpet.[1] The two mosque lamps are appropriately introduced as hanging from the ceiling on either side. The pile is entirely of wool, on silk warps. There are about three hundred hand-tied knots to the square inch, making a total of about 30 million knots for the whole carpet. This represents approximately twenty-four years' work of a single skilled weaver. It is probable, however, that several assistants worked with the master-weaver. Assuming that so many as eight people were able to work together at the loom, even then the carpet would take three years' continuous labour to make.

Another carpet in the Victoria and Albert Museum almost challenges the claim of the Ardabil carpet to the first place in the collection. Both are the most famous examples of the respective classes to which they belong—for they are conspicuously different in design, as well as in colour. Every detail of the elaborate design is planned with the utmost care, and copied by the weaver with consummate skill. The colouring is harmonious, with a simplicity and at the same time a subdued splendour which never wearies the eye. The knotting is very fine, as required by the design. The warps are of silk, and the pile is of wool throughout, with about 450 knots to the square inch. The first plate of this volume reproduces the carpet in colours. It will be seen that the ground is a purplish crimson of a carmine tone, although no coloured plate can do justice to the colouring of the original. Upon this ground is a network of panels in very deep blue, almost black. There is a large circle of lobed outline to the right and left of the centre of the carpet. In the middle of each side is a half-section of this panel, and a quarter-section in each corner. Eight pointed oval compartments unite the central panels with the sections round the edge. This disposition recalls the scheme of the Ardabil carpet, but it is less elaborate and more closely linked up. The panels are filled with a pattern of arabesques and palmettes, and each pointed oval has two

[1] P. Coste, *Monuments modernes de la Perse*, Paris, 1867, Pl. XXI.

flying ducks in addition. The centre of the carpet, often made the most conspicuous feature by the Persian designer, is here occupied by a small round pond with fish. On either side of the pond stands a large two-handled vase supported by two dragons on a lion-pedestal, and containing flowers. One vase and half of the pond is repeated in the middle of each of the short sides of the carpet. The rest of the field is covered with blossoming and fruit-bearing trees and floral stems, amid which are lions (some preying on antelopes and black oxen), gazelles, and falcons pouncing on herons. The wide border is divided in counterchange fashion by slender arabesque stems, with a dark blue and crimson ground matching the middle colours. It has a pattern of slender floral stems, and cloud forms, with animals, birds and dragons. The heads of lions and other animals among the interlaced stems of the narrow outer border should be noticed. There is a restraint and regular sequence both in design and colouring which have induced writers to attribute it to an early period. Dr. von Bode ascribes it to early Safidian times. Martin assigns it to Eastern Persia at an earlier date still—about the middle of the fifteenth century.[1] The place of the design in order of sequence is undoubtedly where these experts put it. We must, however, admit the greater probability of a sixteenth-century origin until more light is thrown on the problem of early Persian carpets. The use of silk warps, and the character of the vases and other details of the pattern, favour that view. This carpet, with that from Ardabil, has an indisputable place in the foremost ranks of the great carpets of the world. Several of the classes of motives used in it are retained as the main theme of Persian carpets in the sixteenth and seventeenth centuries. A remarkably fine carpet belonging to the Earl of Ilchester is of that time (Plate 12). The hunting animals are set in a pattern of floral stems, on a red ground.

One of the best known of the carpets representing roaming animals is in the Museum of the Gobelins, Paris (Plate 13).[2] The lions, tigers and leopards, seen preying on oxen, stags and antelopes, are on a red background, covered with conventional stems in place of the naturalistic trees usually shown. A lobed circular compartment in the middle is in pale blue and red, with animals, floral stems and cloud-bands. On the right and left of this compartment there is a device, half-finial, half-vase, evidently a modified rendering of the vase with two peacocks shown on the carpet just described (Plate 1). The spandrel in each corner is

[1] Bode, *Vorderasiatische Knüpfteppiche*, 2nd ed., p. 33 ; Martin, *O.C.*, p. 33.
[2] Reproduced in colours in Vienna, *O.C.*, Pl. 74.

brownish yellow with floral stems and arabesques interlaced. The longer panels in the border are inscribed with a poem, describing the carpet as pressed by the foot of a world-ruling monarch, and beautiful as Eden, so that it is an object of envy to Chinese art. Its flowery bed shows an ever-lovely spring, that no gales or storms can touch.

Verses which have given the inspiration for the design, or perhaps in some cases have been suggested by it, are inscribed on numbers of Persian carpets. They are usually to be seen, as in this instance, in bold letters on a row of panels in the border. Sometimes they run continuously along narrow bands, or fill smaller spaces. They speak of the springtime, of the stars, the clouds, the winds, the dew and the raindrops; of gardens, flowers and birds; of love, and the wine-bowl; they give expression to good wishes for freedom from care, and for springtime all the year round. Sometimes these verses are borrowed from their national poets, whom the Persians never weary of quoting. A poem in praise of the spring flowers—the rose, narcissus, tulip and violet—is woven in silver thread on a carpet with a similar border to the last, in the Musée des Arts Décoratifs in Paris.[1] There is a large circle in the middle of this carpet with blossoming trees, flowers and peacocks, on panels of different colours. The ground beyond is black, and covered with stems and cloud forms in colours and silver thread. An ode to the nightingale among the rose-bushes is on the inner border of a carpet in wool, gold and silver lent by Baron Nathaniel Rothschild to the Vienna Exhibition of 1891.[2] The bird and the flowers are represented in the middle of the carpet, round a small pond. The rest of the design consists of a formal arrangement of arabesques and palmettes. Verses describing the delights of spring, and others praising the nightingale are inserted on a carpet with arabesque patterns in a private collection in Paris.[3] The most celebrated of all Persian poets, Hâfiz, is quoted at some length on a remarkably fine carpet in the Salting Collection at South Kensington (Plate 14). The materials are wool and gold and silver thread on silk warps, and the texture is very fine. The verses are in silver thread on elongated dark red panels in the border. They have been translated as follows :—

Call for wine and scatter roses : what dost thou seek from Time ?—thus spake the rose at dawn. O nightingale, what sayest thou ?

---

[1] Reproduced in colours, Vienna, *O.C.*, Pl. 71.
[2] Reproduced in colours, Vienna, *O.C.*, Pl. 97.
[3] Illustrated in colours in *Ancient Oriental Carpets*, Leipzig, 1906–8, Pl. 2.

Take the cushion to the garden, that thou mayest hold the lip and kiss the cheek of the beloved and the cup-bearer, and drink wine and smell the rose.

Proudly move thy graceful form and to the garden go, that the cypress may learn from thy stature how to win hearts.

To-day while thy market is full of the tumult of buyers, gain and put by a store out of the capital of goodness.

Every bird brings a melody to the garden of the King,—the nightingale, songs of love, and Hafiz, prayers for blessing.[1]

The pattern of floral stems, cloud-bands and birds, and tigers fighting dragons, betrays Chinese influence. The device of a lion's mask within a palmette, frequently seen on Persian carpets, is repeated several times ; the masks are sometimes merely attached to the stems like flowers. In spite of the wonderful freshness of colour and the fine state of preservation of this carpet, it cannot very well be attributed to a later date than the seventeenth century. It was obtained in Constantinople rather more than thirty years ago, when it was stated to have been in the collections of the Sultan.

Another carpet reputed to have come from the Turkish sultan's palace is of the same class, in the same materials and equally well preserved. It was obtained by Prince Lobanoff-Rostowsky when Russian ambassador in Constantinople in the late 'seventies of last century, and afterwards ceded by him to the Stieglitz Museum in Petrograd.[2] The border has an ode to a conqueror, greater than Darius, Alexander and Feridun, before whose victorious progress throne-carpets are spread. The central panel is similar to that on the carpet in the Salting Collection. The white ground around is covered with delicate interlacing stems of flowers and cloud-bands, amid which tigers, leopards stalking stags, jackals and Chinese dragons are seen. Among the stems in the green spandrels are parrots, pheasants, and a falcon seizing a heron. The alternation of inscribed elongated panels with circular panels to form a border, as exemplified in the carpets just described, is quite often found in other Persian works of art. A segment of a damascened brass dish, showing such a border, is illustrated on Plate 15B. A Persian begging-bowl, of engraved copper, reproduced on the same Plate (15A), shows the Chinese cloud-band as seen on the carpets. These animated forest or park-land

---

[1] Hâfiz, *Divan* (ed. H. Brockhaus, Vol. III, p. 175–6).
[2] Illustrated in colours in Vienna, *O.C.*, Pl. XI. A description of this carpet by M. A. Polovtsoff, Director of the Museum, has been published in the *Burlington Magazine* (Vol. XXXV, 1919, p. 16).

scenes have not always the accompaniment of descriptive verses in gold and silver.

A woollen carpet in the possession of Prince Schwarzenberg [1] has a pond with ducks in the middle. The deep blue ground beyond is closely covered with cypresses and blossoming trees and plants naturalistically drawn, with a great phœnix seizing a small bird in each corner, and more birds and animals below.

Half of a carpet, in wool on silk warps, with a similar design in different colours, is in the Cathedral of Cracow; the other half found its way to Paris, where it is now in the Musée des Arts Décoratifs. [2]

In other examples, which need not be specified, the trees and flowers cover the whole ground, not balanced in opposing directions from the middle, as is usual in carpets with central panels, but continued in an unbroken stretch from one end to the other. The borders of such carpets vary considerably; they are generally wide, with a formal design as a contrast to the free rendering of the middle pattern. [3]

One example, in which the landscape idea is very clearly marked, should not be allowed to pass unnoticed. It is in the Museum of Art and Industry at Vienna. The trees, shrubs and plants are represented with careful fidelity to nature. There are peacocks, pheasants and storks on the ground, and various smaller birds in the foliage. [4]

Much help may be derived from Persian miniature paintings, particularly from those of ascertained date, in the study of carpets. Their rendering of landscape often explains a carpet design, and sometimes an actual carpet is represented. A painting of the seventeenth century, here illustrated, will suffice to show the lines on which comparisons may be made (Plate 16). A Persian prince is seen in a garden with its central pond and ducks, its straight water-channels and vases. Carpets with figures remain yet to be described; the other motives have already been met with. Beyond the enclosure are the cypresses and blossoming trees so often seen on the carpets. Suspended over the prince's head, ignoring in its delineation all rules of perspective, is a floral carpet serving as a canopy. Courtiers are seated on others spread on the ground. Another

---

[1] Illustrated in colours in Vienna, *O.C.*, Pl. XXXI. See also *Meisterwerke*, Munich, Pl. 45.

[2] Vienna, *O.C.*, Pl. 31; G. Migeon, *Exp. des Arts Musulmans*, Paris, 1903, Pl. 73.

[3] There is a specimen in the Victoria and Albert Museum, No. 3—1887.

[4] Reproduced in colours, Vienna, *O.C.*, Pl. I. Dr. Martin (*Oriental Carpets*, Fig. 236) claims an Indian origin for this carpet. It may have been made in India, but the motives are Persian.

miniature of about the same period shows three pile-carpets—one spread on a low platform for a prince to sit on, another forming a canopy over his head, and a third thrown over the back of an elephant (Plate 17).

One of the simplest and most pleasing kinds of Persian carpet-design is based on plant forms throughout. An incomplete carpet of this type in the Austrian Museum of Art and Industry, Vienna, is illustrated in Plate 18. The white ground is covered with an arrangement of trailing floral stems, while another system of slender stems superimposed and carrying large palmettes suggests a partition into panels of regular shape. In the middle of one of these is a vase ; there would have been several others in the entire carpet.[1] In many of these carpets the stems issue from vases, generally disproportionately small, placed at regular intervals. They may seem a little tame after such carpets as have been described hitherto, in which much use has been made of the enlivening effect of animals and birds, but the variety of plant forms and the usual quiet harmony of the colouring make amends. Two examples in the Victoria and Albert Museum show a variation in the design. Instead of the trailing stems, flowering plants are shown entire to the roots, as they would be seen in a garden-bed. They are enclosed by the stems bearing palmettes, as in the carpet just described. The larger one was formerly a valued possession of William Morris. The other was obtained in Constantinople. Each has a deep red ground and a blue border.[2]

The naturalistic floral treatment is somewhat modified, in a fine carpet in the same Museum, by a succession of large lozenge-forms of lobed outline in dark and light blue, purple-brown, salmon pink and white (Plate 19). The carpet is large, and the panels are introduced to give relief to the wide stretch of deep crimson colour. The stems pass through them without interruption. The vases are shown sometimes in the panels and sometimes beyond. There is a deep blue floral border.

When the vases disappear from these carpets, there is sometimes a more assertive arrangement of the floral motives in panels. A carpet belonging to Mr. Lamm of Naesby has a series of panels, each nearly 4 ft. long, in various colours, containing formal floral ornament ; the intervening spaces each contain a blossoming tree on a dark blue ground.[3]

[1] Reproduced in colours in *Ancient Oriental Carpets*, Leipzig, 1906–8, Pl. 11.

[2] The first is illustrated in colours in *Ancient Oriental Carpets*, Leipzig, 1906–8, Pl. 19. Others similar are reproduced in Pls. 5, 9, and 10. Sir Isidore Spielmann has a portion of a very fine carpet of this type (Victoria and Albert Museum, *Catalogue of the Franco-British Exhibition*, 1921, Pl. 32).

[3] Illustrated in colours in Martin, *O.C.*, Pl. 1 ; also in *Meisterwerke*, Munich, Pl. 66.

A very effective design of the type was exemplified by a carpet lent by Count Clam-Gallas to the Munich Exhibition of 1910.[1] The panels are alternately quatrefoil and fan-shaped, with floral and arabesque patterns, cloud-bands and peacocks on grounds of several colours. The background is dark red, with flowering trees. At the same exhibition was to be seen a carpet belonging to the Imperial Ottoman Museum at Constantinople in which the ground is entirely divided up into large lozenge-spaces of various colours containing floral forms.[2] A portion of a very similar carpet is in the Victoria and Albert Museum (Plate 20B) and another is in the Kunstgewerbe Museum, Berlin.[3] These floral carpets are generally attributed to the weavers of the province of Kirman in the south-east. It is not without significance that a favourite type of carpet made there in more recent times shows close rows of vases of flowers, generally on a white ground.[4] The almost entire absence of Chinese motives in these carpets is a strong argument in favour of a South Persian origin. Occasionally carpets of this type have a long looped nap at the back, like a bath towel, for warmth. This would be a very suitable provision at Kirman, where the cold is sometimes severe, owing to its altitude of 6,000 ft. A modern loom from Kirman, with a typical carpet of the district partly woven upon it, is illustrated in Plate 92.

One of the largest Oriental pile-carpets ever made, and one of singular design, was formerly in the Hall of the Forty Columns (Chihal Sutun) at Ispahan. It measured more than 70 ft. long by 30 ft. wide.[5] So wide a loom for a finely knotted carpet must have been a prodigious affair to work at, and the difficulty of keeping the carpet even and straight during its manufacture must have been great. It had a red ground, with a formal arrangement of large white flowers and green stems behind a trellis of yellow stems, each opening being 9 ft. in length. The border, which was 6 ft. wide, was filled with the same ornament on dark blue. This carpet was placed in the great hall behind the throne-room.[6] It has been gradually dismembered by travellers within the last forty years. Three fragments ultimately found their way to the Victoria and Albert Museum, where also

---

[1] Illustrated in *Meisterwerke*, Pl. 50 ; in colours in Vienna, *O.C.*, Pl. 32 ; also in Martin, *O.C.*, Fig. 102, and Bode, *Vorderas. Knüpfteppiche*, 2nd ed., Fig. 19.

[2] *Meisterwerke*, Pl. 52 ; Martin, *O.C.*, Fig. 86.

[3] Reproduced in colours in *Ancient Oriental Carpets*, Leipzig, 1906–8, Pls. 9, 21.

[4] A fine example is in the Victoria and Albert Museum, No. 100. It is inscribed with the name of a Kirman weaver.

[5] See p. 106.

[6] There is a plan of the Pavilion, showing the room in which the carpet was placed, in P. Coste, *Monuments modernes de la Perse*, Paris, 1867, Pl. 41.

may be seen a drawing reconstructing the design (Plate 21). The carpet was of the period of Shah Abbas the Great (1586–1628), who built the hall in which it was placed ; it was probably made during the latter part of this monarch's reign. Dr. F. R. Martin, who emphasizes the approximation of the design to those on Indian carpets at Jaipur, claims it for the Indian weavers. The arguments against such an attribution are formidable. Why should Abbas, under whom carpet-weaving in Persia flourished greatly, have the carpet for the great open pavilion of his own palace woven in India? And assuming that he did, how was the wellnigh insurmountable task of transporting such a bulky object over the difficult country between the Panjab and Ispahan overcome? Dr. Martin claims that all such carpet designs were woven in India. It appears easier, on the whole, to adapt the theory to fit the carpet than the carpet to fit the theory. What was done at Lahore in factories inaugurated by Persian weavers may have been done in Persia as well.

The Persians have not shackled their artistic gifts by notions about the precedence of one kind of art over another. They have ignored all distinctions of the sort, and much of the fine quality of their art is due to this. The range of design seen in their carpets, for example, is no less extensive than that in their paintings, and it includes every class of subject attempted by carpet-weavers elsewhere. Hunting scenes, first shown on the carpets of Persia, are only found outside that country in Indian copies. Figure-subjects form another special group, shared only by India (again as a copyist) and China, if we may pass over the diminutive and grotesque human forms which occasionally fill odd corners in Caucasian and Turcoman work. It has been reserved for the modern Kirman weaver to turn his whole carpet into a picture in semi-European style.[1] In older Persian carpets figures are freely introduced, though with a better sense of restraint. In hunting scenes the theme requires the figures to be generally distributed. In most other cases they appear singly or in small groups—in the border or spandrels, or in compartments upon the central field. In the silk brocades of Persia, where a better opportunity for showing detail renders comparison with

---

[1] A carpet of extraordinarily fine technique, in the possession of Sir Charles Marling, shows a group of figures taken from Watteau's *Fêtes vénitiennes*. An inwoven inscription states that it is from the Atelier of ' Alī Kirmānī, and the dates A.H. 1324 and 1327 (A.D.=1906, 1909) are both woven. It must have taken several years to make. Other Kirman carpets of similar type showing groups of ancient and modern worthies, or single portraits of the Shah, are not rare.

dated miniature paintings an easier task, the weaving of figure-subjects appears to have been in vogue during the reign of Shah Tahmasp (1524–1576), lasting well into the seventeenth century. In the carpets these subjects are found about the same time, and they remain popular throughout the following century. Figures are represented among the trees of a garden, eating fruit, drinking wine, or listening to music. By a strange convention the figures are sometimes winged, but their occupations are still the same, or they are seated alone. By the time these carpets were woven the wings had lost all significance they may ever have had.

A remarkable carpet in the possession of the Duke of Buccleuch (Plate 22) is divided up into pointed oval and lobed compartments. The former contain repetitions of three scenes—a falconer on horseback; two standing figures in a garden, one giving drink to the other; and three seated figures in a garden, one with a tambourine, another with a bottle, and the third with a cup. In the oblong compartments are birds and flowers. The red ground beyond these compartments is covered with beasts of prey—lions, tigers, leopards and wolves—hunting stags, antelopes and goats. The broad border has a succession of elongated yellow panels enclosing dragons and phœnixes, alternating with pairs of dragons intertwining in circles. The dark blue ground is covered with running animals amid floral stems. The narrow outer border has masks of lions and heads of oxen connected by slender stems.

A group of figures drinking and listening to music, seated round a pond with water-fowl, is represented on a carpet formerly in the Bardini Collection at Florence.[1] The seated winged figures in the border of the great hunting-carpet at Schönbrunn (Plate 10) are found again in several carpets. One in the Lyons Museum has them in the border, and scenes similar to those on the Duke of Buccleuch's carpet in the middle.[2] Single-winged figures are to be seen on the spandrels of a remarkable carpet (of which barely one-half is preserved) of the sixteenth century, given to the Victoria and Albert Museum by the late Mr. C. T. Garland. It is in wool and gold and silver thread, with a fine design of hunting animals.[3] A later hunting-carpet, entirely in wool, made in the first half of the seventeenth century, has on each spandrel a group of three

---

[1] Martin, *O.C.*, Fig. 127.
[2] Martin, *O.C.*, Fig. 138 ; R. Cox, *L'Art de décorer les Tissus*, Paris, 1900, Pl. 53.
[3] *V.A.M. Notes on Carpet-knotting and Weaving*, 1920, frontispiece. See also *Burlington Magazine*, XXV, 1919, p. 12.

winged figures, in this case appropriately in clouds.[1] There is one more instance in which some ultra-human attribute is apparently assigned to the winged figures, on the celebrated silk carpet in the Poldi-Pezzoli Museum at Milan.[2] Among the trees and plants two of them are seated before a bowl of flowers overshadowed by a canopy of Chinese form. Perhaps in earlier versions of the motive the bowl was an altar.

There were originally two figures on the spandrels of a carpet in the Kaiser-Friedrich Museum at Berlin ; one is seated and the other, probably an attendant, standing. Nothing more than the lower portion of these figures is preserved. The carpet was formerly in the synagogue at Genoa, and the Jewish objection to the representation of human figures is thought to explain the mutilation.[3]

Two old love-stories of Persia have kept their popularity for many centuries—those of Khusrau and Shīrīn, and Lailā and Majnun. They appear again and again in Persian miniatures and textiles. Both are shown on a carpet in the Musée des Arts Décoratifs in Paris (Plate 23). Each scene is rendered in the traditional manner. In the first, the beautiful Shīrīn has dismounted from her horse to bathe, and she is seated dressing her hair, with her garments hanging on the bough of a tree above, when Prince Khusrau (Chosroes), who has been out hunting, rides past. The hunting-party, from which the Prince has strayed, has the authority of the old story. The appearance among the riders, of Lailā encountering the poor distraught poet Majnun in the desert, may perhaps be explained on the supposition that it was thought appropriate to bring in this story where the other was shown. It will be noticed that two of the huntsmen throw their bows over the necks of antelopes. The ground is deep blue, and that of the border red. The outer stripe of the border is dark blue, and the inner white. The latter has a fantastic pattern of heads of men, lions and horses linked together by blossoming stems.[4]

A strange nautical scene is occasionally found in the spandrels of carpets of a relatively late class, probably made towards the end of the seventeenth century. One example, in the Lyons Museum, shows two

[1] In the Victoria and Albert Museum. Reproduced in colours, *Ancient Oriental Carpets,* Leipzig, 1906–8 (supplementary volume to the great work published in Vienna in 1892), Pl. 22.

[2] W. von Bode, *Vorderasiatische Knüpfteppiche,* 2nd ed., Fig. 5 ; Martin, *O.C.,* Figs. 118, 119.

[3] Bode, *Vorderas. Knüpfteppiche,* 2nd ed., Fig. 12 ; Martin, *O.C.,* Fig. 85 ; Vienna, *O.C.,* Pl. 62.

[4] Illustrated in colours in *Ancient Oriental Carpets,* Leipzig, 1906–8, Pl. 15.

boats filled with figures, and a man apparently drowning among the fishes.[1] The clue to this subject is not known; the boats and figures are European. Another carpet in the Reynolds room at Knole is closely similar. A third, belonging to Mr. Lamm, at Naesby, has the same scene but there is only one boat.[2] Two other carpets of the same class are in the Metropolitan Museum, New York, and the Kunstgewerbe Museum, Berlin. Each carpet shows a singular zigzag arrangement of the central space, with floral patterns on successive grounds of different colours. This expanding zigzag form of ornamentation is to be found on the well-known velvets of Kashan in Central Persia.

This town has long been famous, and is still, for its carpets, and the theory that the carpets with the nautical scenes were made there has much in its favour. Yezd also, the other great centre of velvet-weaving in Persia, made carpets, but the industry there in modern times has declined.[3]

In considering figure-subjects on carpets the remarkable cope of Persian workmanship in the Victoria and Albert Museum should be studied. It is very finely knotted in silk, like a carpet, with details in gold and silver thread. Representations of the Annunciation and the Crucifixion are seen, among the usual floral motives.

The description of the famous carpet of Chosroes (see p. 10), tells of the use of silk, gold and silver, and even jewels, in a floor-covering. It has already been pointed out that this sumptuous work cannot have been a pile-carpet. For many centuries the knotting of Oriental carpets was done in wool, and no material produces a more beautiful pile-surface. When costlier threads began to be introduced, a type of carpet was made which attracts the collector by its richness, though it is unsuitable for placing on the floor. The first step was taken, so far as we can tell, about the beginning of the sixteenth century, when the Persian state, after a long period of alien rule, was becoming unified under the native Safidian dynasty. The epoch was marked by an output of artistic wares on a most generous scale, as the museums of Europe now bear witness. The elaboration of carpet-patterns, involving the tracing of delicate curves and minute details, called for a finer texture, and this necessitated the use of a warp at once thin and strong. The luxury of the times permitted the employment of silk for the purpose, although the thread formed

---

[1] R. Cox, *L'Art de décorer les Tissus*, Paris, 1900, Pl. 52 ; Martin, *O.C.*, Fig. 149.

[2] Martin, *O.C.*, Pl. 6.

[3] It will, of course, be understood that there is no technical affinity between velvets and carpets.

only the foundation of the fabric, and was hidden in the finished texture. The pile was still entirely of wool, the warp threads on which the knots were made and the weft shoots passed through to keep them in line being alone of the richer material. The " Ardabil " carpet, of the year 1540, was thus woven. The next step seems to have been the introduction of gold and silver threads, sparingly at first, for details of the pattern. As the use of metal threads was gradually extended silk was substituted for the wool of the pile, until at last carpets were made entirely of silk on a gold or silver ground. Wool thus disappeared altogether in these sumptuous carpets. Sometimes the metal threads were dispensed with, and the material used was silk throughout. The evolution was completed by the end of the sixteenth century. Meanwhile the making of woollen carpets went on.

The seventeenth-century carpets woven entirely in silk, with metal threads for the ground, have for long been the subject of conflicting views. Attention was first drawn to the problem of their provenance at the time of the Paris Exhibition of 1878. A very fine example, the property of Prince Czartoryski, was then shown in the *Salle polonaise* of the Palais du Trocadéro.[1] The ground of this carpet was of gold and silver thread, not knotted but wrought into the warps by a method analogous to tapestry. The design, of palmettes and floral stems, quite Persian in character though arranged in a somewhat formal manner, was knotted by the ordinary method in coloured silks. In the middle, and again at each corner, was the coat-of-arms of the owner's family. The European heraldry, associated with the unfamiliar materials of the carpet, raised doubts in the minds of the experts of the day as to its Oriental origin, and the theory was advanced that it was the work of a member of a well-known family of weavers established in Poland, Madziarski by name. The appellation of " Polish," given to carpets of this class in consequence, clung to them for many years. Doubts afterwards arose, which were strengthened when it became clear that the weaving establishment of the first of the Madziarski was not in operation early enough. But the theory served a good purpose, for when its foundation was seen to be insecure an incentive was given to further investigation. M. T. Krygowski, writing in the *Orientalisches Archiv*,[2] quoted an inventory of a member of the household of King Albert of Prussia, made

[1] E. Guichard and A. Darcel, *Tapisseries décoratives du Garde-Meuble*, 1877, Pl. 94. It is now in the Czartoryski Museum at Cracow.
[2] II, 1911–12, pp. 70, 106.

in 1578, in which three Polish carpets are mentioned, and another of the Treasury of Prince Ostrogski in Dubno, of the year 1616, with an entry of a Polish carpet inwrought with gold. He also showed that there was a silk factory in Poland as early as the first half of the seventeenth century. All this is useful, but so far it does not involve the assumption that carpets like Prince Czartoryski's are Polish.

The Poles, like the Russians, always had a liking for rich Oriental stuffs, and many must have been imported. So far as Madziarski's weaving establishments are concerned, there is no evidence that they ever made carpets. The first weaver of the family, John, was established about the middle of the eighteenth century at Sluck. The discovery that his signature to an agreement with Prince Radziwill, for conducting a " Persian " factory and teaching Persian art, was in the Armenian language, lent colour to the theory that he was an immigrant weaver of carpets. It appears, however, that the name Madziarski means " Magyar," and it is surmised that the weaver's father may have lived in Hungary, whence he would have been carried as a prisoner to Stambul by a raiding-party of Turks. It was from Stambul that John Madziarski smuggled the first weaving appliances in pieces into Poland. He wove girdles and brocades of silk and gold and silver after Persian models.[1]

It is beyond dispute that carpets woven in gold, silver and silk were made in Persia. These are the materials of the famous Schönbrunn carpet already described (p. 16). The French traveller Jean Baptiste Tavernier, as Dr. Sarre points out,[2] saw " rich carpets in gold and silk " in the Royal Palace at Ispahan in the first half of the seventeenth century. Rather earlier than the date of Tavernier's journey, carpets of these materials arrived in Venice direct from Persia.

Four fine silk and gold carpets are still preserved in the Treasury of St. Mark's at Venice. There is satisfactory evidence that three, at least, were presented to the Doge by Shah Abbas the Great of Persia. An embassy from the Shah, arriving at Venice in 1603, brought a carpet in silk and gold and silver, with the suggestion that the church treasure should be displayed upon it at the time of the annual exhibitions to the public. In 1622 the Persian ambassador brought two more.[3]

---

[1] There is a collection of these in the Victoria and Albert Museum, one having Madziarski's name. Others were shown at the Munich Exhibition of Muhammadan art in 1912 (*Meisterwerke Muham. Kunst*, Pl. 222).

[2] *Ancient Oriental Carpets*, Leipzig, 1906-8, p. 3.

[3] G. Berchet, *La repubblica di Venezia e la Persia* (Turin, 1865). See A. Pasini, *Tesoro di S. Marco in Venezia*, Venice, 1885-6, Pls. 77, 89-92.

HAND-WOVEN CARPETS

A beautiful silk and gold carpet is in the Royal Palace at Stockholm. Like the Austrian Emperor's, it has a " hunting " subject, but much simplified. The huntsmen are afoot—some struggling with lions, and others carrying slain bears on their shoulders. There are also deer, antelopes and other animals. The colours are full and deep. The crimson ground is relieved by a large central panel and spandrels in gold thread. There is a wide pale yellowish border, with an inner and outer stripe, the former black and the other crimson.[1] The famous " Coronation carpet " of the Danish royal house is kept at Rosenborg Castle, Copenhagen. The ground is entirely of gold thread, producing an effect of great richness. The pattern consists of floral stems, palmettes, arabesques and cloud-bands in silk pile with touches of silver thread.[2] Both these carpets have been in Scandinavia since the seventeenth century. They were probably brought by embassies from the East, but there is no precise record.

During the seventeenth century large numbers of carpets in silk pile, mostly with gold and silver thread as well, were made. The patterns show interminable variations of floral stems, palmettes and arabesques, with occasional additions of cloud-bands. A common form of border is the counterchange cresting. There is often a liberal range of colour, with pale, pure tones predominating. Pinks and pale greens are favourites, with deep blue sometimes to give emphasis. Undoubtedly the silk carpets have faded more than the woollen ones, but the contrasts aimed at seem to be rather that between metal and colour than between one colour and another.

An example of the best kind, the property of the royal house of Saxony, is reproduced in Plate 24.[3] The ground of the middle is gold, and of the border silver. The colours are mostly pale in tone ; the dark parts conspicuous in the reproduction are deep blue. The Duke of Buccleuch possesses a very similar carpet.

[1] There is an excellent coloured illustration in Martin, O.C., Pl. 5 (half-tone reproduction of the whole, Pl. 4). The crimson is a little deeper than there shown, and the border paler. The carpet is large, measuring rather more than 18 feet long by 9 ft. 4 in. wide. It is very finely knotted ; Martin computes that there are 20 million knots.

[2] Reproduced in Martin, O.C., Pls. 7, 8. The attribution to Persia of the four embroidered carpets in silk and gold thread at Rosenborg Castle, also illustrated by Martin (Plates 11–14) and considered by him to have been brought from Persia with the Coronation carpet, hardly carries conviction. The Chinese motives are too true to type, and the Persian motives look like the work of an imitator. Their appearance strongly suggests an Indo-Chinese origin.

[3] Reproduced in colours in Vienna, O.C., Pl. 46.

There is a good example, though incomplete, in the Salting Collection at South Kensington,[1] with floral and palmette ornament, and an interlaced border, on gold and silver grounds.   This carpet bears some resemblance to one of those in the Treasury of St. Mark's, Venice.   Other specimens are to be found in the principal museums of Europe and America, and in the possession of wealthy collectors.   Though very sumptuous, they are not altogether satisfactory as carpets.   They are unsuitable for placing on the floor, and the effect of richness is overdone.   Although it is now generally agreed that they were not made in Poland, there is still some mystery about their place of origin.   They are not always entirely true to the Persian tradition of carpet-design.   There can be no doubt, however, that some were made in Persia.   Perhaps, when more is known about carpet-making in India, evidence may be forthcoming that the manufacture was taken there from Persia.   Wherever the weaving was done, it does not seem to have been carried on very long.   This sumptuous manufacture appears to have died out before the end of the century which saw its rise.   A carpet in silk only, without metal threads, belonging to the Gobelins Museum is reproduced in Plate 25.   The central quatrefoil is green and the spandrels white.   The rest of the middle space is red.   The wide border is yellow, with a red outer and blue inner band.

Before returning to the later woollen carpets of Persia, reference may be made to another type, woven in the same materials as those just described, but by the tapestry process.   The thin and delicate texture may perhaps account for the small number now known to exist—hardly more than a dozen altogether.

Carpets of this class, in silk, gold and silver, are occasionally enlivened with human or animal forms.   A fine example, with animals attacking one another, besides grotesque Chinese dragons and phœnixes, is in the Royal Bavarian Collection at Munich.[2]

The colours used are the same as those of the silk pile-carpets, but the different texture produces a much harder effect, more like mosaic-work.

The best known example, and one of the most interesting, is in the Louvre (Plate 26).   A pointed oval in the middle contains a representa-

---

[1] Reproduced in colours in Vienna, *O.C.*, Pl. 96.   The statement, published at the time of its exhibition at Vienna in 1891, that heraldry was represented upon it was incorrect ; it is still repeated.

[2] Munich, *Meisterwerke*, Pl. 55.

tion of a horseman fighting a monstrous serpent—evidently meant for the Persian national hero Rustam, on his horse Reksh, encountering the serpent while on his way to deliver the King Ky-Kâoos from captivity in Mazanderan. The story, taken from the Shah-Namah, the national epic of Persia, may be given in the words of Sir John Malcolm. " In the middle of the night a monstrous serpent, seventy yards in length, came out of its hiding-place, and made at the hero, who was awakened by the neighing of Reksh ; but the serpent had crept back to its hiding-place, and Roostem, seeing no danger, abused his faithful horse for disturbing his repose. Another attempt of the serpent was defeated in the same way ; but the monster had again concealed himself. Roostem lost all patience with Reksh, whom he threatened to put to death if he again awakened him by any such unseasonable noises. The faithful steed, fearing his master's rage, but strong in his attachment, instead of neighing when the serpent again made his appearance, sprung upon it and commenced a furious contest ! Roostem, hearing the noise, started up and joined in the combat. The serpent darted at him, but he avoided it, and, while his noble horse seized their enemy by the back, the hero cut off its head with his sword." [1] The spandrels contain illustrations of the old Arabian love-story of Lailā and Majnun—the scene where Lailā visits the poor poet in the desert. [2]

Three carpets of this kind were lent by the King of Bavaria to the Exhibition of Muhammadan Art at Munich in 1910. One of them has in the middle a shield-of-arms, misunderstood by the weaver, but supposed to be intended for those of a Polish princess married in 1642 at Warsaw. [3] Another shows the usual hunting scene—men on horseback and on foot attacking wild animals. Garden scenes fill the spandrels, with figures by a stream. In the border winged attendants are playing music or offering fruit to a winged prince seated on a throne, and the middle panel contains other winged figures. The third carpet has a conventional floral pattern. An example with a pattern of arabesques, floral stems and cloud-bands is in the collection of the King of Saxony. [4]

In the later woollen carpets of Persia the floral types survive almost alone. Subjects with figures and animals are not common, and when they again achieve popularity during the course of the nineteenth century,

[1] *Sketches of Persia*, 1828, ch. xii.
[2] Another representation of this story, on a carpet in the Musée des Arts Décoratifs, Paris, has already been mentioned (p. 28).
[3] *Meisterwerke*, Munich, Pl. 60. See also Pls. 61, 62.
[4] Vienna, *O.C.*, Pl. 30.

the effects aimed at are more naturalistic if less happy. The varieties of floral patterns are almost endless. While some tend towards the direct imitation of natural life,[1] others show a more or less formal arrangement of palmettes and stems covering the whole ground. A fragment of a carpet reproduced in Plate 27A, made in the seventeenth century, is of the latter class. It shows the usual red colour of the central panel and the dark blue border. A more elaborate example, probably made early in the seventeenth century, is in the Kunstgewerbe Museum at Leipzig (Plate 28). A further stage in the formalizing of the pattern is shown in Plate 29. At last it breaks up into a kind of colour-mosaic, often effective enough, but no longer to be regarded as an organic and intelligible design (Plate 27B).

The later stages of another Persian type, already spoken of as associated with Armenia, may be traced in Plate 20A, where the long leaf-forms covered with floral motives dominate the whole pattern ; and in Plates 132A and 134, where old motives may still be traced. The double prayer-carpet reproduced in Plate 30B belongs to a class of which few examples are known. Knotted prayer-carpets are unusual in Persia, such articles being mostly made of cotton, either embroidered or printed.

The type of pattern in which the design is composed entirely of palmettes and floral stems, sometimes with the addition of cloud-bands (Plates 27 and 28), is one of the best known of all. It is ascribed to the province of Herat, now united to Afghanistan, though under Persian rule during the flourishing days of carpet-weaving. Early in the seventeenth century the province had the reputation of making the best carpets in Persia (see p. 39). The capital city, Herat, was the chief centre of the manufacture. The industry flourished there until the desolation of the province by Nadir Shah in 1731, when many weavers were transported to the western provinces. Although Herat never recovered, carpet-weaving did not entirely cease, and it is still carried on there at the present time. There is evidence that such carpets reached England early in the seventeenth century. King James I is seen standing on one of them in a State portrait, attributed to Vansomer, at Hampton Court. They are also represented in pictures of the Netherlands and Spain in the seventeenth century.

The carpets of Kirman have already been noticed. The French traveller Chardin, who visited Persia in the second half of the seven-

---

[1] Example in the Victoria and Albert Museum, No. 3—1887. Another in Lyons Museum. (R. Cox, *L'Art de décorer les Tissus*, Paris, 1900, Pl. 56.)

teenth century, speaks of the carpets of the provinces of Kirman and Seistan.

Carpets were also made at Ispahan, though apparently not in great numbers. There is little justification, as a rule, for the frequent attribution of old carpets to this former capital of Persia. Other well-known centres of carpet-weaving in Persia have been mentioned in the preceding pages. There is much uncertainty in regard to the locality of manufacture of old Persian carpets, and attributions should be accepted with reserve. It is seldom that they bear the hall-marks of their origin in the unequivocal way of the " Ardabil " carpet.

In this connexion a carpet belonging to Mr. G. Mounsey merits attention (Plate 30A). The inscription has been interpreted by Sir Thomas Arnold as meaning " Jaushaqān work 117 "—apparently locating the carpet as Jushagan work of the year 1170 of the Muhammadan Hegira (=A.D. 1757). The pattern is in red and white. The three elaborated fleurs-de-lys betray European influence—perhaps Florentine rather than French. It is in all respects a singular carpet.

CHAPTER III

INDIA

Abūl Fazl, the devoted admirer and servant of the great Mogul Emperor of India, Akbar (1556–1605), and the author of the *Institutes of Akbar*, in which the events of his reign are set down, writes as follows :—

" His Majesty has caused carpets to be made of wonderful varieties and charming textures ; he has appointed experienced workmen, who have produced many master-pieces. The carpets of Iran and Turan are no more thought of, although merchants still import carpets from Góskhán, Khúzistán, Kirmán and Sabzwár. All kinds of carpet-weavers have settled here, and drive a flourishing trade. These are found in every town, but especially in Ágrah, Fathpúr and Láhór." [1]

In this account we have the record of the real beginning of carpet-knotting in India. It is not difficult to suggest a reason why India was late in the field. Pile-carpets were devised to meet the needs of colder climates than that of India, and in such climates suitable wool for making them can be more easily grown. Before Akbar's time the floor-coverings in India would have been for the most part the cotton daris or tapestry-mats such as are still made and used. The implication in Abūl Fazl's chronicle that before Akbar's reign Persia and Turkestan (" Iran and Turan ") provided such pile-carpets as were required to satisfy the demands of wealth and luxury is confirmed from other sources. Even when the new Indian factories were started, their output did not meet all needs. Persia still continued to send supplies. Abūl Fazl says they came from Jushagan (near Ispahan), Khuzistan (S.W. Persia), Kirman (S.E. Persia) and Sabzwar (in Khorassan, N.E. Persia), places where carpets have continued to be woven down to the present day.

On the other hand, there was a small export trade in Indian carpets which began, if not in the reign of Akbar himself, at any rate in that of his successor. In the latter half of the seventeenth century the number sent out of the country must have been considerable.

---

[1] The *Ain i Akbari* by Abul Fazl 'Allahmi, translated by H. Blochmann, Calcutta, 1873, Vol. I, p. 55. He goes on to give particulars of prices and sizes in the Imperial Workshops. The writer was born in 1551, and died in 1602.

HAND-WOVEN CARPETS

In spite of the labours of such competent authorities as Colonel Hendley, Vincent Robinson, Sir C. Purdon Clarke [1] and others, the subject of Indian carpets still offers a field for study and investigation. Besides the valuable, but somewhat equivocal, witness of Akbar's chronicler, there is the account of Sir Thomas Roe, the first English ambassador to the Mogul Court, who arrived in India in 1612, when Akbar's successor Jahangir was on the throne. He states that he saw Persian carpets spread before the Emperor on the festival of the New Year, and he records a promise of Jahangir to send Persian carpets to England. That the ambassador took pains to discriminate between Persian and Indian carpets may be doubted. [2]

So far as actually existing specimens of the seventeenth century are concerned we have chiefly those in the palace of the Maharaja at Jaipur, so fully described by Col. Hendley; a few similar carpets noted as being in mosques at Berhampur and Bijapur, besides some at Ahmedabad; the Girdlers' Company's carpet; the "Fremlin" carpet; and a number of others scattered about the world which are ascribed, on one plea or another, to the factories started by Akbar.

The most characteristic of the carpets at Jaipur seem to be certainly Indian, though not of Akbar's time. The design of these represents rows of flowering plants each delineated separately and entire to the roots as if planted in a garden, or else set in the interstices of a trellis as though climbing. They were brought to the Treasury at Jaipur from the old Palace at Amber near by, about the year 1875. Col. Hendley, who examined the old tickets upon them, points out that some are described as Lahore carpets, and that the dates, where given, are not earlier than the middle of the seventeenth century, though it is not clear whether such dates are those of manufacture or of the inventories. The shapes of some are unusual. One is circular and others have a polygonal inset contour on one side. These have been ascertained to have been specially made for an apartment of the palace at Amber built in 1630. In view of this evidence, it seems quite safe to assign the carpets of this class at Jaipur

---

[1] Colonel T. H. Hendley, C.I.E., *Asian Carpets : Sixteenth and Seventeenth Century Designs from the Jaipur Palaces*, London, 1905. V. Robinson, *Eastern Carpets*, London, 1882. *Oriental Carpets*, Vienna, 1892–4. F. R. Martin, *Oriental Carpets*, Vienna, 1908.

[2] The language of these days took little heed of geographical precision in matters of the kind. The minutes of the Girdlers' Company, of 1634, describes the carpet then given to them by Sir Robert Bell as a Turkey carpet, though it was known to have come from India. Later in the century, the terms Chinese, Japanese and Indian are applied almost indiscriminately to artistic imports from the East.

to the Indian looms in the seventeenth century. Two of the carpets from Jaipur, with flowers on a red ground, have recently been brought to England. They are reproduced on Plate 31. The further claim which has been put forward that all existing carpets showing such patterns are Indian seems more open to question.[1] If that be so, then very troublesome points must arise in regard to velvets, brocades and other works of art with plant designs treated in the same way. In fact, these motives were long popular with Persian craftsmen. They may even have been carried into India by the Persian weavers who, as all authorities agree, worked in Akbar's factories.

A fine carpet showing plant-forms similar to those on the carpets from Amber, and done in similar colours, is in the Salting Collection, Victoria and Albert Museum (Plate 32). It will be seen that the plants are each in a separate compartment. This example is incomplete. Another in the Düsseldorf Museum is probably part of the same carpet. It has a broad border of floral forms resembling the middle pattern.

Another class of carpets in the Jaipur treasury shows palmettes and floral stems disposed in a somewhat formal manner on a red ground, with a wide border of palmettes and leaves on dark blue or green. Sometimes there are hunting-animals in the middle field, and occasionally Chinese phœnixes and dragons. Such designs are obviously modifications of the finer and freer patterns of Persia in the sixteenth century. The scheme of colouring often has a quality of its own in warmth and depth; but are we to say that these phenomena were peculiar to India? Until a score of years ago, these carpets were all attributed to Herat, and the attribution to that celebrated centre of Persian carpet-weaving must still be allowed to have been often correct.

Olearius, who went to Persia with the embassy of the Duke of Holstein-Gottorp about 1639, says that in the city of Herat the most handsome carpets of Persia were then made.[2] At the same time, it is a plausible theory that if any of the carpets actually made under Akbar exist today, some of this class are among them. Herat was favourably situated for transporting either its carpet-weavers or their products to Akbar's Court.

The most completely authenticated of all Indian carpets has already been briefly referred to—that in the possession of the Girdlers' Company

[1] F. R. Martin, *Oriental Carpets*, p. 89.
[2] Adami Olearii, *Reisebeschreibung nach Muskow und Persien*, Hamburg, 1696. **Quoted by** F. R. Martin, *O.C.*, p. 69.

of London (Plate 33). The elucidation of the history of this carpet a few years ago threw a new light on the problem of Indian carpet-weaving. It measures about 8 yards in length by 2½ yards in width. The coat-of-arms and motto of the Company are represented in the middle. At each end is a shield azure, an eagle displayed argent, in chief three fleurs-de-lys or. Between each of these and the central coat is seen a bale of goods with the monogram R.B. and a merchant's mark. The researches in the books of the Company and in the records of the India Office recovered all material facts. The arms at the ends were identified as those borne by Robert Bell, master of the Girdlers' Company in 1634, and a director of the East India Company. The records of the India Office showed that the carpet was made for him in the royal factory at Lahore, and those of the Company recorded the gift by him in the same year.[1] The middle of the carpet is red, the wide border being in dark blue. The identification of the Girdlers' carpet helped towards that of another carpet which left England for America some years ago. A coloured illustration in Vincent Robinson's *Eastern Carpets* preserves a record of the design (Plate 34). The middle has a pattern somewhat like that of the Girdlers' carpet, but with the addition of hunting animals among the stems. The wide border is blue, with the arms of the Kentish family of Fremlin at intervals with palmettes and stems between.[2] The points of resemblance between this carpet and the Girdlers' prompted a reference to the published literature of the East India Company, where the name was found to occur several times. The conclusion that a member of this family arranged for the carpet to be made in India through the agents of the company seems fairly safe.

There is little else but conjecture to aid in carrying farther forward the record of the factories in India founded under Akbar. An interesting fragment in the collection of Dr. Friedrich Sarre of Berlin is shown to be Indian by the pattern of two fighting elephants ridden by their mahouts.[3] Two other fragments—one in the possession of Dr. Roden of Frankfurt, and the other formerly in the collection of M. Jeuniette, and now in the

[1] Information collected and published by the Company. See also *Art Workers' Quarterly*, Vol. III, July, 1904, p. 97 ; T. H. Hendley, *Asian Carpets*, 1905, p. 8.

[2] Or Framlingham, of Hartlip, Kent. Gules, a chevron between three close helmets argent plumed or. Crest, an elephant or, armed gules, gorged with a chaplet vert. The arms were identified by Mr. Van de Put, and first published in *The Times* special Textile number, June, 1913. In V. Robinson's book (London, 1882, Pl. 9) the carpet is attributed to the weavers of Alcaraz in Spain.

[3] Illustrated by Martin, *O.C.*, Fig. 235. His attribution of the carpet to the sixteenth century seems rather too early.

Louvre, have fantastic patterns of heads of elephants, lions, oxen and horses with diminutive serpentine bodies, and floral sprays interspersed. They are probably of the seventeenth century, contemporary with Dr. Sarre's piece. A singular carpet in the Museum of Fine Arts at Boston in America has, in a medley of motives, a hunting-cheetah driven to the chase on a bullock wagon covered with a brightly-coloured textile, to which it is chained.[1] This recalls Abūl Faẓl's account of Akbar's hunting expeditions, where he says that the hunting leopards got Jushagan carpets to sit on, and even had carts made for them.[2] The French traveller François Bernier, who visited India in 1656–68, refers to the practice of keeping the hunting-leopards chained on a small car.

The importation of carpets into England through the East India Company appears to have been considerable in the seventeenth century. Great families, notably that of the Duke of Buccleuch, whose ancestor the Duke of Montagu was a director of the Company, still possess fine specimens. They are mostly of the " palmette " or " Herati " type. Whether any were brought into India from Persia it is difficult to say, but it is to be remembered that the Company traded in Persian goods, thus supplanting the more difficult route of communication with Persia established by the English Mucovy Company by way of Archangel in the reign of Queen Elizabeth.

The weaving of pile-carpets in India appears never to have quite ceased from the time of Akbar onwards.

The types of the nineteenth century are varied. On the one hand there are the sumptuous silk carpets of Warangul, with floral patterns, made about the middle of the century ; on the other, the exceedingly coarse wool carpets, with animals, birds and floral forms, of Tanjore and Malabar. A carpet made at Tanjore in the Madras Presidency is illustrated in Plate 35. Its principal interest lies in the fact that the design is typically Indian in character, without Persian influence. The compartments enclosing the floral sprays are red, buff and pale blue. The border is white. The knotting is coarse and the colours are dull.

Soon after the middle of the century, carpet-knotting was begun in the jails, with the object of providing useful and remunerative employment for those detained there. This object was to some degree attained. The scheme had another aspect—whether it tended to raise or depress the standard of the industry in India. That question need

[1] Martin, *O.C.*, Fig. 234.
[2] Blochmann, *Ain i Akbari*, I, p. 287.

not be discussed here. Most of the " jail-carpets " were copied from old patterns.

The cotton pile-carpets made in several districts of India in the latter half of the last century are, it is to be hoped, unique.

CHAPTER IV

TURKEY

Beyond all question the best carpets in the world are the Persian, whether the point of view taken be that of design, colour, or craftsmanship. Little imagination is needed to appreciate the skill demanded of the weaver in keeping a great carpet like that from Ardabil straight and even in the making, and to give it a texture which should outlast five hundred years of use. Such mastery of the technicalities of the craft is often combined, as in that carpet, with resourcefulness in design and true genius for colour. Every other carpet-weaving country has felt the influence of Persia. In Asia Minor that influence prevailed to such a degree that it almost becomes a question whether the best carpets made there should properly be called Turkish.

This designation is not altogether satisfactory for the art of Asia Minor, but there is no better comprehensive term. Traces of the native Turkish art of their old home in Central Asia are rare, although they are sometimes to be found in nomad carpets. The art was the outcome of a more advanced civilization. In the course of history, successive waves of humanity have been pressed into the narrow limits of Asia Minor after a fashion which may be compared, in another element, with those bays into which the waters of the ocean rush from time to time in a tidal wave. An enumeration of the races represented in Asia Minor includes Turks, Greeks, Jews, Persians, Turcomans, Tartars, Yuruks, Circassians, Armenians, Nestorians, Syrians, Kurds, Cossacks, Bulgarians, Arabs and gypsies. Not all these people are carpet-weavers, but several of them are. The pressure of the Mongolian horsemen which set the Seljûks moving westward, and after them the Ottoman Turks, drove Persian craftsmen and poets to seek the same asylum, and the latter brought with them a proficiency in the arts of which the Turks were not slow to take advantage. In 1514 the conquest of Tabriz was effected by the Turkish Sultan Selim I, and that city was again entered by his successor Suleiman I twenty years later. Craftsmen were carried away into Asia Minor by the conquerors. Some, indeed, have attributed the brilliant height attained by Turkish art in the sixteenth century to that event.

The Turk was a Sunni—an orthodox and literal observer of the precepts in the sacred writings. He could not therefore permit the representation of figures of men and animals, which the sectarian Persian allowed. But for this, the most accomplished of the carpets of Asia Minor might be regarded as an offshoot of Persian art. The mixture of races in Asia Minor finds expression in a variety of types often having little relation one to another. The "Turkey" carpets used in Western Europe during the last five centuries are the work of the uplands of Anatolia behind the port of Smyrna, whence so many were shipped. For a long time these were practically the only pile-carpets brought to Europe. The relative inaccessibility of Persia, and the almost insuperable difficulties of transport rendered the Persian carpets practically unknown until the seventeenth century, and even after they began to be imported they were called "Turkey" carpets like the rest.

The seafaring communities of Italy had trading settlements dotted along the coast of Asia Minor as early as the thirteenth century. With the abandonment of these posts under pressure from the Ottoman Turk during the course of the fifteenth century, commercial activity was not put an end to. A lively trade still went on between the Venetians and the Turks. The Italian traders also had their agents in the countries of Western Europe, and by such means the carpets were obtained which are seen represented in early pictures. The carpets of Asia Minor first became known in the West in the fourteenth century, and in the two following centuries they were imported in large numbers. Their strange exotic beauty rendered them popular at once with the painters, who obviously copied them with much fidelity. These pictorial representations of the fourteenth, fifteenth and sixteenth centuries have greatly simplified the task of classification.

The first essay on this subject was contributed by Dr. Julius Lessing of Berlin. His book,[1] published at Berlin in 1877, reproduces a series of illustrations in colour from carpets represented in paintings by, or attributed to, Jan van Eyck, Memlinc, Van der Goes, Mabuse, Holbein, Ghirlandajo, Pinturicchio, Montagna, Moroni, Girolamo dai Libri and others.

Most later writers on Oriental carpets have either made use of Lessing's work or made further comparisons for themselves. The subject requires

[1] *Alt Orientalische Teppichmuster nach Bildern . . . des XV–XVI Jahrhundert.*

careful handling, for Oriental motives often have a long life, and similarities between representations in old pictures and actual carpets obviously of far more modern times are occasionally quite startling. Even these cases afford useful evidence, for they tend to confirm the conclusions made on various grounds that the old painters were remarkably true to their models, and that the origin of designs still in use must be traced to a remote past. An example is afforded among the illustrations in the present volume. The painting at Vienna by Hans Memlinc (Plate 36) shows a carpet with a central pattern almost identical with that of the carpet reproduced on the same plate—yet the picture is of the fifteenth century and the carpet is of the nineteenth.[1] Relatively few carpets of the time of the paintings are now to be seen in the land of their origin, although some of the greater mosques contain important specimens. On the other hand, it is not beyond the bounds of probability that a few carpets depicted by the European artists mentioned above are actually in existence to-day. Considerable numbers found their way into the churches of Italy, where infrequent use has guarded them from destruction. Many have been sold during the last forty years, and are now to be found in the museums and private collections of Europe and America.

The earliest Turkish carpets we know of are in the mosque of Ala-ed-Dîn at Konia (the ancient Iconium). That city was the capital of the Seljûk Sultans of Rûm, and Dr. Martin, who was the first to detect their significance, attributes the carpets to the reign of the sultan whose name the mosque bears (A.D. 1219–36). The question whether they are as old as that may be debatable, but there need be no hesitation in ascribing them to the times of the old Seljûk line at Konia, before it was superseded in the fifteenth century by the Ottomans, whose capital was far to the west at Brûsa.

There are four carpets, all somewhat dilapidated, and two fragments. The patterns are primitive diapers and interlacings of geometrical form, and two of them have archaic Kufic lettering in the borders. The colours are chiefly shades of blue and red, and yellow.[2]

---

[1] A very similar carpet is reproduced in a French romance of the fifteenth century at Vienna, *Cœur d'Amour épris*, Cod. 2597. (See *Kunst und Kunsthandwerk*, V, 1902, p. 307.)

[2] Martin, *O.C.*, Pl. 30.
Their resemblance to the heraldic carpets made in Spain in the fifteenth century is quite striking (see p. 68). It seems likely that some of the motives of the Spanish carpets were borrowed from the successors of these Konia carpets in Asia Minor which have since disappeared entirely. See also article by F. Sarre in *Kunst und Kunsthandwerk*, Vol. X, 1907, p. 503.

A carpet preserving a tradition no less remote is here illustrated (Plate 37A). In its present incomplete state it shows two octagonal compartments, each filled by an angular and disguised, though unmistakable, rendering of a Chinese dragon and phœnix in red and blue on a yellow ground. The pattern is obviously archaic, and the difficulty of assigning a date to the carpet itself is considerable. Dr. von Bode, who obtained this carpet many years ago in Rome, has pointed out the remarkable similarity to the pattern of a carpet represented in Domenico di Bartolo's fresco of the " Marriage of the Foundlings," painted between the years 1440 and 1444 in the Hospital of Sta Maria della Scala at Siena. Animal forms, even thus disguised, are rare in Turkish carpets. Restrictions in regard to such representations were not so rigidly observed under the Seljûks as under the later Ottomans, and it is probable that the tradition of this carpet goes back to Seljûk times. There is no difficulty in accounting for such Chinese motives. They found their way to Asia Minor in the first instance through the Mongolian conquests, but they were reinforced afterwards by the immigrant Persian craftsmen. However early in origin the patterns may be, few existing carpets from Asia Minor were actually made before the sixteenth century. The finest in texture and the most intricate in design of all Turkish carpets were made during that time. Like some of the contemporary woollen pile-carpets of Persia, they are generally woven on silk warps to secure a closer texture, although at times a fine woollen warp is used. They show such uniformity in design and colouring that it seems almost beyond doubt that all were the work of a single locality. Some of them are of large size. It has been suggested that the factory was an Imperial one, and this seems likely, for the carpets must have been too costly for the general markets.[1] The location is not known ; perhaps it was in the neighbourhood of Brûsa, the Asiatic capital. The best work was done in the sixteenth century, although some examples appear to belong rather to the seventeenth. The patterns are floral and very gracefully drawn, with roses, carnations, tulips, irises and hyacinths, and long curving leaves, rendered in the same manner as on the exquisite painted pottery of the time (see Plate 38). The colouring of the ground is almost always a bright crimson of a characteristic tone, though blue is occasionally used. There is often a central panel and

---

[1] A later Imperial factory was situated at Hereke on the eastern shore of the Sea of Marmora, at a short distance both from Constantinople and Brûsa. A modern Hereke carpet is reproduced in Plate 97.

spandrels in dark or light blue, green, yellow or white, or border-panels in the same colours. Floral ornament, contrasted with the rest of the design by its formal character, and arabesques generally fill these panels. A carpet, unfortunately not complete, in the Victoria and Albert Museum (Plate 39) has the crimson ground with a typical pattern.

Another carpet which falls within the same group is illustrated in Plate 40. The distribution of the floral stems here shown is unusual for a carpet, although parallels may be found in the painted tilework. The ground is again red. The salience of the small white flowers is due to the use of cotton instead of wool for those parts, giving a dead white in place of the softer tones of the wool.

Several examples are illustrated in colours in the great Austrian book. Two are in the Museum of Art and Industry at Vienna, one in the museum at Leipzig, and a fourth in the Musée des Arts Décoratifs in Paris.[1] Another in the last-named collection is on a blue ground, which is very exceptional.[2]

A few prayer-carpets of this class are known. One, in the Austrian Imperial Collection, was shown at Vienna in 1891, and again at Munich in 1910. Two more were shown in the latter exhibition. The first belongs to the Kunstgewerbe Museum, Berlin, and the second to Prince Liechtenstein.[3] It is a point which may not be entirely without significance that two of these prayer-carpets have borders from which those most frequently seen on the later prayer-carpets of Ghiordes (see Plate 53) are obviously derived. Thus the possibility of an origin in the same locality is suggested.

A different type of carpet is illustrated in Plate 41. These contrast so forcibly with the kind just described that it seems almost beyond belief that both should have been made in the same part of the world at the same time. The knotting is coarser and of another kind; the colouring is simpler and quite different in tone. The designs are stiff and formal where the others are free and natural, and the motives are geometrical rather than floral.[4] Persian influence is strong in the first group. In

---

[1] Vienna, *O.C.*, Pls. 40, 85, 15 and 68. See also Martin, *O.C.*, Figs. 328–30.

[2] Reproduced in colours in *Ancient Oriental Carpets*, Leipzig, 1906–8, Pl. 25. See also Martin, *O.C.*, Fig. 327.

[3] *Oriental Carpets*, Pl. 14 ; *Meisterwerke*, Munich, Pls. 74, 75 ; Martin, Fig. 331.

[4] Dr. F. Sarre, in an illuminating paper on early Turkish carpets (*Kunst und Kunsthandwerk*, X, 1907, p. 513) suggests that the border of the first example on Plate 41 is a modified Kufic inscription. It appears rather to be a counterchange cresting like Plates 118A and 141.

the latter the type of design is Turkish, and in modified forms its continuity is traceable down to the present day. Large numbers must have been exported to the West. The two in question were both obtained in Italy, and such carpets are not now found in Asia Minor. They are often to be seen in pictures of the Italian, Flemish and German schools in the fifteenth and sixteenth centuries. Ghirlandajo, Memlinc, and Holbein, among others, certainly had access to carpets of the kind.[1] There is almost a suggestion of primitive austerity in these large and uncompromising geometrical forms, and there can be no doubt that they are descended from an early type. Another geometrical type popular with these painters is reproduced on Plate 42, in a carpet belonging to Mr. George Mounsey. The interlaced border associates this carpet also with the well-known rugs showing arabesques in the middle field (see Plate 43B). The carpet illustrated in Plate 37B represents a step towards greater freedom of design. Small shaped panels in dark blue on a red ground are distributed over the surface.

The " Oushak " carpet, the real forerunner of the " Turkey carpet " of to-day, was much in demand in Western Europe in the sixteenth and seventeenth centuries. The name is derived from a town situated in the middle of the carpet-weaving districts of the Anatolian uplands some distance due east of Smyrna. These carpets are generally of convenient size for transport, perhaps 6 ft. wide and twice as long, though far larger examples are sometimes met with. The colours are generally brilliant and pure but not in great variety. A succession of large panels occupies the middle space, either in blue on red or red on blue ; sometimes there are two shades of blue. One well-known form of design is illustrated on Plate 43A. The large star-shaped panels are dark blue and the ground is red. Carpets of this type are to be found in pictures. A well-known example is in a painting by Paris Bordone, in the Academy at Venice, representing the Fisherman restoring the lost ring to the Doge. King Henry VIII stands on another carpet of similar style, in a portrait at Belvoir Castle.[2] Sometimes large pointed-ogee panels are substituted for the star-forms ; they are generally placed close together, with half-

---

[1] A very good example is Holbein's great painting of the " Amabassadors " in the National Gallery, London ; another is seen in a painting by Memlinc in the same gallery. Several patterns of the type are illustrated in J. Lessing's *Alt Orientalische Teppichmuster nach Bildern . . . des XV–XVI Jahrh.*, Berlin, 1877 ; see especially Pls. 1, 19, 26 (Memlinc); 9, 11 (Holbein) ; 13, 14 (Ghirlandajo) ; 21 (Anguissola).

[2] *Connoisseur*, Vol. VI, 1903, p. 67. This shows that such carpets reached England before the middle of the sixteenth century.

panels at the sides. An example in the Victoria and Albert Museum is reproduced (Plate 44).[1]

In the sixteenth and early part of the seventeenth century there was a large output of these "Oushak" carpets. At the same time, smaller rugs with a class of pattern of their own, were carried to Italy in considerable numbers. These, like the Oushak carpets, were probably made principally for export. There are two chief kinds of design—one in which the middle is covered with repeating arabesques (Plate 43B), and the other with a plain middle space relieved only with a small central ornament and spandrels in the corners. The colour of the ground is generally brick-red, sometimes blue. Yellow enters largely into the pattern as a rule, relieved by blue and white. Chinese cloud-bands are not unfrequently used in the borders, repeated at close intervals, and occasionally in the middle. The most usual border is the conventionalized Kufic lettering, generally interlaced. The arabesques are drawn in an angular manner and closely packed to cover the surface. The Kufic border is found so frequently in the Italian, Flemish and German paintings of the fifteenth and sixteenth centuries that there is no need to single out examples. The arabesques, too, are often seen—more especially in the paintings of the Venetian Lorenzo Lotto. The Kufic border continued to be used until the eighteenth and even the nineteenth century with little change (see Plates 63 and 64).

A small carpet in the Victoria and Albert Museum, obtained from a church in Italy, has the same pattern of floral ornament and cloud-bands carried through the middle and the border alike. The ground of the middle is blue, and of the border red.

The demand for these carpets by the Venetians and other seafaring traders calling at Smyrna was considerable. Evidences of concessions to Western taste may be seen not only in the subdued colouring, but also in the general uniformity of shape and size and to some extent in the design. A carpet lent by Frau Limburger to the Munich Exhibition of 1910 had the usual yellow and blue arabesques covering the red ground everywhere except in the top left-hand corner, where there was a shield-of-arms of the Genoese families of Centurione and Doria impaled.[2]

---

[1] Other examples, mostly in private possession, are illustrated in Vienna, *O.C.*, Pl. 17 ; Martin, *O.C.*, Figs. 315, 317–20 ; *Meisterwerke*, Munich, Pls. 70, 71. There is a carpet with the star-shaped panels in the Victoria and Albert Museum (No. 138), and two with ogee-shaped panels (Nos. 135 and 136).

[2] *Meisterwerke*, Munich, Pl. 72. The arms have been identified by Mr. A. Van de Put. Cardinal Wolsey's insistent demand for these carpets is referred to later (p. 76).

HAND-WOVEN CARPETS

The rugs with the space of plain colour in the middle convey more forcibly still the impression of having been made to suit the taste of the European customer. The eye of the Oriental is not so partial to those monotonous spaces, which might have been relieved by a simple pattern with very little extra trouble. We have in these rugs the first signs of an adaptation, as early as the sixteenth century, to the exigencies of the foreign market for which they were destined. In later days those influences were so potent that the survival to the present day of the beautiful craft of carpet-weaving as a native industry is almost to be wondered at. Yet it would be hard to point out any great branch of the artistic handicrafts now practised in the East with better results. It is true that we cannot hope to see carpets made again to rival the great work of the past, any more than we can look for a revival of the conditions under which it was produced. The royal patron, with the resources of the whole kingdom at his command, has given way to the commercial trader. It is due to the latter to say that he has done much to keep the industry alive, but whether modern conditions are favourable to the development of the highest qualities in design and craftsmanship is another matter. At any rate it may be justly claimed that surprisingly beautiful modern carpets may still be bought at a trifling cost.

Other types of carpets made in Asia Minor are contemporary with the small rugs just described. Somewhere about the end of the sixteenth century a white ground was used. The choice of colour may again have been a concession to Western taste. White grounds are occasionally found in old Persian carpets (e.g. Plate 18), but they do not cover the whole carpet, border and all; and where used they are more broken up by close patterns. The colours are chiefly red, blue and yellow. The carpets illustrated on Plates 45 and 46A are of this kind. It will be noticed that the former has the cloud-band repeated at intervals in the border. Various explanations have been given of the nondescript forms in the middle, but they are nothing more than angular renderings of the S-shapes often found in Persian design. The other carpet has in the middle repetitions of the double stripe and the group of three discs below (see Plate 205), which appears so often in the art of Asia Minor in the sixteenth century. The double stripes may have originated either in cloud-forms or in the fur-markings of animals. The three discs appear to have been devised, or at any rate adopted as a badge by the great Mongol conqueror Timur in the latter part of the fourteenth century.

When Ruy Gonzalez de Clavijo, who went with an embassy from

Castile to the Court of Timur at Samarcand in 1403, arrived at the town of Kesh, 36 miles from Samarcand, he was shown a palace which had been many years in building, and was not then finished. Over a doorway he noticed " the figure of a lion and a sun, which are the arms of the lord of Samarcand ; and, though they say that Timour Beg ordered these palaces to be built, I believe that the former lord of Samarcand gave the order ; because the sun and lion, which are here represented, are the arms of the lords of Samarcand ; and those which Timour Beg bears are three circles like O's, drawn in this manner $^{oo}_{o}$, and this is to signify that he is lord of the three parts of the world. He ordered this device to be stamped on the coins, and on everything he had."

Later the ambassador mentions that the judges in the city of Samarcand use " the seal of the lord, having three marks upon it, like this, $^{oo}_{o}$."[1]

Timur penetrated into Asia Minor, but it is not necessary to connect the appearance of his device there with his invasion. The use of the three discs was rendered so widespread by his orders that in course of time they must have become merely a trite motive of ornamentation.

Another kind of pattern, an arrangement of interlacings in star-form, generally surrounded by diminutive trees and floral stems, placed in radiating fashion, sometimes covers the middle of the carpet. These carpets seem to form a link between those of the mosque at Konia and the Anatolian examples described above. There is something in them which suggests North Africa or even an approximation to the carpets of Spain, but they may be Asia Minor work of the fifteenth to the seventeenth centuries (Plate 47). A more intricate design, with similar tendencies, is of equally uncertain origin (Plate 48). Three specimens of a class of carpets not unfrequently seen, both in actual examples and in pictures, are reproduced in this volume (Plates 49–51). Carpets of this group are singularly uniform in design. There can be little doubt that they were made in a single district of Asia Minor, though it is not known where. They have acquired the name of Transylvanian carpets from the accidental circumstance that considerable numbers have been found in that province, which lies at the south-eastern corner of the old Austro-Hungarian lands, separated by the Carpathian Mountains

---

[1] *Narrative of the Embassy of Ruy Gonzalez de Clavijo to the Court of Timour, at Samarcand*, A.D. 1403–6. Translated by Clements R. Markham (London, Hakluyt Society, 1859, pp. 124, 175). Dr. F. R. Martin first drew attention to this passage in connexion with the appearance of the device on works of art.

from Roumania. While the latter country remained annexed to the Turkish Empire these carpets were imported by way of Kronstadt, thus making Transylvania a centre for their distribution farther afield.[1] The earlier type is represented by Plate 49. This carpet resembles closely a specimen in the Victoria and Albert Museum; the chief difference is that the spandrels of the latter carpet are filled with a kind of arabesque design instead of the floral motives, indicating an earlier date. Examples must have reached the Low Countries by the seventeenth century, for they are to be found faithfully reproduced in pictures. There is a good example in the London National Gallery, a painting of two men in a room (called " A Merchant and His Clerk "), by Thomas de Keyser.[2]

The colouring of the earlier specimens is subdued and varied, the central field being usually of a deep purple tone, and the border panels in four or five different colours. The relatively numerous examples extant afford a very good opportunity of tracing first their Persian derivation, then the gradual appearance of Turkish colouring and motives, and finally the complete subordination of the original design. For this reason it is proposed to discuss these examples more fully. If the four spandrels of the carpet reproduced in Plate 49 had been united into a star, they would have formed quite a good central pattern, and this treatment of the spandrels is more Persian than Anatolian in origin. The method of treatment of the central field and of the spandrels, however, shows a tendency to geometrical conventionalization which is aided by the coarse knotting employed in this type of carpet. It will be seen that the middle space is occupied by two vases placed in the niches formed by the spandrels and still provided with the chains which betray their derivation from hanging lamps. The shape and filling of the narrow border panels show quite clearly their relation to the well-known Persian border pattern in which arabesques surround a flower. Specimens of more recent date do not have the small star-panels in the border and the narrow panels are immediately adjacent to each other. Later on the central vase-pattern with the conventionalized floral stems disappears. In its place we sometimes find a central ornament of a totally un-Persian character, surrounded with flowers (Plate 50). In the spandrels appears a geometric pattern which can scarcely be recognized as consisting of

[1] Several examples in the Victoria and Albert Museum actually came from Transylvania about forty years ago. Dr. Martin states that the Transylvanians retained a percentage of the carpets passing through, as a tax (*O.C.*, p. 130).

[2] Lessing reproduces the border of another in a portrait by Cornelis de Vos at the Brussels Museum (*Alt Or. Teppichmuster*, Pl. 29).

flowers or leaves. After a lapse of only a few years the flowers in the narrower panels of the border lose their natural character, while the arabesques become stiffened almost beyond recognition. In order to leave no doubt that these carpets come from Anatolia, we find sometimes those conventionalized carnations springing from the spandrels and reaching into the central panel which are so common in the Anatolian prayer-carpets.

The last carpet of this type here illustrated (Plate 51) shows these motives. The central panel reveals its connexion with its predecessors (Plates 49, 50), and there are other traces of good tradition—but there is hardly anything in this carpet to remind us of its original Persian ancestry.

Prayer-rugs have already been briefly referred to. They were nowhere so popular as in Asia Minor.

Every Muhammadan has to perform five ablutions daily, which are followed by five prayers. Just as specially shaped vessels have to be used for these ablutions, so have all particulars for the prayers been laid down. The prayer-rug in the mosque is placed immediately in front of the prayer-niche (Qiblah), which indicates the direction of Mecca, towards which the faithful have to pray. For this reason the carpet has a special design, which in itself is reminiscent of the niche, so that the apex may be pointed towards Mecca. The true believer has to step on to the farther end in order that, after bowing towards the angels on the right and on the left, who record his good and his evil deeds respectively, and murmuring several prayers, he may kneel down and, while resting upon his hands, touch the earth, that is to say the carpet, with his head.

The type from which the Anatolian prayer-carpets are derived is a niche supported by one or two columns at each side, and provided with a lamp of vase-form hanging from the apex, and perhaps having two pricket-candlesticks below.[1] Several of these constituent parts have undergone radical change at the hands of the carpet designer, no doubt due to successive copying through the centuries. If the earliest prayer-carpets had come down to our times the original type would have been shown more clearly. The niche is the most constant feature. The lamp becomes a hanging vase of flowers with the chains still seen, though the vase is inverted (see Plate 49). Sometimes a spray of flowers hangs

[1] See an early carved wood panel belonging to M. Gillot, in *Exposition des Arts Musulmans*, by G. Migeon, Paris, 1903, Pl. I.

alone (Plates 53 and 54). Quite often the lamp is replaced by an inverted ewer with handle and spout, generally containing flowers (Plate 98).[1] Occasionally it is transformed into a nondescript ornament (Plate 102), and in a few instances a central panel is connected by a line with the head of the niche, as though it too were derived from the hanging lamp. The supporting columns remain as a rule in some form or another (Plate 55). At times they become ornamental stripes sprouting into floral forms at top and bottom (Plate 54); or the niche head may even be provided with the unsubstantial support of a mere succession of floral forms (Plate 53). Floral sprays or stripes may also represent the pricket-candlesticks, which are not found in an intelligible guise on existing carpets.

The three best-known types of these prayer-carpets have been associated with the localities of Ghiordes (Gordium?), Kula and Ladik (Laodicea), but this classification (for it cannot safely be regarded as a precise statement of geographical fact) takes no account of some important specimens of which the carpet reproduced in Plate 52 is an excellent example. Here the spandrels are a deep red, and the niche itself a very dark blue, but the colour reverts to red again below the large pale blue cloud-band which in form almost repeats the niche-head, though this is perhaps accidental.[2] The carpet is Anatolian. In some respects it resembles the small rugs imported into Italy in the fifteenth and sixteenth centuries (see p. 44). It has been attributed to the end of the fifteenth century by Bode, and to the middle of the sixteenth by Martin. Much depends on whether the exaggerated angularity of the pattern is a sign of primitive origin, or whether the impression that it may be a good design breaking up, is altogether without foundation. The carpet is a fine one, but the possibility of an origin in the seventeenth century cannot safely be overlooked. The three classes of prayer-carpets referred to above are mostly of the eighteenth and nineteenth centuries, though a few examples are as early as the seventeenth. The most familiar type of Ghiordes prayer-carpet is illustrated in Plate 98.

It shows a well-known border with palmettes and rosettes and numerous little stripes of conventional ornament. The extra stripes

---

[1] A Ghiordes prayer-carpet belonging to the Duke of Buccleuch has in the niche a lamp, with foliations springing from it, suspended by chains, and beneath that an inverted ewer containing carnations. A Turkish prayer-carpet is usually woven upside down; this may account for the inversion.

[2] There is an excellent coloured illustration in Vienna, *O.C.*, Pl. 3. See also W. von Bode, *Vorderasiatische Knüpfteppiche*, coloured frontispiece to 2nd edition.

above the niche will also be noticed. The hanging lamp has become an inverted ewer. A simpler and more unusual form of Ghiordes prayer-carpet is shown on Plate 54. The carpet reproduced in colour on Plate 53 is again more elaborate. It is one of a few examples woven with inscriptions. That in the two panels above the niche is as follows : " My lord, my august Padishah—may you be joyful and happy unto the days of the last judgement." This inscription shows that the carpet in question may have been intended as a present for a sultan or some other dignitary. There is also an inscription within the niche, as follows : " I come before thy throne heavily laden with sin and pray that my sins and guilt may be forgiven me." [1] It is in Turkish but contains a few Persian words, a circumstance which has no bearing, however, on the theory held by some that these carpets were actually made by Persian workmen in Anatolia, because a number of Persian words, especially religious terms, are used by the Turks.

An inscription in the open space of the prayer-niche is rare. The suggestion of lion-masks in each alternate palmette of the border (to be seen also on Plate 98) may be accidental. On the other hand, it will be recalled that masks of lions are often found in the palmettes of Persian carpets of the sixteenth and seventeenth centuries, or even attached independently to the stems. [2] The same border is seen in the curious prayer-carpet illustrated on Plate 56, although in that example the palmettes are obviously quite floral in character. The elongated form of the niche-head is unusual. This carpet must be classed with the Ghiordes group. It belongs to Mr. George Mounsey. The hyacinth sprigs within the niche may be compared with those on Mr. Mounsey's small mat illustrated on Plate 46B. The mat is knotted in wools like a carpet, although the design is evidently taken from the well-known silk-velvet divan covers of Asia Minor.

The Kula prayer-carpets are generally inferior to those of Ghiordes. The knotting as a rule is not so fine, the design shows a tendency towards monotonous diapers, and the colour is paler and less pleasing, with a predominance of yellow. The blue niche with the strings of blossoms shown on Plate 100 is common in Kula carpets. The wide border is filled with rows of carnation blossoms. It is more usual for the border to be broken up into many narrow stripes ; more than a dozen may be

[1] Translated by Professor Dr. von Kaelitz.
[2] See Pls. 1, 10, 14 and 22. Two Ghiordes prayer-carpets are reproduced in colours in Vienna, *O.C.*, Pls. 57, 60.

counted in some instances. The carpet illustrated on Plate 101 has eleven, and it is classified as a Kula, although the little patches of landscape within the niche do not properly belong to such carpets.

The difficulties which beset any local classification of the carpets of Asia Minor are demonstrated in an example reproduced on Plate 57. The most conspicuous motive of the pattern is the series of four small landscapes within the niche, with a representation of a mosque in the arch at the top. Such little plots of ground with cypress-trees and buildings are generally supposed to have been intended to represent a Muhammadan cemetery, and from the circumstance the name usually applied to such carpets is derived. Apart from this feature, the design has ingredients both of the Ghiordes and Kula types. The border, with its row of " lion-mask " palmettes and flowers alternating, resembles those of the Ghiordes carpets just described (Plates 52 and 56). The narrow stripes outlining the border on each side, and the filling of the space above the niche, are typical of Kula (see Plate 100). The carpet is Anatolian, and it is unsafe to specify the actual locality of production more closely. The same may be said of another carpet belonging to Mr. George Mounsey, in which the landscape motive is again rendered (Plate 58). The ground is bright red, with rows of houses and trees in strongly contrasting colours.

The last of the three principal types of these later Anatolian prayer-carpets is the " Ladik." A good example is seen on Plate 102. A row of long inverted stems ending in blossoms is generally to be found below the niche in this group. The device filling the niche, with its four ewers precariously balanced, has lost all meaning. A yellow panel under the central arch bears the date 1211 of the Hegira, corresponding to A.D. 1797.[1] The fantastic forms of this type of carpets are again exemplified in Plate 103, which has a ewer poised in the niche and two more in the spandrels. Another variation, much simpler, with three distinct arches, is shown on Plate 55. In some Ladik carpets even the niche is reduced to an absurdity (Plates 104 and 105). There are several other types of prayer-carpets of Asia Minor bearing geographical names. These are described in a later chapter (see p. 155 foll.).

Carpets such as that reproduced on Plate 114 seem like intruders among the carpets of Anatolia. Their strange barbaric design, their exclusive use of geometrical forms and the multiplicity of hooked

[1] A Ladik prayer-carpet reproduced by F. R. Martin (*O.C.*, Fig. 340) is dated A.H. 1110=A.D. 1699.

contours give them an unsophisticated air which tells of nomad life. They are the work of the Yuruks—nomad shepherds of Asia Minor.

Before turning to the consideration of the carpets of the Caucasian region, two examples of uncertain provenance should be referred to. The first (Plate 59) has the form of an Anatolian rug with a niche at each end, but in some respects it resembles still more nearly the carpets of Western Persia. Were it not for the stiff conventionalization of the floral border, and the trivial diaper-filling of the spandrels, the carpet might almost have been attributed to the weavers of Kurdistan.[1] It was probably made in Eastern Asia Minor. The other (Plate 60) conforms still more closely to Western Persian types, but the border is found in Caucasian work, and it should be borne in mind while considering the carpets to be discussed in the next chapter.

[1] Cf. Vienna, *O.C.*, Pl. 66.

Chapter V

THE CAUCASUS

In a present-day classification of Oriental carpets the segregation of a group which it is convenient to describe as " Caucasian " is inevitable. After very little acquaintance with the subject this term calls up quite a definite image, though the carpets to which it is collectively applied vary as much as the people do in that part of the world. Few of the carpets placed in this group are older than the eighteenth century, and most are of the nineteenth, though carpet-weaving was carried on among the Caucasian people considerably earlier than that. The anomaly thus involved may be explained first of all by its practical convenience, and again to some degree by the gradual southward advance of Russia over the Caucasian region, and an apparent localization and fusion of patterns which followed. The predecessors of these " Caucasian " carpets must be looked for among those assigned to Asia Minor, Armenia and Persia.

The territories in question lie between the Caspian and the Black Sea, with the Caucasus Mountains running obliquely across from the one to the other. This range forms a natural boundary between Europe and Asia, and until the beginning of the nineteenth century it marked approximately the frontier between Russia on the one side and Persia and Turkey on the other. From time to time the two latter people disputed for a larger share of the southern borderland, but ultimately Russia shifted her own frontier by conquest southwards, and a Trans-Caucasian province of Russia was constituted. In the first year of the nineteenth century the King of Georgia abdicated in favour of the Czar. In 1827 during a campaign against Persia, Erivan and Tabriz were conquered, and in the following year the Russian frontier was fixed by Treaty at the Aras River. The boundary between the Russians and the Turks was thrust forward in the next year, and in 1878 Russia obtained Batûm. The whole of this relatively narrow strip of land between the two great inland seas is peopled, as might be expected, by a mixture of racial elements.

The carpets are mostly made on the south side of the mountain-range, but there are carpet-weavers in the narrow angle between the mountains and the Caspian shore on the north side. Motives descended from the old designs of Persia, Armenia, Asia Minor and nomad tribes are to be discerned. Generally speaking, these carpets show a stiff conventionalization of floral patterns, and geometrical forms much bolder in scale than those of most nomad carpets. The almost playful introduction of little figures of men, animals or birds, usually in odd corners, is quite frequent.

The task of differentiating the various local groups now recognized must be left to a later section of this book, to which it properly belongs. A few general considerations are all that need be set down here.

The carpet reproduced on Plate 61 shows roughly what may be expected in the group. The middle design renders the old Persian palmettes and large floral motives in a fashion almost unrecognizable, while the stems have been transformed into a random medley of zigzags. The border is less broken up, forming a strong contrast with the middle pattern.

A less drastic change is seen in another carpet (Plate 62) showing the transformation of an entire pattern, not only of single motives, when transplanted to Caucasian soil. The Persian stems and palmettes and cloud-bands are here marshalled into a rigid order quite alien to the old Persian tradition. Although there is no central medallion and no corner spandrels, one need only visualize the stems, flowers and cloud-bands in a freer rendering and a well-known Persian design of the seventeenth century lies before our eyes. The angularity of the design in this case is by no means due to clumsiness or want of technical ability; on the contrary, it is perfectly intentional. It will be noticed that the ends of the cloud-bands which are repeated so often in the carpet, both horizontally and vertically, have been treated as conventionalized leaves. The local touch which is seldom missing in old imitations of famous patterns, because they were copied in all innocence, without any intent to deceive, may be seen here in the flower consisting of eight curves, which is repeated five times, once almost in the middle of the carpet, and again towards each corner. This motive may often be found in Caucasian carpets (see Plates 125, 132A).

The carpet shown in Plate 27B is another link between the Caucasian work and the traditional designs of Persia. Another carpet attributed to the Caucasian region is reproduced on Plate 20A. Its elongated leaf-forms on an unusually large scale, overlaid with conventionalized floral stems, have an obvious affinity with the dragon-carpets shown on Plates 5 and 6, and the Armenian carpet dated A.D. 1679 (Plate 7). The border is an angular rendering of one of the type shown in Plate 165. It will be remembered that the extension of the Russian boundary brought Armenia partly within the territories of Turkey, Persia and Russia.

A well-known group of Caucasian carpets is represented by Plates 63 and 64. These carpets, with their compressed and angular renderings of Persian floral patterns, usually on a deep blue ground, are admirable from a decorative point of view. The borders are almost invariably of white interlinked bands derived from Kufic lettering. It is a curious fact that the earlier forms of the border pattern are as typical of the art of Asia Minor as those of the middle design are of Persia. Occasionally carpets of this class have in the middle field an interlaced design in which the forms of Kufic letters appear. The carpet illustrated on Plate 119 shows a similar middle pattern but a different border—of conventionalized floral motives. The narrow stripes edging the borders of these carpets are filled with rows of carnation blossoms turned alternately to right and left—a motive found earlier in Anatolian prayer-rugs.

This edging is seen on the border of the carpet reproduced in colour on Plate 121. The middle pattern with its row of bold octagons and its uncompromisingly geometrical treatment belongs to a class usually ascribed to the province of Shirvan on the north side of the Caucasus Mountains. The carpet is not older than the nineteenth century, but it is instructive to compare it with Anatolian examples such as those illustrated on Plate 41. A comparison, with the former of these especially, will leave little room to doubt of the derivation of the one from the other, allowing for three centuries of change. It also provides a valuable commentary on the origin of the typical modern Caucasian patterns. It is also the favourite pattern of the pileless " Soumak " rugs, an example of which is reproduced in Plate 146. The latter again should be compared with the Anatolian rugs above mentioned ; in this case it is the second example which shows the greater similarity. The various types of Caucasian rugs of the nineteenth century, with their territorial names, are dealt with in a later chapter.

Chapter VI

EASTERN ASIA

(a) Turcoman Tribes

Although few existing Turcoman carpets are likely to have been made before the eighteenth century, there are no carpets of more primitive type. Carpets of Asia Minor and the Caucasus recall them at times, and the earlier these carpets are the more likely are they to do so. It is the same with the carpets reproduced in pictures; the oldest are most like them. There can be no doubt that the craft among the Turcoman people dates back many centuries. Had there been an export trade, it might have led to the preservation of a few early examples in the West.

The Turcoman carpets follow a line of their own in matters of design, colour and technique. They are made in a greater variety of forms, and they serve more purposes, than those of other lands. The tradition they follow is no doubt of great antiquity, and if the carpets themselves are of no great age, the reason must be sought in the daily use to which they were all alike subjected. They are made in the regions beyond the farther shore of the Caspian Sea, in a tract extending eastwards as far as Bokhara, northwards to the Sea of Aral, and southwards to the boundary of Persia. There are also Turcoman nomads in Afghanistan, Beluchistan, Persia and Asia Minor, most of whom weave carpets. The sedentary population are not carpet-producers, but the nomads for the most part are skilled in carpet-weaving, and different tribes have their own special patterns. The principal equipments of their large movable tents (*kibitka*) are made by these weavers. Rugs for the floor are never large. The most characteristic production is the tent-band, usually about a foot wide and sometimes as much as 50 ft. long, which is hung round the tent where the sides join the roof. The designs, sometimes including rude figures of men, besides camels and other animals, are usually in knotted pile on a pileless ground of light tone (see Plate 177). Bags of carpet-weaving are hung round the tent to contain the family belongings. There are also portières, narrow fringed borders for tent-entrances, camel-collars and other articles of the same material. The work is done by the women. The ground is almost invariably a deep purple-red, except in those cases where it is pileless and of a natural pale tone. The pattern is mostly in dark blue, white, and shades of red; sometimes green or yellow are added. The basis of the pattern is usually polygons, star-shapes, lozenges or crosses, containing, and separated by, interlacings, chequer-patterns and geometrical forms perhaps derived from floral motives. The carpets are excellently well made, the wool of fine quality, the dyes good, the knotting close and regular, and the work durable. The different patterns are specified in a later chapter. Rugs with the prayer-niche are not common, although perhaps the specimen illustrated on Plate 190 may be intended to show this feature. There is a prayer-rug in the Victoria and Albert Museum, with a plain niche, apparently of undyed camel-hair; the row of dark blue cones in the border is a little unusual in Turcoman rugs. It almost seems as though the nomad weaver had borrowed some ideas, for once, from an Anatolian prayer-carpet. The Turcoman carpets made in Afghanistan and Beluchistan are usually rougher and poorer in technique, and simpler in pattern (see Plates 187 and 193).

(b) *China and Chinese Turkestan*

The history of Chinese carpets has not yet been written, and the task cannot be undertaken with any approach to finality just yet. There is still need for careful research on the spot and for more representative collections to be formed in Europe so as to provide a field for comparative study. A few Chinese carpets, picked up by travellers, were brought to the West during the course of the last century. More recently still, the vogue which arose for Chinese art generally focused attention on the carpets and large numbers were shipped to America and Europe by commercial agents. For the most part, it was as novelties that they gained their popularity.

Reference has already been made to the fragments of pile-carpets found within the last few years in the Gobi desert region (see p. 6). Further developments must be awaited, and proper facilities for study afforded, before a reliable estimate of their age and nationality can be formed.

Marco Polo, who makes frequent references to the textile industry of China, says nothing about the weaving of pile-carpets there, although on his way out he remarks how good the carpets of Asia Minor are.

Chinese carpets to-day form a group of very pronounced individuality. The main characteristics of this group are common to a large area of Asia extending in a wide belt from the westernmost limits of Chinese Turkestan at the apex of India, through Tibet, and across the northern provinces of China as far as the Yellow Sea.

There are grounds for believing that pile-carpet making among those peoples is not of great antiquity. They seem rather to have picked up the craft from their neighbours. The most vital point of contact would be Turkestan, where they were in touch with the Turcoman and Persian weavers. Carpets have long been made in Kashgar, Yarkand and Khotan, but they are woven also in Turfan and in other outlying parts of the province. The line of advance towards the Eastern seas would be that sketched out above, and the craft appears to have spread gradually from one point to another along the route.

The industry in Chinese Turkestan, Tibet and the neighbouring parts of China is carried on chiefly by the women in their homes. As it advances through North China it is taken up by the men, and factories have been established in recent years.

The Chinese carpets usually regarded as showing the best evidence of age are those in silk, or silk and gold, commonly attributed to the time of the Ming dynasty, but with small justification as a rule. Silk is not an ideal material for carpet-knotting, and its use for such a purpose, though natural in China, is probably no older there than elsewhere in carpet-weaving countries.

The designs of these carpets have an archaic appearance, due largely to the stiff and angular treatment of the floral motives usually forming the pattern. The Chinese way of putting in the gold thread, where that is used, adds emphasis to this angularity, and the pale and faded tones of the silk strengthen the illusion of age. The example illustrated on Plate 65 is typical. The conventionalization, to a point almost past recognition, of the circular dragon-and-phœnix motive will be noticed. The carpet was originally wider, with the motive in each corner and another in the middle. Blue, the colour of the ground, is the prevailing tone. Much of the pattern is in gold thread. In these carpets the floral motives are usually closely packed to cover the whole ground. A remarkable example acquired in the year 1919 by the Stockholm Museum showed repetitions of two plant forms in lobed compartments on a gold ground, and a border of interlaced floral stems on a silver ground, recalling Persian design.[1] Sometimes other motives appear as well. Blue is usually

[1] Described and illustrated by Dr. Eric Folcker in *Burlington Magazine*, Vol. XXXV, 1919, p. 61.

the dominant colour of the silk. Where gold thread is used, it is poor in quality and loosely woven into the texture. The carpet partly illustrated on Plate 66A is a good example of this type. It has a row of eleven niches, all containing floral patterns in silk on a gold-thread ground. Silver thread forms the ground in the spandrels. There is a similar carpet, but smaller, with only six niches, in the Austrian Museum of Art and Industry, Vienna.[1] An example of later date, without the metal threads, is shown on Plate 67.

The silk and gold carpets form a strong contrast to the majority of the Chinese woollen-pile carpets, which show a great variety of motives, often in the bright clear colours characteristic of Chinese art. At times the designs show an originality not beyond criticism. Relief effects cannot be banished from carpet-design, and it is no use making the attempt; but when flower-pots, incense-vases, table-ornaments and the like are rendered as though they were actual objects placed on the carpet, the result is not entirely free from a suggestion of incongruity. The carpet illustrated on Plate 68 is a very favourable example of this class of pattern, on a white ground. The artistic sense of the Chinese, when the balance is not disturbed too much by purely commercial motives, is still genuine and good, and they know well how to harmonize what would appear as absurdities in other hands. The handicap from the beginning in regard to their carpet industry seems to have been that its lineage was not very ancient, and as a late-comer it was pressed into a mould fashioned for other uses. Figure-subjects have been freely used in Chinese carpet-design. For the most part they represent divinities, saints, sages or priests, often with an inscription in Manchurian, Mongolian or Tibetan. These carpets are intended for use in the temples.

Most of the designs are drawn from the repertory of traditional Chinese art. We find dragons and phœnixes, sometimes together, " unicorns " (ch'i-lin), deer, horses, cranes, bats and butterflies. " Corean lions " and various emblems associated with Buddhism are found, as well as emblems of the Taoist philosophy. Landscape effects with trees and animals are sometimes suggested, and the various forms of the " long life " character are introduced. Corean lions and floral sprays in colours on a red ground, form the sole motive of the carpet shown on Plate 69. The dragon-headed horse (lungma) and the phœnix are represented in the middle of the small rug reproduced on Plate 70B. The ground of this carpet is red, and the pattern chiefly in blue and white.

[1] Vienna, *O.C.*, Pl. 52.

A peculiar arrangement of rocks and waves is sometimes disposed round the middle space based on the inner border of the carpet, and converging towards the centre. Carpets with simpler patterns, of floral, diaper, or fret motives are often very decorative. The carpet, in white and two shades of blue, with a simple lotus pattern (Plate 71), is an excellent example.

The Chinese, and with them the Tibetans, have used the pile-knotting method for a variety of purposes. Some of their carpets are of large dimensions; others are little mats varying from about 3 ft. to only a few inches square, never intended for the floor. Sometimes two mats are made in one continuous texture to cover the seat and back of a chair —square for the seat and shaped for the back. An example, with a floral pattern in colours on a red ground, is illustrated on Plate 70A. A similar double arrangement of two oblong panels is intended for a long seat. Where three panels are thus woven together, the third is intended to hang down in front. Saddle-cloths are also made in a curved shape. Designs evidently intended to be seen upright, and not suited for a horizontal position, are generally meant to be used as temple-hangings for the wall or altar, or as table-hangings. A species of carpet peculiar to the Chinese and kindred peoples of the Far East is made to be placed round pillars, in such a way as to bring the two side edges together and so complete the design. Sometimes these carpets have standing figures; more often they have dragons, which appear to be coiling round the columns. There is generally a line of waves and rocks with spray breaking over them below, and a festooned arrangement of jewels and tassels above. The examples on Plates 72 and 73 are shown both flat and in the way they are meant to be used.

The carpets of Eastern Turkestan were the first among the Chinese group to find their way to Europe, and as they became familiar in the West before others made farther afield were seen, a habit grew up of assigning all Chinese carpets to this region.

Though preponderatingly Chinese in design and colour, they have a character of their own which renders them distinguishable, as a rule, from the carpets of Northern China. A typical example is shown on Plate 74, and a small mat of very similar design, on a red ground on Plate 75A. The pattern of sea waves in the border is very common in these carpets. The fret-ornament in the corners and the rosettes in the middle are motives also frequently found. Sometimes these carpets are more definitely based on those of Western Asia, although the colour-scheme and the details of the pattern are still Chinese. A carpet shown at the Vienna Exhibition of 1891 had a pattern of flowering stems in the middle, partly issuing from two vases at either end, and a border of counterchange cresting.[1] The effect is that of an interpretation of an Anatolian design, though delineated quite in Chinese fashion.

In the north-eastern provinces, Shan-si, Chi-li and Shantung, the industry appears to have been well established in the eighteenth century. Two small mats reproduced (Plates 75B, 66B) are probably from those provinces. The latter was brought from North China by the owner, Colonel Croft-Lyons.

Many carpets find their way to Tientsin for export, and on that account the term " Tientsin carpet " has come into use. The place was merely the emporium for the Far East, like Bokhara for Middle Asia, or Smyrna for the Near East.

Ninghsia and Peking have a name for making the best carpets. Kalgan in Chi-li is also mentioned, and at Tsinanfu in Shantung the craft is taught. Fifty years ago, Colonel Yule, the editor of Marco Polo's travels, recorded that in the city of T'ai-yuan fu, northern Shan-si province, fine carpets " like those of Turkey " were made.[2] The phrase probably means no more than that the carpets were of knotted pile.

The wool of the sheep, goat, camel and yak are used. The material comes chiefly from Mongolia, but local supplies are used where obtainable.

A common practice among the Chinese carpet-weavers of cutting into the pile in order to round-off the angular contours produced by the knotting process shows that they do not submit willingly to its limitations. The result is that many single tufts are cut away on one side down to the knot itself, thereby impairing the durability of the carpet. This practice is not followed elsewhere and it tends to show that in devising it the Chinese were endeavouring to adapt a foreign process of weaving to their own favourite types of design. The colours used by the Chinese are few in number and generally of strong tone. The ground is mostly red, yellow, blue or white, and a few other colours are used. Blue is greatly employed, as in their pottery; quite frequently shades of blue and white form the entire colour-scheme. The native dyes are said to be by far the best, and where poor dyes have been used, it is to be assumed that they were derived from foreign sources.

The brisk trade in Chinese carpets in recent times has arisen partly

[1] Vienna, O.C., Pl. 49.
[2] Sir H. Yule, The Book of Ser Marco Polo, 3rd ed. 1903, Book II, ch. 37.

from an awakened interest in Chinese art generally. At the outbreak of the war an impetus was given by the cutting off of the carpet-weaving centres of Western Asia, resulting in the organization of the industry in Northern China for export purposes. Experiments in setting the craftsmen there to imitate the patterns of Western Asia have not been an unqualified success.

CHAPTER VII

EUROPE

(a) Spain

It has been known for many years that pile-carpets were made in Spain, but the long record of the industry there, and the extent to which it has been carried on, were unsuspected until recent times. On the one hand, the Spanish weavers had attributed to them typical Oriental carpets with devices, such as heraldry, for instance, betraying Western connexions, while some of their own carpets were ascribed to the East ; and on the other hand it has been hinted that they were slavish copyists of Eastern work, and poor at that. Sheer weight of facts gradually coming to light is correcting such views by the best of all methods, that of demonstrating the truth of contrary ones. During the past forty years the spoils of many churches, convents and mansions have found their way into the market, and although the necessity is to be deplored, there is at least one advantage—that museums have been provided with the material for arriving at a truer understanding of Spanish art. So far as carpets are concerned, we do not know everything yet, but the main facts have been made clear. Not every pile-carpet known to have come from Spain, or still there, is Spanish. Carpets were imported from Anatolia ; many such have been found in Spain, and others may be seen represented in old Spanish paintings. Like all other European countries where carpet-knotting has been carried on, Spain learnt the craft from the East, but she learnt it early, and developed at once on independent lines. There is a decidedly individual character in Spanish carpets, both as regards design and technique.

Some of the oldest carpets now in existence are Spanish. This conclusion, which sounds improbable at first, is provided with a sound historical basis by the heraldry usually found on these early carpets. They are mostly abnormally long in proportion to their width, a characteristic pointing to a local and domestic origin. A carpet may be as long as the weaver desires, but its width is determined by that of the loom, and domestic looms are usually narrow for convenience. It is quite likely that these long heraldic carpets were convent work. Two very important examples, shown at the great exhibition of Muhammadan art at Munich in 1910,[1] came from the Convent of Sta Clara in Valencia, Old Castile. One has a shield-of-arms three times repeated in a line down the middle, on a dark blue ground of diaper ornament. There is an inner geometrical border, and an outer border of slim formalized Kufic characters [2] with human figures, animals and birds filling the spaces between the letters. Along each end outside the border there is a white strip with a design of wild men attacking animals in a wood. The inscribed outer border is a special feature of these early Spanish carpets, and the extra white band at the ends will be met with again. The arms are those of the family of Enriquez. The anchors flanking the shield show that the bearer held the rank of Admiral of Castile, and this places the carpet between the year 1405 and the end of the fifteenth century. The other carpet generally similar, but much larger, is partly reproduced on Plate 76. There are three shields, each several times repeated. They refer to Marina de Ayala and Fadrique Enriquez, Admiral of Castile (d. 1473).[3] The carpets may therefore be dated approximately in the middle of the fifteenth century. A few other carpets of the kind are known. One similar to the two described, but without heraldry, was shown at the Munich Exhibition.[4] Two more are in the Kunstgewerbe Museum, Berlin. One of these has shields-of-arms at present unidentified, on a blue ground, and the other has elaborate palmette forms branching on either side from a central stem, in blue, red and white on a dull red ground (Plate 77A). The latter is reputed to have come from a church in the Tyrol. Both appear to be of the fifteenth century. Although the Victoria and Albert Museum has not yet succeeded in obtaining one of these rare carpets, some useful fragments, acquired by gift from Mr. Lionel Harris, show the character of the work.

Another type, of which a few examples still exist, is no less early in origin. A representative example is illustrated (Plate 78). The arrangement of octagons enclosing geometrical forms recalls that of Anatolian carpets illustrated in early pictures—those of Memlinc and his school

---

[1] Lent by Mr. Lionel Harris, of London. It is understood that they are now in America.
[2] Sir Thomas Arnold states that there can be no certainty as to the actual significance of letters on carpets of this type.
[3] The identification of the arms on both carpets is due to Mr. A. Van de Put (see *Burlington Magazine*, XIX, p. 344). See also *Meisterwerke Muhammedanischer Kunst*, Munich, 1910, Vol. I, Pls. 85, 86; Museum, I, 1911, p. 431. The sizes are: (1) L. m. 5.90, W. m. 2.64; (2) L. m. 8, W. m. 2.30.
[4] *Meisterwerke*, Pl. 87.

(Plate 36), or Holbein, for example.   The octagonal spaces which occur so frequently in carpets illustrated in pictures of the fifteenth, and even the fourteenth century, are probably primitive and convenient renderings of circles.   In the Spanish carpets, the form is shown in its stiffest convention, but redeemed by the variety and brilliancy of colouring. The example illustrated has a row of three large red octagons enclosed by rectangular compartments.   Within each octagon is a large and elaborate star-device in polychrome on a bright red ground.   The star is filled with a variety of diaper patterns and modified Kufic letters.   The space around each octagon has a trellis pattern on dark green.   There are borders of conventional ornament on pale blue and black.   Another example, the property of Dr. Ludwig von Buerkel, was shown at the Munich Exhibition of 1910.   It had a double row of octagons, but otherwise it was very similar though less varied in detail.   It was probably a few years later in date than the London carpet.[1]   The later development of this pattern of octagons in Spain is exemplified in a carpet with a red ground in the Victoria and Albert Museum (Plate 77B).

Both the types of Spanish pile-carpets hitherto described have originality enough to render them fairly easily recognizable.   A third group, now to be discussed, is quite unique.   There is nothing in the whole range of carpet-knotting like them.[2]   They reproduce the patterns of contemporary Spanish woven silk stuffs, much enlarged in scale, but with no further modification beyond that required by the technique.   Such patterns make considerable demands upon the skill and patience of the carpet-knotter where fine lines and curves have to be rendered.   The adoption by the Spanish weavers of a single-warp knot (see p. 95), perhaps invented for the very purpose, made the task easier, though it involved great manipulative skill.   The earliest-known example of the class is the fine carpet in the Victoria and Albert Museum with a pattern found in several variations among Hispano-Moresque silks. Two lions stand to right and left of a pointed fruit device from which branch downward two long stems which curl round to enclose the lions, uniting above where they end in elaborate foliations.   The design is in red and yellow on a dark blue ground.   There is a narrow border of dragons, with interlinked necks, in yellow.   This carpet has the early Spanish characteristic of inordinate length in proportion to its width.

[1] *Meisterwerke*, Pl. 88 ; Museum I, 1911, p. 429.   See also F. R. Martin, *O.C.*, Fig. 342.
[2] The nearest approach, in principle though not in detail, is made by the English carpets yet to be described.

The collection of Spanish carpets in the Victoria and Albert Museum is the largest and most varied existing, and it includes other remarkable examples. Reference must be made to a few of them in tracing the later development of the craft. One of these (Plate 79) has a variation of the familiar " artichoke " pattern in green and blue on a red ground. The white outer edging at the two ends, with the pattern of primitive tree-forms and birds, links this carpet with the long heraldic ones described above. It was probably made in the last years of the fifteenth century. A very fine strip, with the lobed pattern so familiar in Italian and Spanish silk velvets of the fifteenth century, belongs to the Hon. H. D. McLaren, M.P. The colours are unusually subdued, on a black ground (Plate 80). Reverting to the Museum collection, a carpet with another rendering of the " artichoke " pattern in green, has a flame-coloured ground, of glowing red dying off into orange—a most beautiful effect of colour. A typical example of the sixteenth century has a fine blue-and-white damask pattern in the middle, with five yellow shields superimposed (Plate 81). Upon that in the middle is the Sacred Trigram I H S, while those in the corners have the familiar *memento mori*, a skull and cross-bones. The conventional renaissance border is principally in red and yellow.

In the seventeenth century the design of Spanish carpets becomes a little uncertain. On the one hand there are the true successors of the frankly Spanish carpets of the sixteenth century, and side by side with these there are deliberate adaptations of the Turkish carpets which were probably to be found in considerable numbers in the peninsula at the time. One example in the Museum has a copy of a floral Turkish carpet-design in the middle, done in blues and greens and yellows, and a border of double-headed eagles. Another with an Oriental design throughout has the word " Trinidad " wrought into the border—no doubt representing the name of the church or convent for which it was made. The carpet reproduced in colours on Plate 82 is perhaps one of the Spanish adaptations of an Eastern design.

An interesting carpet of the early eighteenth century given to the Museum by the late Sir Charles Dilke returns to the heraldic tradition. The central field is taken up with a shield-of-arms and an inscription apparently referring to the title Vizconde de los Villares, created in 1708.[1]

Two other types of carpets were made in the Spanish peninsula in considerable numbers. One has a looped pile surface in wool or silk

[1] The identification of the arms is due to Mr. A. Van de Put.

on a linen ground. These were made in the Alpujarra Mountains near Granada and perhaps in other districts. As they are not hand-knotted they need not be described in detail. Others are boldly embroidered on linen and therefore they do not concern us here.

(b) Poland

Some reference to the question of carpet-knotting in Poland has already been made, in connexion with the mistaken attribution to Poland of the Persian silk-and-gold carpets. There is ample evidence, however, that pile-carpets were made in Poland.

Both Polish and Persian carpets are mentioned in old inventories, and examples undoubtedly of Polish origin exist to-day. Two are preserved in the Museum at Lemberg. One has shields-of-arms and the date 1698. The other has a floral pattern. Another carpet with heraldry is in a private collection at Cracow.[1]

The carpet illustrated here (Plate 83) is the property of Dr. Friedrich Sarre. The pile is wool, and the pattern is in colours on a white ground. The general appearance of these Polish carpets recalls the English work, but the treatment of the design is more angular.

(c) Finland

The making of hand-knotted carpets probably dates back several centuries among the peasantry of Finland. The question whether the carpet-knotting method is indigenous there, or whether it was borrowed from neighbouring peoples is considered as debatable by investigators of the national arts of the country.

Considerable numbers of pile-carpets of local origin exist to-day. They are invariably of modest dimensions, mostly about the size and proportions of a hearthrug. The knotting is not very fine, and the carpets consequently have a rough and fleecy appearance. The patterns are mostly simple peasant designs based on floral motives, done in bright and varied colours. One of these rugs usually formed part of a bride's trousseau, and many have the initials of the owner and the date. Examples with dates earlier than the middle years of the eighteenth century appear to be unknown, but the craft goes back very much farther.

At one time the work declined, but in recent years efforts have been made, not altogether without success, to revive it. The example here

---

[1] *Orientalisches Archiv*, II, 1911–12, Pls. 11–13.

illustrated, with the date 1799, is in the Victoria and Albert Museum (Plate 84). The colours are red, green, blue and white on a black ground. The broad border is in blue, white and black on a red ground; there is a narrow edging in blue. Tapestry-woven mats of Finnish origin are known, although they are rare. Others have been made in Norway and Sweden, but they may be more suitably classed with tapestries, and they hardly come within the scope of the present work.

(d) France

The makers of hand-woven carpets in France, as elsewhere in Europe, borrowed the processes from the East. In regard to design they followed a course no less independent and original than the English craftsmen. The real beginning of carpet-knotting in France cannot be traced to an earlier date than the opening years of the seventeenth century. A guild of carpet-makers existed in Paris four centuries before, but nothing now remains of their handiwork, and we are even ignorant of its nature.

In the year 1601 a craftsman, Jehan Fortier, claimed to be the originator of a process of carpet-making which was described as being after the manner of Turkey and the Levant, and a similar claim was made by Pierre Dupont in 1605. Privileges were granted for carrying on the work. A factory was established by Henry IV in the Louvre under Dupont, and artists of repute were commissioned to make designs. These were probably from the beginning in the style of contemporary French decorative art, like those made under Louis XIV and later. In consequence, French carpets have a very distinct originality.

The factory of the Savonnerie, which has provided a generic name for all French hand-knotted carpets, was founded in 1626. Its site was a building originally used as a soap-works, on the banks of the Seine at Chaillot, then a suburb of Paris, but since united with the city. Simon Lourdet, a pupil of Dupont's, was the first director. In 1672 the Louvre *atelier* was transferred to the Savonnerie, where work for Louis XIV was already in progress. Ninety great carpets were ordered for the Louvre, many measuring as much as 30 ft. in length by 16 ft. or more in width. These commissions kept the looms at work for the greater part of the long reign of Louis XIV. The designs were characterized by the magnificence and splendour associated with that monarch's name. They were based largely on the acanthus foliage and scrollwork belonging to the period, forming a setting for the royal arms and emblems, the trophies of arms, the gods and goddesses and other devices. The effect aimed at, and attained, can only be properly gauged in their appropriate surroundings, lying on the floors of the great saloons of Louis XIV, and associated with the ponderous boule-work and inlaid furniture of the time. More than thirty of these great carpets are still in the French Mobilier National.

By the kind dispositions of the administrator, M. Dumonthier, and with the sanction of the French Government, a fine series of these carpets, numbering eleven in all, was placed on public view in the Victoria and Albert Museum in London, in the years 1912 and 1921. Two of these carpets in the Mobilier National are here illustrated, with the permission of M. Dumonthier (Plates 85, 86).

The existence to-day, in a remarkably good state of repair, of so many of these carpets witnesses to the high quality of the craftsmanship and materials.

Work at the Savonnerie went on during the course of the eighteenth century, and under the First Empire. Numerous carpets in the Mobilier National are of those times.

In 1825, after a career of two centuries at the Savonnerie, the works were united with the national tapestry-factory of the Gobelins. In these new quarters carpets were made for the palaces of the Louvre, the Tuileries, the Elysée, St. Cloud, Compiègne and Fontainebleau, for the Cathedral of Notre Dame and for the Panthéon.

The work is still carried on at the Gobelins. The modern carpets not infrequently exceed the older in weight and size. At times their designs are based on earlier traditions, in order to adapt them to their destined entourage.

Chapter VIII

ENGLAND

The making of pile-carpets by hand in England followed very closely upon the first importation of Oriental examples. In the sense in which the term " carpet " is used to-day, and in any sense cognate to it, carpets were unknown in this country five hundred years ago. In the West their gradual adoption has kept pace with progressive ideas of comfort. In the East they are the outcome of the conditions of daily life, and they have always been indispensable. There are very few carpets now in the world more than five hundred years old, but that fact provides no clue to the antiquity of the carpet, since such goods were liable by their nature to perish in the using. Whatever our uncertainties may be in regard to the East, we can be pretty sure that practically nothing was known in England of the pile-carpet before the reign of Henry VII at the earliest, if not that of his successor. There are many illustrations of interiors in English paintings and miniatures executed before those times, but in none of them is a pile-carpet represented. As late as the fifteenth century a flooring of stone or earthenware tiles, or, perhaps, wood-boards, was considered to need no covering for the sake of comfort or appearance. The occupants of the more modest dwellings probably had often to be content with the bare earth ; and, indeed, some of our country churches were no better off at a much later time. A " foot-cloth," a piece of rich stuff of some kind, would be laid down before the altar of a church or before the throne in the royal presence-chamber.

These cloths, spread out in special places on occasions of ceremony, were only in a very limited sense the predecessors of the modern carpet. They did not entirely meet the problem of the treatment of the floor in mediæval times. In the houses of the well-to-do, sweet rushes, hay, straw, foliage, fragrant herbs or flowers were scattered over the floor. These could be renewed at will, and the broom might be more or less drastically used, at regular or irregular intervals, according to the taste of the individual.

An illustration from a celebrated manuscript in the Library of Lambeth Palace, entitled *Dictes and Sayings of the Philosophers,* a Latin book translated into English by Earl Rivers, shows the translator offering the book to King Edward IV. The cloth of honour is brought forward so as to pass under the feet of the king, while loose rushes, painted bright green in the picture, cover the whole of the rest of the floor.[1]

Even after another century had passed, at the end of Elizabeth's reign, the state of affairs was very much the same. Paul Hentzner, a German who came to London in 1598, states that Queen Elizabeth's presence-chamber at Greenwich was strewn with hay. In fact, the interior economy of our houses seems to have been in harmony with their outward appearance. We recall the picturesque exclamation of the Spaniard in Queen Mary's time : " These English have their houses made of sticks and dirt, but," he is careful to add, " they fare commonly as well as the king."

Rush-matting, although used to cover the floor by our nearest neighbours, the French, at the beginning of the fifteenth century, does not appear to have been adopted in England before Henry VIII's reign, and its general use cannot be ascribed to an earlier time than that of James I. One of the earliest representations of rush-matting in an English picture is in a portrait of Henry VIII at Belvoir Castle.[2] The rushes are simply plaited in a diagonal fashion. In this reign the pile-carpet first comes on the scene. Cardinal Wolsey was probably the first Englishman, for a subject at any rate, to bring pile-carpets into use. They had long been known, though only as rare and valuable commodities, on the Continent. A minister who, if rumour spoke truly, fed his aspiring soul with dreams of the papal tiara, and who at one time would have rejoiced to secure the imperial crown for Henry, must not be chargeable with insular habits. He must be equipped in the fashion of the times, and carpets must be got. The foreign trade of the country being then largely in the hands of Continental merchants resident in London and the seaports, he could apply to the Venetian factors ; but that course would be tedious and slow. The steps he did take lifted the question out of the sphere of commerce into that of international diplomacy. The dispatches and reports of Sebastian Giustinian, then Venetian Ambassador in England, show how much significance that dignitary attached to a request from the Cardinal for some carpets.[3] Negotiations went on for

[1] Allen, *Selections from Erasmus*, p. 126, gives a criticism of the practice.

[2] The Drapers' Hall is said to have had mats in the Chequer Chamber, and rushes in the hall, in 1495, but we have no information as to the material of the mats.

[3] *Four Years at the Court of Henry VIII. Selections of dispatches, etc.* Vol. II, pp. 198 foll.

more than a year. In June, 1518, Giustinian writes home to the Signory from Lambeth that the Cardinal had promised to take him before the Council and obtain audience for his arguments in regard to the repeal of the duties on Candian wines imported into England by the Venetian traders. " After these colloquies," the ambassador proceeds, " his right reverend lordship requested me very earnestly to contrive with the magnifico the captain and the masters that, paying for the same, he might have certain choice carpets and some other articles, but above all the carpets. I told him that I did not know whether there were any, but that if there were, his lordship should have them. I suspect he will not be accommodated, which will prove of serious detriment to us ; whereas had he received twelve or fifteen small handsome carpets, he would have been extremely satisfied. Should your Excellency think fit, you might see either to forwarding them by land, or promise that he should receive some by the next galleys." In November of the same year the ambassador writes again from Lambeth. The Cardinal, he says, was extremely angry with the Venetian merchants in London, who appear to have done something which led him to believe that they thought too lightly of his authority in the kingdom. Giustinian had been to see him with the object of arranging the dispute. He appears to have been in some degree successful. The Cardinal sent for the merchants, who offered him seven very handsome Damascene carpets. He was willing to accept this present from the ambassador, but not from the merchants. In the end, he agreed to regard them as the joint gift of both. These carpets were but a drop in the ocean. The autumn of the next year came, and still the request for the carpets, and the contingent question of the duty on the Cretan wines remained as before. Giustinian is by this time back in Venice. In October, 1519, he makes a report in the Senate on his legation in England. The Cardinal is still very anxious, he says, for the Signory to send him one hundred Damascene carpets, for which he has asked several times. The Senate is urged to make the gift, and even if the Signory does not choose to incur the expense, the London factory will take it on themselves. The gift might easily settle the affair of the wines of Candia, whereas it would be idle to discuss that matter further until the Cardinal receives his hundred carpets. In October, 1520, Wolsey received sixty carpets from Venice. Doubtless they were similar in character to that shown in the full-length portrait of Henry VIII at Belvoir Castle, to which reference has already been made. The king stands on a carpet with a pattern of arabesques in large compartments. A royal portrait-group, painted by Holbein, in the Privy Chamber at Whitehall, after that palace had been handed over to the king by Wolsey, perished in the fire of 1697–8, but copies made before that date show the king standing on a carpet somewhat similar to that at Belvoir.[1] Still another portrait of Henry, in Earl Spencer's collection at Althorp, claims our attention. The king is seated at a table with the Princess Elizabeth; the jester Somers stands behind them. On the table is spread a small Oriental rug. It will be remembered, of course, that for a long time after Oriental carpets were first brought into Europe it was far more common to use them as tablecloths than as floor-coverings. Evidence on this point meets us continually in Flemish, Dutch, and Italian pictures of the fifteenth to the seventeenth century.

The actual making of pile-carpets in this country followed hard upon their first importation from the East. A carpet represented in part on Plate 87A has in the middle the royal arms of England, with the initials of Queen Elizabeth and the date 1570. On the left are the arms of the borough of Ipswich, and on the right those of the family of Harbottle. The whole of the pattern is thoroughly English and typical of Elizabethan times. In particular, the borders of honeysuckle and oak-stems are to be noticed. The carpet is the property of Lord Verulam. It is probably the oldest existing example of carpet-knotting in England. Attempts at carpet-weaving may have been made at an earlier date, even under Wolsey himself; for among his household goods at Hampton Court were several woollen " table-carpets of English making." The patterns of these are described, and they are not inconsistent with the idea that the carpets may have been of knotted work; but, still, we cannot be sure. It may be taken for granted that, in view of the wide disparity as regards the cost of labour, the English craftsman in the days of Elizabeth was no better able to enter the lists against the skilled Oriental weaver than he is to-day. But for all that, the English worker had his own sphere, and the craft, once taken up, was long kept alive.

Before the end of Elizabeth's reign, the English Turkey (or Levant) Company had begun direct trading with the Eastern Mediterranean, and carpets were more easily obtained. Some of these were copied, more or less faithfully, in England. A carpet in the Victoria and Albert Museum has a stiff geometrical pattern (Plate 88). The shield-of-arms

[1] There is a copy by Remigius van Leemput at Hampton Court.

in the middle of three of the borders is that of Sir Edward Apsley. An unusual feature is the inscription, along one of the short sides, in beautiful Elizabethan characters in knotted pile, like the rest of the carpet. It reads as follows: " Feare God and keepe his commandements made in the yeare 1603." The knighthood was conferred in that year, and the carpet may have been made to commemorate the event. The design is Eastern in origin, but the carpet is English. In the same museum there is a small panel bearing the arms of Queen Elizabeth, with her initials and the date 1600 (Plate 87B). The design is typical throughout of the English art of the time. It is not a large piece, and it could hardly have been intended for the floor. This knotting process came to have the name of " Turkey work " in England. The knot is quite a simple one—the same as that generally used in Turkish carpets. Panels made in this way were often used for upholstery, and numbers of them exist to-day.[1]

The carpet reproduced in colours on Plate 89 is a very fine example of the time of James I. The date 1614 will be found in the border, and the whole design is characteristically English of the period. The carpet is in the possession of Lady Hulse. There is an English carpet of similar design at Knole. A second example at Knole has the arms of the Countess of Dorset, who died in 1645.

English travellers got to Persia early in Elizabeth's reign, and a little later an effort was made to find a Persian carpet-weaver who might be induced to come to England.

A chapter in Hakluyt's *Voyages* is entitled " Certaine directions given . . . to M. Morgan Hubblethorne, Dier, sent into Persia, 1579." In this chapter we read as follows: " In Persia you shall finde carpets of coarse thrummed wool, the best of the world, and excellently coloured : those cities and towns you must repair to, and you must use means to learn all the order of the dyeing of those thrums, which are so dyed as neither rain, wine, nor yet vinegar can stain. . . . If before you return you could procure a singular good workman in the art of Turkish carpet-making, you should bring the art into this realm, and also thereby increase work to your Company."

We have no evidence that Hubblethorne secured his Persian workman. Carpet-knotting in the old style went on, however, until

---

[1] In the Inventory of 1679 there were mentioned four Turkey-work carpets in the Wardrobe, and twelve Turkey-work chairs and one Turkey-work carpet in the lower offices. (Mrs. Charles Roundell, *Ham House*, pp. 50, 51.)

the middle of the seventeenth century. By that time the country was richer, and the trade of the East India Company having developed, there was no real difficulty about getting carpets from India and Persia, though it was a costly business. The Girdlers' carpet, as already stated (p. 39), was obtained through the East India merchants in 1634. The quantity of carpets of this Indo-Persian class still to be seen in old English houses bears witness to the extent of this commerce, and, incidentally, to the national wealth in the latter half of the seventeenth century. As a consequence, the industry at home seems practically to have died out; and when, as we shall see in a moment, it was revived in the middle of the eighteenth century, it was regarded as a new industry.

Meanwhile, experiments in carpet-knotting " after the manner of Turkey and the Levant " had been made in France, as already related. Two craftsmen in the Savonnerie at Chaillot, having some difference with the administration, removed to London in 1750, and began making a carpet in a room at Westminster. They had raised some money by subscription, but they soon got into difficulties. In the end they applied to a fellow-countryman in London, Pierre Parisot, a tapestry-weaver. Parisot succeeded in interesting the Duke of Cumberland, and engaged the men in 1751. The factory was removed to Paddington, and the first carpet made was presented by the Duke to the Princess of Wales. After two years the works were removed to Parisot's tapestry-factory at Fulham. Great expectations were raised by the undertaking, but its career was short. The entire works of the Fulham factory were sold by auction in London in 1755. It is the usual story of such enterprises in England. The work was costly, and there was only a limited demand. Perhaps had the factory been able to pull through the first few years of effort and financial straits, its career might have been assured; but even that is doubtful.[1]

The models and appliances thus fell into other hands, and so the failure of Parisot's venture must have helped towards the success which attended other efforts made about that time.

In 1756, the year following the sale of the Fulham works, the Society of Arts offered a premium for making carpets in England in imitation of those made in Turkey and Persia. The name of Thomas Moore, of Chiswell Street, Moorfields, is the first on the list of recipients. A carpet he produced to the Society was considered to be " in many respects equal, and in some respects superior, to those imported from Persia

[1] See the *Gentleman's Magazine*, Vol. XXIV, 1754, p. 385.

and Turkey." [1] He received a premium of £25 in 1757, and a like sum was awarded to Thomas Whitty of Axminster. The next year Whitty received £25 again ; while Passavant of Exeter received an equal amount. Again, the following year (1759) the Society made an award of £50, giving £30 to Whitty and £20 to William Jesser of Frome.

More than twenty years later the good results of these awards were apparent. There is a note in the first volume of the Society's *Transactions* (1783) that by them the manufacture of carpets " is now established in different parts of the kingdom, and brought to a degree of elegance and beauty which the Turkey carpets never attained." That expression of opinion is coloured by the tastes of the day, which would have discovered more beauty in the Græco-Roman elegancies of the brothers Adam than in anything the East ever had, or ever could have, produced. But we are in a position to judge for ourselves.

Not much appears to be known of the subsequent career of Jesser's factory. In regard to Passavant's at Exeter, the carpet illustrated on Plate 90 was doubtless made there. It bears the inscription EXON and the date 1757. A carpet very similar in character, but different in design, is at Petworth House. It has the same inscription, with the date 1758.

The other two recipients of the Society of Arts' awards, Moore and Whitty, attained a greater celebrity. Moore seems to have attracted the favourable notice of Robert Adam, and this brought him commissions for carpets for mansions built or enlarged by that celebrated architect. The carpet illustrated on Plate 91 is in the red drawing-room of Syon House. The design is in the style which we have learned to associate particularly with the brothers Adam. There can be no doubt as to the craftsman responsible for the weaving. His name, " Thomas Moore," with the date 1769, is woven into the border. At Osterley, another house associated very extensively with Robert Adam's activities, the Earl of Jersey possesses several carpets which are shown by the records to have been made by Moore. The designs for four of these are in the Soane Museum. Those for the Tapestry Room and Etruscan Room are dated 1775 ; that for the State bedroom is dated 1778. There is no date on the design for the drawing-room. The Soane Museum has an extensive collection of Robert Adam's designs for carpets.

Thomas Whitty's factory outlasted the others. The industry which

[1] *A Concise Account of the Rise . . . of the Society. . . . By a Member of the said Society*, 1763, p. 58.

still flourishes at Wilton traces its origin to him. He first started carpet-making at Axminster, in the Court House near the church, in 1755. There carpets continued to be made for about eighty years. That factory was succeeded by Moody's, at Wilton, where carpet-making has gone on ever since.

Among the Axminster products were some very elaborate and costly carpets made for the Pavilion at Brighton. The expenditure on the building and equipment of this royal residence was very lavish, and the carpets were in keeping with the general scale of magnificence. An enormous carpet was made for the Saloon about 1823. It was shaped at the ends to fit the room. A portion is still preserved at Buckingham Palace. The pattern is on a light ground, and shows the influence of the Chinese taste so conspicuous in the decoration of the Pavilion.

In another carpet, made for the Music-Room, the pseudo-Chinese style is still more marked. It is now only a fragment, but an account is given by Nash and Brayley,[1] who describe it as " one of the largest in the kingdom, its dimensions being 61 ft. by 40 ft., and its weight about 1,700 lb."[2] It was made at Axminster to fit the room, costing £700. The Saloon carpet cost £620. Another carpet, for the Banqueting Room, was made at Axminster to Mr. Jones' design, costing £735.

An account of the carpet-knotting industry in this country would lack its natural counterpart if all reference were omitted to the weaving of carpets in Scotland and Ireland. The manufacture of carpets in the south-west of Scotland was carried on with much success in the second half of the eighteenth century. The industry has had an unbroken and prosperous career ever since. It seems likely that hand-knotting was not adopted there at first, but in 1831 the Trustees for Manufacture in Scotland awarded two premiums—of £150 and £30—for four Turkey-carpets to a Kilmarnock firm. These are said to have been the first of that luxurious and costly type manufactured in Scotland.[3] Hand-knotted carpets continued to be made in the south-west of Scotland for about twenty years. Early in the present century efforts were made to start carpet-knotting among the fisher-folk of Sutherland and Caithness, but in the end it was found impossible to induce the girls to settle down to regular work. The looms were removed to Glasgow, where they

---

[1] *Illustrations of Her Majesty's Palace at Brighton*, 1838, p. 9.
[2] This is completely outclassed by a carpet lately made in Donegal, weighing $2\frac{1}{4}$ tons.
[3] British Association Reports, Glasgow, September, 1876. *The Textile Industries*, by James Paton, pp. 204–6.

were kept going until the outbreak of the war. There are still deft fingers ready to make carpets to-day, whether knotted after the Turkish or the Persian manner. But the mainstay of the carpet industry of Scotland has ever been the use of those ingenious contrivances for producing a pile-surface by mechanical means.

When we come to Ireland we must begin a little farther back. Irish " rugs " were in demand in this country in the sixteenth and seventeenth centuries. But the " rug " of those days was a rough material, shaggy in appearance, perhaps like a modern blanket. Holinshed has a story of a man who went to a bear-baiting in London on a frosty morning wearing a Waterford rug. " The mastiffs," says the Elizabethan chronicler, " had no sooner espied him than they set on him, thinking him to be a bear." It is a long stride from the Waterford rug of Queen Elizabeth's days to the Donegal carpets of our own times. Perhaps the chief link connecting them is the quality of the Irish wool. The hand-knotted carpet industry was introduced, or revived, in Ireland about twenty years ago. A factory was opened at Killybegs in 1898, and the work was soon extended to other centres in North and South Donegal. Before long, hundreds of workers were employed. Some very good results have been obtained. An imposing product of the Donegal factories is in the Library of Australia House in London. It measures 46 ft. 6 in. by 23 ft. The general tone of the ground is brown. There is a fine border of wattle and vine-leaves. This carpet is matched by others of the same manufacture now in this country. Others are also to be found in Scotland and Ireland and on the Continent, as well as in Canada, the United States, Egypt and South Africa. Fine carpets have also been made in Kildare and in Queen's County.

In conclusion, the carpets made by our great craftsman William Morris must not be forgotten. It was in 1879 that his first experiments in carpet-knotting were made in Queen Square. Then carpet-looms were set up at Hammersmith, and finally the work was transferred to Merton. A careful study of the old productions of the East was the foundation of his work. " They show us the way to set about designing such things," he said. Modern carpets, " while they should equal the Eastern ones in material and durability, should by no means imitate them in design, but show themselves obviously to be the outcome of modern and Western ideas."

Morris made some noble carpets. The large carpet made for the Earl of Carlisle's drawing-room at Naworth, was finished in 1881. It took nearly a year to make, and " weighed about a ton." Another fine carpet was made for the late Earl of Portsmouth. It was arc-shaped, made so as to fit the place for which it was destined at Hurstbourne. The floral pattern is interrupted by three large shields bearing the arms of the Earl and the Countess.

PART II
TECHNICAL

CHAPTER I

THE TECHNIQUE OF HAND-WOVEN CARPETS

(a) Knotting and Weaving

It is essential to students to have some knowledge of the technique of carpets, for not only does it help in understanding and appreciating at its proper worth any particular specimen standing alone, but it is also of the utmost importance in grouping together kindred pieces, and in associating with such groups, when made, any fresh carpet that may be met with. In this latter respect technique is of even more importance than design itself, at least so far as the finer subdivisions are concerned. The connoisseur who identifies a carpet by its general appearance really pays more attention to technique than he is usually aware of, for the same design looks very different when it is rendered in various textures ; and the texture, apart from the design, produces an impression more valuable for purposes of diagnosis than may be realized. This impression is made much more vivid and reliable by an understanding of the knotting, weaving and other technical details of the specimen under consideration. Apart from this, moreover, it is easy to understand that a weaver is more inclined to change his designs than his methods. The demand of the market may be for certain patterns at the time popular ; or the beauty of rugs made in other places and following other traditions may appeal to him so strongly that he will copy their designs ; but there are no such reasons to induce him to depart from his accustomed methods of weaving. So far as unorganized production is concerned the technique is a very reliable indication of the place or people responsible for the rug. On the other hand, in the case of a highly organized factory system, both the design and technique of some other district may be copied, and then the question of the identification of the product may be a very difficult or unanswerable one. Luckily it is in these circumstances that the answer is of the least consequence.

In the first place one requires to distinguish a hand-made from a machine-made carpet. It is not easy to give a simple rule to decide the point ; but the inspection of a few pieces, especially from the back, soon makes the difference obvious even to the untrained eye, and the

87

perusal of the following pages describing the making of hand-knotted carpets should afford positive indications by which the matter can be placed beyond all possible doubt. Leaving the question of machine-made carpets for a subsequent brief mention, the whole field of hand-made carpets can be divided into two great classes—those with smooth faces, and those with a pile. Both classes are textile fabrics; which means that they consist essentially of two sets of threads—the warp and the weft—which cross each other at right-angles and are interwoven so as to make a coherent tissue. The smooth-faced carpets consist of warp and weft alone: the pile carpets have, in addition, short extra pieces of thread knotted to the warp-threads, so that their free ends stand up and form a surface similar to that made by the blades of grass in a meadow.

Like other textile fabrics carpets must be made on a frame, which is known as a loom. This consists essentially of two horizontal beams or rollers, kept a proper distance apart by side-pieces. The threads of the warp are stretched between these two beams and all lie parallel to each other and usually in a vertical position. When they are placed on the loom the weaving can begin. The weft-threads are put in one by one: the first thread passes in front of alternate warp-threads (suppose the first, third, fifth, etc.), and behind the remaining warp-threads (the second, fourth, sixth, etc.); the second weft-thread reverses the arrangement of the first, passing behind the odd-numbered and in front of the even-numbered warp-threads; the third weft-thread repeats the arrangement of the first, the fourth of the second, and this alternate reversal is carried throughout the whole of the fabric (Fig. c, p. 92).

The loom need not be an elaborate structure. In its simplest form it may consist of two round pieces of wood, tied or otherwise fixed to two adjacent trees, one piece being near the ground and the other as much higher as the length of the warp requires. On such a loom the necessary tension of the warp can be obtained by wedging the beams further apart, or by tightening the cords which lash them to the trees. A more convenient arrangement is to have for beams two rollers capable of rotation, fixed in a permanent framework (Fig. A). This plan has the advantage that the loom need not be the full height of the carpet; for a supply of warp can be wound round the upper beam (thus often called the warp-beam) and unwound as the finished part of the carpet is, bit by bit, rolled round the lower, or cloth-beam. With such an arrangement the weavers can sit all the time in about the same position, though it is still often found convenient to accommodate them on a plank that can be placed at various heights on the rungs of two ladders. At the Victoria and Albert Museum there is a Persian Carpet-loom which was in actual use in a house in Kirman a few years ago. It has on it a small rug, partly finished, and it is accompanied by all the usual implements of the carpet weaver (Plate 92A). A typical form of Turkish loom accommodating several weavers is shown in Plate 92B. The loom is not always vertical, though in the majority of cases it is so. Among nomad weavers, and especially in the districts of Central Asia, a horizontal loom is quite common. The two beams rest on the ground and mostly have slots in them through which the side-pieces pass, the whole arrangement strongly resembling the common embroidery-frame. The weavers squat on the finished part of the carpet, which lies a few inches above the ground but can easily be supported by placing under it pieces of wood or other objects. The necessary attitude is, however, an uncomfortable one for persons unaccustomed to it.

The laborious method of guiding the weft-thread in its proper course round each warp-thread separately can be avoided by a simple contrivance added to the loom. A thick stick is thrust through the warp in exactly the same manner as a weft-thread, only it is placed far above the place where the actual weaving is taking place. This stick divides the warp-threads into two sets or *leaves*, and forms what is called a *shed* (Fig. A). All the odd-numbered warps are in one leaf and all the even-numbered in the other. The weft-thread, wound on a shuttle, can now be easily passed between the two leaves of the shed and at once takes its right position in relation to the warp. For the next passage of the weft a reverse shed has to be made. This is effected by attaching all the warp-threads of the back leaf of the shed to a strong rod, by means of short cords of equal length—an arrangement called a *heddle*. If then the rod is drawn forward or suitably rotated, the warp-threads attached to it will be drawn in front of the other set and so a reverse shed is formed, through which the weft-thread can be passed as before (Fig. B). It is clear that one shed is permanently set on the loom, but the other can be temporarily substituted for it at will.

Some other accessories of the weaver must be mentioned here. One is a heavy comb-like implement for beating the weft down. Its teeth pass between the warp-threads, and a few blows consolidate the latest rows of weft and knots with the finished part of the carpet. For severing the pile-yarn a knife is mostly used, which is held in the right hand while the knot is tied with the left. Shears with long and slightly-curved blades are employed for trimming the pile of the carpet to a uniform level. Balls or skeins of coloured yarn for the pattern hang in a row from the upper beam or heddle-rod within easy reach of the weavers. All these accessories are illustrated in Plate 92.

As implied already smooth-faced carpets are simpler in construction than pile-carpets and, consequently, it is convenient to describe the details of their technique first. They are called Kilims (Gilîm), and the most common kind —which are essentially similar in technique to the tapestry-hangings of Europe —are often called Karamani, after the province of Karaman in Southern Asia Minor, though their production is by no means confined to that locality but indeed extends through almost the whole of the carpet-making regions of the East.

The warp does not show in the finished Kilim, but the pattern is entirely formed by the weft which is beaten down sufficiently to hide the former completely. To make a varied

FIG. A.—CARPET-LOOM.

pattern the weft-threads of course must be of different colours and so cannot be passed right across the loom, but each thread is taken only so far as that particular colour is needed and then passed back again, and so on until a patch of colour of the desired shape is formed, the whole pattern being composed of many such coloured patches. If in any place the boundary between two patches of colour is vertical (i.e. parallel to the warp), it is clear that a vertical slit must result there (Fig. c), for no weft-thread passes from one patch to the other to bind the fabric together. This defect is commonly avoided by designing the pattern so that vertical lines either do not occur or else are very short, but the weavers of Karaman and Kurdistan often make a feature of this very limitation and allow an open-work effect to give an added beauty to their work.

From the manner of their manufacture Kilims are practically alike both back and front. Sometimes, it is true, short ends of the weft lie loose at the back ; but more often these are inwoven so as to make the two sides indistinguishable. The peculiarities of the technique of Kilims have a great influence on the patterns adopted. Fine details are rarely seen, and the constant use of diagonal or stepped outlines is a feature which mostly enables them to be distinguished at a glance.

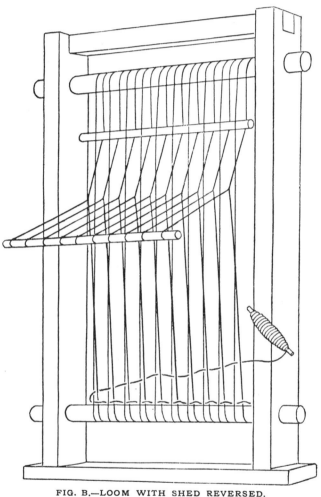

FIG. B.—LOOM WITH SHED REVERSED.

Smooth-faced carpets of another kind are known as Soumaks. These differ from ordinary Kilims and from all other carpets in the way the weft is interlaced with the warp. Each weft-thread is passed forwards in front of four and then backwards behind two warp-threads (Fig. D). Thus the stitches, as they may be called, overlap each other on the front of the carpet, and as they usually slope in opposite directions in consecutive rows, a kind of herring-bone effect is produced. At the back, the shorter stitches form a series of ridges ; but the back is not intended to be seen and no attempt is made to keep it free from loose ends of yarn. The normal texture of a Soumak has often to be slightly modified near the boundaries of the pattern, for the long stitch across four warp-threads would sometimes interfere with the finer details. Another difference between Soumaks and other Kilims is that the former have after every one or two rows of stitches an extra weft-thread, which passes right across the carpet but is not visible when the latter is finished.

The fineness of texture of Kilims depends upon the closeness of the warp-threads, which are usually spaced so that from five to twenty-four fall within one inch. The weft-threads lie considerably closer together than this, but whereas each warp-thread forms in the fabric a fine rib, which is easily perceptible, the exact size of the weft does not to any considerable extent affect the appearance of the carpet. It may be said that there are about six times as many weft-threads as warp-threads in a given distance.

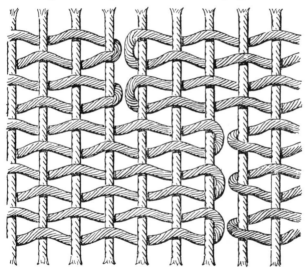

Kilims are made more quickly than pile-carpets and are generally lighter in substance, as a result of which their wearing qualities are not equal to those of the latter. In the East they are largely used on the floor, but in Western countries, where perhaps the conditions are more severe, they are often reserved for hangings or furniture coverings, for which purposes they are admirably adapted.

Useful and beautiful as the smooth-faced carpets are, they are much excelled in importance by the larger class of carpets with a pile surface. In these the warp and weft foundation is completely hidden, as far as the front is concerned, by the more or less upright pile. The effect of use is gradually to wear away this pile, but as long as any is left the vital threads forming the foundation of the carpet are protected from serious injury. Even the back of the carpet, though it gets far less wear than the front, is protected by the pile-yarn passing round the warp-threads. This is by no means the only advantage that a pile gives. In a Kilim the surface is composed of the fibres of the yarn lying flat in the plane of the carpet; in a pile-carpet it is the countless cut-ends of the fibres that are presented to the eye, an arrangement which gives to the surface a quality that no other can. The colours of the yarn become richer and more transparent; the contours of the pattern are made softer and more mysterious, and the tone of each coloured area not only varies subtly from point to point, but often changes completely as the spectator views it from different positions.

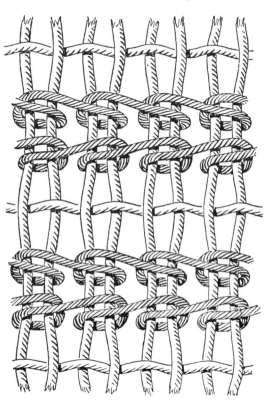

The pile is formed from short pieces of yarn, rarely more than one inch long, tied to, or twisted round, the warp-threads —the whole piece, including the free ends, usually being called a knot or tuft. The knots are tied in rows right across the carpet, each row being finished and secured by weft-threads before another row is begun. With few exceptions the knots are attached to two adjacent warp-threads,

FIG. D.—SOUMAK WEAVING.

but there are various ways in which they may be tied. In all Eastern carpets, and nearly all Western ones, only two kinds of knots are found. They are known as the Ghiordes, or Turkish knot, and the Sehna, or Persian knot. The names are those of carpet-weaving villages in Asia Minor and Western Persia respectively.

In the case of the Ghiordes knot the yarn lies across and in front of the two warp-threads and its free ends pass round behind them and then emerge again between them. As each pair of warp-threads has its own knot it will be understood that consecutive warp-threads have either two, or no yarn-ends passing forward between them, and that what may be called the collar of the knot is seen lying across a pair of threads (Fig. E).

In the case of the Sehna knot the yarn completely encircles one warp-thread of a pair; one yarn-end emerges between them, while the other passes behind the second warp-thread and comes to the front outside it (Fig. F). Thus, with the Sehna knot one yarn-end emerges

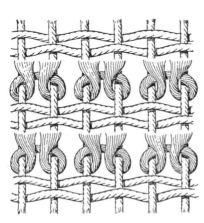

FIG. E.—GHIORDES KNOT.

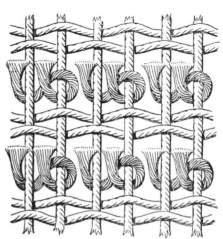

FIG. F.—SEHNA KNOT.

between each pair of warp-threads right across the loom, and the collar of the knot is seen crossing one warp-thread only; in both knots the free ends come below the collar so that the pile inclines to the lower or first-woven part of the carpet.

The Ghiordes knot is symmetrical from side to side while the Sehna knot is unsymmetrical; it follows that the latter may be tied in two ways, for the encircled warp-thread may be either the right-hand or left-hand one of the pair, as seen by the weaver. The right-hand Sehna knot is much more common than the left-hand, and its pile tends to lie towards the left, while the pile of the left-hand inclines towards the right (Fig. G). If the knot is known to be of the Sehna variety, passing the hand across the carpet will usually tell at once of which kind it is.

When the warp-threads are spaced very closely on the loom it may be impossible for them to lie all in one plane, in which case alternate threads fall towards the back, and the warp lies on two levels. Sometimes the depression of the back set is only slight, but it may be so pronounced that only half the warp-threads are seen at the back of the carpet. A Ghiordes knot tied on a warp on two levels may incline either to the right or to the left; but in the case of the Sehna knot, the encircled warp-thread is always the one lying nearer to the front of the carpet (Fig. H). In a tightly-woven carpet with a warp on two levels it is often very difficult to be sure which kind of knot is used, because in either case two yarn-ends emerge between every pair of warp-threads of the front set. If the knot is a Ghiordes, a little probing will

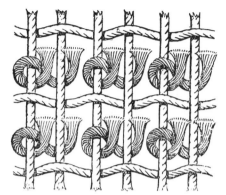

FIG. G.—LEFT-HAND SEHNA KNOT.

usually show its collar crossing two warp-threads; but if this cannot be found, then, though a Sehna knot may be strongly suspected, the proof may be quite difficult. It may be said, however, that the Ghiordes knot is rarely found with a warp on very different levels, and a Sehna knot still more rarely with a warp strictly on one level. Both these knots are sometimes found tied on four instead of on two threads, though rarely throughout the whole of a carpet. In such a case the knot itself is not really different, for it only means that two warp-threads are taken together and treated as one.

The adoption of one or other of these knots is rather due to custom than to any inherent advantage of either. It is true that carpets of very fine texture usually have the Sehna knot, and distinctly coarse ones almost invariably have the Ghiordes, but it is quite possible to use the latter for very close knotting.

A third kind of knot, tied on a single warp-thread, is much less com-

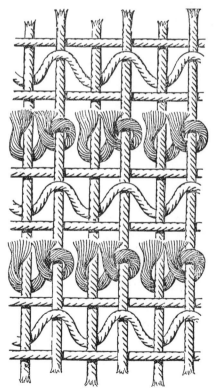

FIG. H.—SEHNA KNOT.

95

mon than the two already described, being found only, but almost exclusively, in early Spanish carpets. The yarn completely encircles the single warp-thread, one end crosses the other at the back and then the ends come to the front, one at each side (Fig. I). It is tied only on alternate warp-threads ; and on that account, as will be seen later, is very easy to recognize.

When a row of knots, of whatever kind, has been tied, one or more weft-threads are put in. The most usual number is two, in which case the thread is taken from side to side right across the loom, and then without being severed taken back through the reverse shed. If only one *shoot* (as it is called) of weft is made after a row of knots, then the shoot after the next row is taken through the reverse shed. Three or more shoots of weft may be found after a row of knots, but the larger numbers are not often used throughout the whole of a carpet.

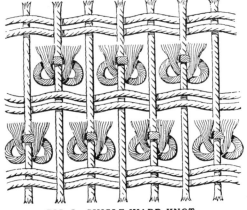

FIG. I.—SINGLE-WARP KNOT.

The weft when beaten down usually takes a more or less sinuous course in the thickness of the carpet, for the warp is too strong and tight to be much deflected from a straight line. If the warp lies on two levels the weft-threads through one shed are necessarily more sinuous than those through the reverse shed ; and if the levels are very distinct then it will happen that the weft-thread through one shed is quite straight and undeflected while the other is very sinuous indeed. In many of the finer Persian carpets with a warp on two levels, a common plan is to have uniformly three shoots of weft after each row of knots, the middle shoot being very sinuous and the other two straight (Fig. H).

To ensure a carpet having even edges and being free from bulges or puckers, and of equal width throughout, it is necessary to allow the weft a proper and uniform amount of slack and then beat it down so that its tension is the same in each part of the width of the carpet.

When a line of weft, consisting of one or more shoots, is completed the carpet is ready for another row of knots. The Ghiordes and Sehna knots are tied on the same pairs of warps as before, that is they come vertically above each other : on the other hand the single-warp knots

96

are tied on those warps left blank in the previous row, and so fall into diagonal instead of vertical lines. A carpet with the single-warp knot therefore has the easily-noticed peculiarity that diagonal lines in the pattern are much smoother in contour than those in a truly vertical direction.

The fineness of knotting in a pile carpet is a feature of great influence in determining the beauty of its texture and the amount of labour necessary for its production. It depends primarily upon the closeness of spacing of the warp-threads on the loom. The number of these to the linear inch may vary from about eight to more than sixty, giving from four to thirty or more knots to the inch in a horizontal line. The number of knots in a vertical line (i.e., in the direction of the warp) depends upon the fineness of the yarns employed, the number of shoots of weft after each row of knots and also upon the thoroughness with which the beating-down is carried out. These details are mostly arranged so that the height of the knots is roughly equal to their width, but it mostly happens that the latter dimension is the smaller and the ratio of height to width is commonly about four-fifths, though sinking as low as one-half in some groups of carpets.

The simplest way of estimating the fineness is to compute the number of knots in a square inch of surface. This number will vary from about 16 to nearly 1,000, though in the vast majority of carpets it lies between 50 and 100. If there are more than 100 knots to the square inch the texture may be considered fine. Carpets with more than 300 knots are rarely met with and there appears to be no advantage to the appearance of the carpet in pushing the fineness beyond 400 knots to the inch, though phenomenal pieces of such texture are occasionally seen. As far as durability is concerned, a coarser carpet, provided it is well knotted and not extremely coarse, is more satisfactory than a finer one.

Whether a bit of yarn just long enough for a knot is used in making it, or whether, as is a common practice, the end of a long piece is taken and cut off when the knot is tied, it is impossible to ensure all the free ends being of the same length, so that a final operation is to clip the pile level with shears. Here the Chinese show some of their peculiar ingenuity, for by cutting down the knots nearest to the contours of the pattern, they cause a distinct furrow to be formed which not only serves to round off the angularities of the contour but also throws the design into relief. This effect of relief is often increased by trimming somewhat closer the whole of the pile of the ground.

In carpets other than Chinese, though the usual practice is to have the pile as even as possible, yet its length varies considerably in different specimens. In some rugs, notably those from Sehna and Ghiordes, the pile is so short that the collars of the knots are scarcely hidden. In such cases the rug itself is thin, and the pile stands upright, which makes the surface lustreless and harsh to the touch.

The Nomadic tribes of the Caucasus and Kurdistan, on the other hand, prefer a long and sometimes almost shaggy pile, a choice which results in thick and mostly very durable rugs. Such a pile of necessity lies flat, and exhibits to the utmost the lustre of the wool. A long pile of a dull wool, as seen too much in India, has the least satisfactory appearance of any.

The treatment of the sides and ends of a carpet still remains to be mentioned. At the sides the returning weft-threads by themselves form a selvedge and prevent the fabric from becoming unravelled, but in use they would soon get worn through. It is customary, therefore, to have at the edge one or more stouter warp-threads and to leave these free from knots, but to serve them with extra turns of weft, and then to fortify the whole with an overcasting of extra threads which may form one or several cord-like lines along the side.

As the ends of the warp-threads are loose when the carpet is removed from the loom, unravelling is a danger which must be provided against. Usually before the knotting begins a piece of plain, or of tapestry-weaving is done at the beginning of the carpet, and a similar piece is added at the top when the knotting is finished. When the carpet is taken from the loom the loose ends of the warp are either braided in various ways or they are taken in groups of about four to eight, which groups are next taken in pairs and knotted together, and this process often is repeated until there are several rows of knots. In either case the carpet usually terminates in a loose fringe. The lower end of the warp may consist of loops instead of cut-ends, owing to the way in which it was originally put on the loom. These loops may be treated as above, but an alternative plan when they exist is to fill them up with a few rows of ordinary weaving so that a true selvedge is formed. This cannot be done at the upper end of the carpet, for it would be almost impossible to have the loops of warp there all of the same length.

Many smaller points of technique, as well as some variations from the normal methods described above, may be very useful in identifying carpets; but they can be mentioned more conveniently with the groups in which they are found.

THE TECHNIQUE OF HAND-WOVEN CARPETS

The structure of machine-made carpets is generally quite different from that discussed above. It is notoriously difficult to devise a machine to tie a knot, though recently it has been found possible to reproduce the Ghiordes knot on a machine, and the method is employed commercially. The process most in use, however, is one founded on the technique of velvet-weaving. In this, besides the foundation-warps, other warps of much greater length are woven into the fabric and allowed to stand up in a series of loops. These are cut through in " Wilton " and left uncut in the " Brussels " carpets. In other methods loops of the pile-yarn are held in position by being pinched in various ways by the foundation threads : or lengths of chenille are first made separately and then woven with other foundation threads in such a way that they lie in the face of the fabric. It is by such a method that the " patent Axminster " carpets were made.

(b) Group Characteristics of Early Carpets.

The technique of the oldest carpets known does not differ in essentials from that of those of the present day, and all the details found in them have already been described in the preceding chapter, but it may still be useful to take each of the well-defined early groups in turn and give a short account of their technical construction.

The early Persian carpets with a woollen pile may be divided into two groups—those made in the periods roughly corresponding to the sixteenth and seventeenth centuries.

Persian carpets of the earlier of these two groups invariably have the Sehna knot. The warp is on two levels and there are three shoots of weft after each row of knots. The warp is sometimes of silk, but more often of cotton. The middle or sinuous shoot of weft is either of silk or cotton, and the other two shoots are mostly of cotton but not infrequently of wool and occasionally of silk. The texture is very fine, there being on the average about 230 knots to the square inch. The pile is generally of wool, though some metal thread, inserted by the tapestry method, is found in a few examples.

The selvedges and ends of these early carpets rarely remain now, but it appears that the sides were usually finished with a single over-casting, and that the ends had a simple warp-fringe—in fact that the treatment was the same as that of the best modern Persian carpets. The number of different colours used was fairly constant and rather large, being on the average nine or ten. The colours most frequently occurring,

99

placed in order of the amount used of each, are :—crimson : dark blue : yellow : orange : ochre : white : blue : light blue : green : black. Other colours, placed in order of frequency of occurrence, are :—light red : green-blue : red : brown : pale green : light crimson : pale brown. In this and the following lists, shades and colours not included are occasionally found.

Persian Carpets of the later group also have the Sehna knot and a warp on two levels and in most respects resemble the earlier ones. The warp, however, is generally of cotton : the sinuous shoot of weft is mostly of cotton and the other two shoots are either of cotton or wool. The texture is not so fine as in the earlier group, but still the average number of knots to the square inch is as high as 175. Metal thread is not used. The average number of colours used is nine or ten as before. Those most frequently occurring, placed in order of the amount used, are :—dark blue : crimson : blue : white : yellow : light blue : green : orange : red : black. Other colours placed in order of frequency of occurrence, are :—green-blue : ochre : red : brown : purple : pale green.

It will not be supposed, of course, that the foregoing descriptions apply to the average standard of the carpets made in the periods in question, for they are, and can only be, based on the carpets which have come down to us and which were therefore the most precious or the most durable of those made.

The carpets usually called Indo-Persian (see p. 39) which in point of date probably centre about the beginning of the seventeenth century, or a little later, also have the Sehna knot, a warp on two levels and three shoots of weft. The warp is either of silk or cotton, and for the weft cotton is generally used for all three shoots. There are on the average about 165 knots to the square inch. The pile is of wool with occasionally a little white cotton. The colours, which are very bright, rich and transparent, number ten on the average. Those most frequently occurring, placed in order of the amount used, are :—crimson : deep green-blue : green : yellow : orange : dark blue : white : pale crimson : blue : light blue : black. Other colours, placed in order of frequency of occurrence, are :—pale brown : deep yellow : deep purple : light red : purple : dark brown.

The carpets of Asia Minor, of the kind called Ushak, which date from the fifteenth to the seventeenth centuries, are invariably woven with the Ghiordes knot. The warp is of white wool and lies on one level or on two levels very slightly separated. The weft is of red wool and there are two shoots after each row of knots. The pile is of wool with occasionally a little white cotton, and the texture is rather coarse. The sides and ends have rarely been preserved, but it seems that the former were usually finished with a selvedge consisting of several cords. Traces of wide coloured webs at the ends of many carpets make it appear that this was the usual way of treating them.

The earlier of these Asia Minor carpets—that is, those up to about the end of the sixteenth century, have on the average about 70 knots to the square inch. The number of different colours is on the average seven. Those most frequently occurring, placed in order of the amount used, are :—red : dark blue : yellow : white : black. Other colours, placed in order of frequency of occurrence, are :—light blue : green : green-blue : dark blue : light red : purple.

The later of these Asia Minor carpets have an average of about 85 knots to the square inch. The average number of different colours is seven as before. Those most frequently occurring, placed in order of the amount used, are :—red : dark blue : blue : yellow : green : light blue : black. Other colours, placed in order of frequency of occurrence, are :—green-blue : white : purple.

The Asia Minor carpets commonly called Transylvanian differ in some respects from those already described. The warp is mostly dyed, yellow being the usual colour ; and the weft is more often yellow than red. The average number of knots to the square inch is 70. There are six different colours on the average. Those most frequently occurring, placed in order of the amount used, are :— red : yellow : white : blue : black. Other colours, placed in order of frequency of occurrence, are :— light blue : purple-red : light red.

A group of Turkish carpets dating from the sixteenth century are woven with the Sehna knot, which is never used in other Turkish rugs. They may be divided into four classes, but it is not certain that carpets of the last two were made in Turkey (see p. 51) though the technique considered alone points that way.

Those of the first class (see p. 46) have a warp of very fine yellow wool, apparently that of the Angora goat. The warp has a right-handed twist, and lies on two levels. There are three shoots of weft, which is of wool usually yellow in colour. The pile is of wool, and there are on the average 85 knots to the square inch. The average number of different colours is seven. Those most frequently occurring, placed in order of the amount used, are :—crimson : yellow : yellow-green : blue : green : light blue : white. Other colours, placed in order of frequency of occurrence, are :—deep yellow : dark blue : black.

The carpets of the second class (see p. 47) resemble those of the first in most respects. The warp (also with a right-handed twist) is, however, often of silk, and is crimson, green or yellow. The knotting is much finer, there being on the average 205 knots to the square inch. The average number of different colours is six. Those most frequently occurring, placed in order of the amount used, are :—crimson : yellow : light blue : white : green. Other colours, placed in order of frequency of occurrence, are :—blue : dark blue : black : yellow-green : deep yellow.

The third class consists of carpets with arabesque patterns of the kind shown in Plate 48 (see also p. 51). Technically, they resemble the first group very closely though the texture tends to be rather finer. The average number of different colours is five or six. Those most frequently occurring, placed in order of the amount used, are :—crimson : green : light blue : yellow : white. Other colours, placed in order of frequency of occurrence, are :—blue : black : purple.

The fourth class comprises carpets with arabesque pattern of the kind shown in Plate 47 (see also p. 51). Apart from having the Sehna knot, they resemble in technique the ordinary Ushak carpets. The warp is of coarse white wool with the usual left-handed twist, and lies on one level. There are two shoots of woollen weft—mostly red in colour. The knots average about 80 to the square inch. The average number of colours is seven or eight. Those most frequently occurring, placed in order of the amount used, are :—red : light blue : blue : white : yellow : black. Other colours, placed in order of frequency of occurrence, are :—brown : purple : dark blue.

Spanish carpets of the sixteenth and seventeenth centuries are made entirely of wool and the single-warp knot is generally used. The warp is white, and the weft, which usually consists of three or four untwisted strands, is red, white or yellow. The average number of knots to the square inch is 110. The sides are finished with a narrow web of plain weaving, which no doubt was turned under the carpet. The ends, apparently, had wide webs and fringes. There are on the average about six colours. Those most frequently met with, placed in order of the amount used, are :—red : blue : yellow : green : white : light blue. Other colours, placed in order of frequency of occurrence, are :—dark green : light red : dark brown : bright yellow : black : orange.

THE TECHNIQUE OF HAND-WOVEN CARPETS

The carpets made in England during the sixteenth and seventeenth centuries were clearly based, as far as their technique is concerned, upon Asia Minor models, though important differences are found. The warp is of hemp, or perhaps coarse flax, and it lies on one level. The weft is of the same material as the warp and there is one shoot after each row of knots. The Ghiordes knot is used, and the pile is of wool. The texture is rather coarse, there being on the average about 65 knots to the square inch. The sides were finished with a narrow band of plain weaving and there appears to have been a similar web at the ends in most cases. The colours used were often bright and each was used in several shades so that the total number of differently-coloured wools was high. Apparently in the seventeenth century there was a tendency to replace the hempen warp with one of wool, and in still later times the warp was more generally of the latter material.

The following are descriptions of the technique of those carpets illustrated in this book, which it has been possible to examine closely. In each case the colours have been placed, as far as could be judged, in the order of the amounts occurring in the particular specimens described. After a colour the most important parts of the design where it is used are sometimes specified and in this connexion it may be noted that the border-stripes are numbered from the outer edge of the carpet.

PERSIAN CARPET (Victoria and Albert Museum). 15th–16th century. 18 ft. × 9 ft. 10 in. (See Plate 1 and p. 19.)
 Warp : Two-ply green silk. On two levels. 45 to 1 inch.
 Weft : White silk. Three shoots after each row of knots.
 Knots : Wool. Sehna. 21 to 1 inch. 470 to the square inch.
 Colours : Nine. Crimson (field ; outer part of 2nd border) : dark blue (inner part of 2nd border) : orange (1st border) : white (3rd border) : blue : light yellow : light green : black : light brown.

PERSIAN GARDEN CARPET (Wagner Collection). 16th–17th century. 17 ft. 5 in. × 14 ft. 2 in. (See Plate 3 and p. 12.)
 Warp : Four-ply white cotton. On two levels. 33 to 1 inch.
 Weft : Wool, or occasionally silk, of various colours. Three shoots after each row of knots.
 Knots : Wool. Sehna. 14 to 1 inch. 240 to the square inch.
 Colours : Nine. Blue (field) : light blue : white : yellow (border) : crimson-red : blue-green : brown : dull green : black.

HAND-WOVEN CARPETS

ARMENIAN CARPET (Victoria and Albert Museum). 17th–18th century. 6 ft. 11 in. × 6 ft. (See Plate 5B and p. 16.)
Warp : Two-ply white wool. On two levels. 16 to 1 inch.
Weft : Red wool. Two shoots after each row of knots.
Knots : Wool. Ghiordes. 12 to 1 inch. 100 to the square inch.
Colours : Eight. Red (field) : blue : white (1st border) : yellow : light blue : dark blue : brown-black : purple.

ARMENIAN CARPET (Victoria and Albert Museum). Probably 17th century. 11 ft. × 6 ft. 4 in. (See Plate 8 and p. 16.)
Warp : Two-ply whitish brown wool. On two levels. 18 to 1 inch.
Weft : Red-brown wool. Two shoots after each row of knots.
Knots : Wool. Ghiordes. 9 to 1 inch. 80 to the square inch.
Colours : Seven. Brown-black (field) : white (border) : blue : yellow : crimson-red : light blue : purple.

PERSIAN CARPET (Victoria and Albert Museum). 16th century. 19 ft. 10 in. × 13 ft. (See Plate 9 and p. 16.)
Warp : Four-ply white cotton. On two levels. 22 to 1 inch.
Weft : Buff cotton. Three shoots after each row of knots.
Knots : Wool. Sehna. 11 to 1 inch. 120 to the square inch.
Colours : Ten. Crimson (field) : ochre (2nd border) : dark blue : white : green-blue (3rd border) : blue : green : light blue : light red : black.

THE ARDABIL CARPET (Victoria and Albert Museum). Persian ; dated 1540. 34 ft. 6 in. × 17 ft. 6 in. (See Plate 11 and p. 17.)
Warp : Two-ply yellow silk. On two levels. 35 to 1 inch.
Weft : Yellow silk. Three shoots after each row of knots.
Knots : Wool. Sehna. 19 to 1 inch. 340 to the square inch.
Colours : Ten. Dark blue (field) : crimson (4th border ; long panels in 2nd border) : white (3rd border) : black (2nd border) : orange-red (1st border) : yellow (central medallion and corner pieces) : green (round panels in 2nd border) : blue : light blue (pattern of 1st border) : light crimson.

PERSIAN CARPET (The Earl of Ilchester). 16th–17th century. 20 ft. × 8 ft. (See Plate 12 and p. 20.)
Warp : Six-ply white cotton. On two levels. 28 to 1 inch.

Weft : Pale red cotton. Three shoots after each row of knots.

Knots : Wool. Sehna. 16 to 1 inch. 230 to the square inch.

Colours : Thirteen. Dark blue (field) : deep crimson (2nd border) : blue-green (pattern on ground of field) : light crimson (pattern on ground of 2nd border) : buff (1st and 3rd borders) : yellow (pattern on ground of 1st and 3rd borders) : white : light blue : crimson : brown : blue : black : light blue-green.

PERSIAN CARPET (Victoria and Albert Museum). Probably 17th century. 7 ft. 7 in. × 5 ft. 5 in. (See Plate 14 and p. 21.)

Warp : Yellow silk. On two levels. 54 to 1 inch.

Weft : Yellow silk. Three shoots after each row of knots.

Knots : Wool. Sehna. 27 to 1 inch. 730 to the square inch.

Metal Thread : Gilt-silver strips wound on a core of white or yellow silk. Tapestry-woven on the upper layer of the warp, three shoots being equivalent to one row of knots.

Colours : Eleven. Crimson (medallion and border panels) : dark blue (field) : green (2nd border) : light crimson (1st border) : white (3rd border) : light blue : brown : yellow : light green : black : orange.

PERSIAN CARPET (Victoria and Albert Museum). 17th century. 24 ft. 6 in. × 9 ft. 5 in. (See Plate 19 and p. 24.)

Warp : White cotton. On two levels. 31 to 1 inch.

Weft : Two shoots of white wool and one shoot of white cotton after each row of knots.

Knots : Wool. Sehna. 12 to 1 inch. 180 to the square inch.

Colours : Eleven. Dull crimson (field) : dark blue (outer border) : blue (inner border) : white : yellow : green-blue : light red : light blue : light purple : black : purple-brown.

PERSIAN CARPET (Victoria and Albert Museum). 17th century. 5 ft. 5 in. × 10 ft. 4 in. (See Plate 20B and p. 25.)

Warp : White cotton. On two levels. 18 to 1 inch.

Weft : White cotton. Three shoots after each row of knots.

Knots : Wool. Sehna. 7 to 1 inch. 60 to the square inch.

Colours : Nine. Red : blue : yellow : white : green : dark blue : light crimson : blue-green : black. The compartments are variously coloured upon no fixed plan.

PERSIAN CARPET from the Palace of the Forty Columns at Ispahan (fragments at the Victoria and Albert Museum). Late 16th century. Original size 71 ft. × 33 ft. (See Plate 21 for design and p. 25.)
> *Warp :* Three-ply white cotton. On two levels. 24 to 1 inch.
> *Weft :* White cotton. Three shoots after each row of knots.
> *Knots :* Wool. Sehna. 15 to 1 inch. 180 to the square inch.
> *Colours :* Eight. Crimson (field) : dark blue (2nd border) : yellow-green : white (1st and 3rd borders) : light crimson : black : brown (? black of a different dye).

PERSIAN PRAYER-CARPET (Mr. George Mounsey). 18th century. 5 ft. 11 in. × 4 ft. 5 in. (See Plate 30A and p. 36.)
> *Warp :* White cotton. On two levels. 21 to 1 inch.
> *Weft :* White cotton. Three shoots after each row of knots.
> *Knots :* Wool. Sehna. 9 to 1 inch. 100 to the square inch.
> *Colours :* Two. White (ground) : copper-red in various shades.

INDIAN CARPETS (Mr. Lionel Harris). Early 17th century. A. Shaped piece, 14 ft. 7 in. × 9 ft. B. Square piece, 24 ft. 2 in. × 9 ft. 2 in. (See Plate 31 and p. 39.)
> *Warp :* White cotton. On two levels. 26 to 1 inch.
> *Weft :* Pink cotton. Three shoots after each row of knots.
> *Knots :* Wool. Sehna. 13 to 1 inch. 170 to the square inch.
> *Colours :* Nine. Crimson (field) : Green-blue (2nd border) : light blue : white : deep purple : yellow : light crimson : black : dark green.

INDIAN CARPET (Victoria and Albert Museum). Early 17th century. 4 ft. 8 in. × 2 ft. 11 in. (See Plate 32 and p. 39.)
> *Warp :* Two-ply silk (red, green or white). On two levels. 46 to 1 inch.
> *Weft :* Red silk. Three shoots after each row of knots.
> *Knots :* Wool. Sehna. 26 to 1 inch. 600 to the square inch.
> *Colours :* Twelve. Crimson (field) : yellow-buff (serrated leaves) : light green (border) : blue-green : dark blue : white : blue : light red : deep yellow : light blue : purple : dark purple.

INDIAN CARPET (The Girdlers' Company). Dated 1634. 24 ft. × 8 ft. (See Plate 33 and p. 40.)

Warp : Probably cotton. 30 to 1 inch.
Weft : Probably cotton.
Knots : Wool. Sehna. 16 to 1 inch. 240 to the square inch.
Colours : Twelve. Crimson (field) : dark blue (4th border) : white : blue : light crimson : light blue : yellow : light brown : very light crimson : dark brown : light green : purple-brown.

ASIA MINOR CARPET (Victoria and Albert Museum). 16th century. 9 ft. 6 in. × 5 ft. 6 in. (See Plate 37B and p. 48.)
Warp : Two-ply white wool. On two levels. 17 to 1 inch.
Weft : Red wool. Two shoots after each row of knots.
Knots : Wool. Ghiordes. 10 to 1 inch. 85 to the square inch.
Colours : Ten. Red (field) : dark blue (panels) : green : white : light red (border) : dark blue-green : light blue : blue : black : greenish yellow.

ASIA MINOR CARPET (Victoria and Albert Museum). 16th century. 7 ft. × 6 ft. 7 in. (See Plate 39 and p. 47.)
Warp : Four-ply yellow wool. On two levels. 32 to 1 inch.
Weft : Crimson wool. Two shoots after each row of knots.
Knots : Wool. Sehna. 13 to 1 inch. 210 to the square inch.
Colours : Eight. Crimson (field) : deep yellow : light blue (1st border) : white : yellow (2nd border) : yellow-green : green : dark-blue.

ASIA MINOR CARPET (Victoria and Albert Museum). 16th century. 9 ft. 4 in. × 8 ft. 3 in. (See Plate 40 and p. 47.)
Warp : Two-ply green silk. On two levels. 41 to 1 inch.
Weft : Crimson silk. Two shoots after each row of knots.
Knots : Wool and white cotton. Sehna. 16 to 1 inch. 330 to the square inch.
Colours : Seven. Deep crimson (field and border) : white : dark blue (panels in border) : yellow : green : light blue : black.

ASIA MINOR CARPET (Mr. George Mounsey). 16th century. 6 ft. 11 in. × 6 ft. 1 in. (See Plate 42 and p. 48.) This carpet is made up from a larger one, of which there is another piece in the Circulation Collection of the Victoria and Albert Museum.
Warp : White wool. On one level. 15 to 1 inch.

Weft : Red wool. Two shoots after each row of knots.
Knots : ⁷⁄₂ Wool. Ghiordes. 9 to 1 inch. 70 to the square inch.
Colours : Nine. Red (alternate squares of the field) : dark green
   (alternate squares of the field) : white (pattern of border) :
   deep crimson-red (1st border) : green : black : light blue :
   blue : greenish yellow.

ASIA MINOR CARPET (Victoria and Albert Museum). 16th century.
5 ft. 8 in. × 3 ft. 7 in. (See Plate 43B and p. 48.)
Warp : White wool. On one level. 16 to 1 inch.
Weft : Red wool. Two shoots after each row of knots.
Knots : Wool. Ghiordes. 12 to 1 inch. 95 to the square inch.
Colours : Seven. Red (field ; 1st border) : yellow (pattern on
   ground ; 2nd border at sides) : white (pattern of 2nd border) :
   green-blue (2nd border at ends) : light blue (3rd border) :
   blue : black.

ASIA MINOR CARPET (Victoria and Albert Museum). 16th–17th
century. 17 ft. 4 in. × 8 ft. 2 in. (See Plate 44 and p. 49.)
Warp : White wool. On two levels only slightly separated. 18 to
   1 inch.
Weft : Red wool. Two shoots (sometimes three) after each row
   of knots.
Knots : Wool. Ghiordes. 11 to 1 inch. 100 to the square inch.
Colours : Six. Red (field and 2nd border) : dark blue (central
   medallion, pattern on ground, and 1st border) : dark green-
   blue (side medallions) : yellow (3rd border) : light blue : black.

ASIA MINOR MAT (Mr. George Mounsey). 17th century.
3 ft. 6 in. × 2 ft. 1 in. (See Plate 46B and p. 55.)
Warp : Two-ply white wool. On two levels. 17 to 1 inch.
Weft : Brown wool. Two shoots after each row of knots.
Knots : Wool. Ghiordes. 11 to 1 inch. 90 to the square inch.
Colours : Eight. Red (field) : white (end-border) : blue : light
   red : light blue : green : purple : grey-brown.

ORIENTAL CARPET (Mr. George Mounsey). 16th century. 6 ft. ×
4 ft. 6 in. (See Plate 47 and p. 51.)

Warp : White wool. On two levels. 22 to 1 inch.
Weft : Brown and red wool. Two shoots after each row of knots.
Knots : Wool. Sehna. 8 to 1 inch. 80 to the square inch.
Colours : Nine. Red (field) : light blue (2nd border) : blue (1st and 3rd borders) : white : yellow : brown : black : dark blue : purple.

ORIENTAL CARPET (Mr. George Mounsey). 16th century. 6 ft. 3 in. × 4 ft. 10 in. (See Plate 48 and p. 51.)
Warp : Fine yellow wool. On two levels. 23 to 1 inch.
Weft : Red wool. Two shoots after each row of knots.
Knots : Wool. Sehna. 10 to 1 inch. 120 to the square inch.
Colours : Six. Crimson (field and 1st and 3rd borders) : green : light blue (central medallion and 2nd border) : yellow : white : black.

ASIA MINOR PRAYER-CARPET (Mr. George Mounsey). Late 17th century. 5 ft. × 3 ft. 9 in. (See Plate 56 and p. 55.)
Warp : Two-ply white wool (ends dyed yellow). On one level. 17 to 1 inch.
Weft : Red wool. Two shoots after each row of knots.
Knots : Wool. Ghiordes. 8 to 1 inch. 65 to the square inch.
Colours : Five. Red (field) : yellow (2nd border) : white (1st border and spandrels) : black : light blue.

ASIA MINOR CARPET (Mr. George Mounsey). 18th century. 13 ft. 1 in. × 3 ft. 7 in. (See Plate 58 and p. 56.)
Warp : White wool. On two levels not much separated. 17 to 1 inch.
Weft : Red wool. Two shoots after each row of knots.
Knots : Wool. Ghiordes. 10 to 1 inch. 160 to the square inch.
Colours : Eight. Red (field) : green (border) : purple (extra end-borders) : dull yellow : blue : white : black : dark blue.

CHINESE CARPET (Lady Cunliffe). 17 ft. 11 in. × 4 ft. (See Plate 66A and p. 64.)
Warp : White or pale blue cotton. On two levels. 19 to 1 inch.
Weft : White cotton. Three shoots after each row of knots.
Knots : Silk. Sehna. 6 to 1 inch. 60 to the square inch.
Metal Thread : Woven on the upper leaf of the warp by a process similar to Soumak weaving.

Colours : Seven. Rose-red, faded (border) : blue : green : yellow : light blue : white : black. The ground of the niches is in gold, and of the spandrels in silver thread.

CHINESE SILK CARPET (Lieut.-Col. G. B. Croft Lyons, F.S.A.). 5 ft. × 3 ft. 2 in. (See Plate 66B and p. 66.)
Warp : White cotton. On one level. 17 to 1 inch.
Weft : White cotton. Two shoots after each row of knots.
Knots : Silk. Sehna. 8 to 1 inch. 70 to the square inch.
Colours : Four. Yellow (field) : green-blue (border) : blue (pattern on border) : black.

CHINESE CARPET (Victoria and Albert Museum). 18th century. 6 ft. 2 in. × 8 ft. 5 in. (See Plate 68 and p. 64.)
Warp : Four-ply white cotton. On one level. 14 to 1 inch.
Weft : White cotton. Two shoots after each row of knots.
Knots : Wool. Sehna. 7 to 1 inch. 55 to the square inch. Clipped round some of the contours.
Colours : Eight. White (field) : dark blue (3rd border and edging) : rose-red (1st border) : light rose-red : yellow : blue : deep yellow : light purple-red.

CHINESE CARPET (Victoria and Albert Museum). 18th century. 9 ft. 3 in. × 7 ft. 1 in. (See Plate 69 and p. 64.)
Warp : Four-ply white cotton. On one level. 12 to 1 inch.
Weft : White cotton. Two shoots after each row of knots.
Knots : Wool. Sehna. 5 to 1 inch. 30 to the square inch.
Colours : Six. Rose-red (field) : dark blue (2nd border and edging) : yellow (1st border) : blue : white : deep yellow.

CHINESE KNOTTED SEAT-COVER (Victoria and Albert Museum). 18th–19th century. 4 ft. 10 in. × 2 ft. 3 in. (See Plate 70A and p. 65.)
Warp : Three-ply white cotton. On one level. 13 to 1 inch.
Weft : White cotton. Two shoots after each row of knots.
Knots : Wool. Sehna. 7 to 1 inch. 45 to the square inch. Clipped round many of the contours.
Colours : Eleven. Orange-brown (field and border) : dark blue : blue : light purple-red : light red : yellow-green : greenish yellow : light blue : white : grey : purple-grey.

CHINESE CARPET (Victoria and Albert Museum). 18th century. 4 ft. 4 in. × 2 ft. 2 in. (See Plate 70B and p. 64.)
Warp : Four-ply white cotton. On one level. 13 to 1 inch.
Weft : Cream-coloured cotton. Two shoots after each row of knots.
Knots : Wool. Sehna. 7 to 1 inch. 45 to the square inch.
Colours : Eight. Salmon-red (field) : dark blue (border) : blue : yellow : deep yellow : white : light blue : light salmon-red.

CHINESE CARPET (Victoria and Albert Museum). Probably 18th century. 11 ft. 8 in. × 8 ft. 4 in. (See Plate 71 and p. 65.)
Warp : White cotton. On one level. 13 to 1 inch.
Weft : White cotton. Two shoots after each row of knots.
Knots : Wool. Sehna. 5 to 1 inch. 35 to the square inch.
Colours : Six. White (field) : dark blue (pattern on field, 1st border and edging) : blue : deep yellow : apricot-red : yellow.

CHINESE PILLAR CARPET (Victoria and Albert Museum). 18th century. 8 ft. 3 in. × 3 ft. 3 in. (See Plate 72 and p. 65.)
Warp : White cotton. On one level. 12 to 1 inch.
Weft : White cotton. Two shoots after each row of knots.
Knots : Wool. Sehna. 6 to 1 inch. 38 to the square inch. Clipped round many of the contours.
Colours : Eleven. Purple-red (ground) : yellow : deep yellow : greenish yellow : white : red : light red : very light red : blue : dark blue : grey-brown. Some colours are hard to distinguish owing to fading.

CHINESE PILLAR CARPET (Victoria and Albert Museum). 18th century. 7 ft. 8 in. × 4 ft. 2 in. (See Plate 73 and p. 65.)
Warp : White cotton. On one level. 13 to 1 inch.
Weft : White cotton. Two shoots after each row of knots.
Knots : Wool. Sehna. 5 to 1 inch. 32 to the square inch. Clipped round many of the contours.
Colours : Twelve. Yellow (ground) : dark blue : white : light blue : red : greenish yellow : deep yellow : light red : light yellow : purple-red : very light red : grey-black. Some colours are hard to distinguish owing to fading.

III

HAND-WOVEN CARPETS

EASTERN TURKESTAN RUG (Victoria and Albert Museum). 18th–19th century. 3 ft. 7 in. × 2 ft. 9 in. (See Plate 75B and p. 66.)
Warp : Five-ply white cotton. On two levels. 15 to 1 inch.
Weft : Three-fold white cotton (some brown wool). Three shoots after each row of knots.
Knots : Wool. Sehna. 6 to 1 inch. 40 to the square inch.
Colours : Seven. Red (field) : blue (2nd border) : yellow : dark brown (1st and 3rd borders) : ochre : light blue : white.

SPANISH CARPET (Victoria and Albert Museum). 16th century. 14 ft. 11 in. × 6 ft. 10 in. (See Plate 77B and p. 70.)
Warp : Two-ply white wool. 25 to 1 inch.
Weft : White wool. One shoot after each row of knots.
Knots : Wool. Single-warp. 11 to 1 inch. 135 to the square inch.
Colours : Eight. Red (field and 2nd border) : dark green (1st border) : white : blue : yellow : orange : light blue : black.

SPANISH CARPET (Victoria and Albert Museum). 15th century. 6 ft. 8 in. × 4 ft. (See Plate 78 and p. 69.)
Warp : Two-ply white wool. 21 to 1 inch.
Weft : Threefold white wool. One shoot after each row of knots.
Knots : Wool. Single-warp. 10 to 1 inch. 110 to the square inch.
Colours : Seven. Red (field) : blue (2nd border) : dark green-blue : yellow : black (1st border) : white : orange.

SPANISH CARPET (Victoria and Albert Museum). Late 15th century. 7 ft. 6 in. × 5 ft. 4 in. (See Plate 79 and p. 71.)
Warp : White wool. 20 to 1 inch.
Weft : White wool. One shoot after each row of knots.
Knots : Wool. Single-warp. 11 to 1 inch. 110 to the square inch.
Colours : Seven. Red (field) : green : dark blue : white (3rd border and 1st extra end-border) : blue (2nd border) : black (1st border and 2nd and 3rd extra end-borders) : yellow.

SPANISH CARPET (the Hon. H. D. McLaren, C.B.E., M.P.). Late 15th century. 15 ft. × 2 ft. 11 in. (See Plate 80 and p. 71.)
Warp : White wool. 16 to 1 inch.

Weft : White wool. One shoot (fourfold) after each row of knots.

Knots : Wool. Single-warp. 10 to 1 inch. 80 to the square inch.

Colours : Seven. Black (ground) : light blue : yellow : white : light red : purple : green.

SPANISH CARPET (Victoria and Albert Museum). 16th century. 9 ft. 7 in. × 5 ft. 11 in. (See Plate 81 and p. 71.)

Warp : White wool. 33 to 1 inch.

Weft : Red wool. One shoot (threefold) after each row of knots.

Knots : Wool. Single-warp. 16 to 1 inch. 270 to the square inch.

Colours : Six. Blue (field) : red (border and panels) : yellow (pattern on border and panels) : white (pattern on field) : light blue : green.

FINNISH RUG (Victoria and Albert Museum). Dated 1799. (See Plate 84 and p. 73.)

Warp : White flax. On one level. 10 to 1 inch.

Weft : Fine white wool. Four shoots after each row of knots.

Knots : Wool. Ghiordes. 2 to 1 inch. 11 to the square inch. There is also a pile at the back of the rug, formed by white woollen knots tied after every 8 shoots of weft.

Colours : Eight. Rose-red (border) : black (field) : blue : light blue : white : green : yellow : light crimson.

TWO FRENCH SAVONNERIE CARPETS. Late 17th century. (Mobilier National, Paris.) 15 ft. 10 in. × 29 ft. and 12 ft. 7 in. × 28 ft. 9 in. (See Plates 85 and 86 and p. 74.)

Warp : Flax. On two levels. 22 to 1 inch.

Weft : Flax. Three shoots after each row of knots.

Knots : Wool. Ghiordes. 10 to 1 inch. 110 to the square inch.

Colours : Many.

ENGLISH KNOTTED PANEL (Victoria and Albert Museum). Dated 1600. 1 ft. 9 in. × 3 ft. 6 in. (See Plate 87B and p. 79.)

Warp : Three-ply hemp. On one level. 13 to 1 inch.

Weft : Three-ply hemp. One shoot after each row of knots.

Knots : Wool. Ghiordes. 8 to 1 inch. 55 to the square inch.

HAND-WOVEN CARPETS

Colours : Nine. Dark green (ground) : blue : crimson : red : yellow : white : orange : light crimson : black.

ENGLISH CARPET (Victoria and Albert Museum). Dated 1603. 16 ft. 8 in. × 7 ft. 8 in. (See Plate 88 and p. 79.)
Warp : Hemp. 20 to 1 inch.
Weft : Hemp. One shoot after each row of knots.
Knots : Wool. Ghiordes. 9 to 1 inch. 95 to the square inch.
Colours : Seven. Dark green-blue (field) : green : yellow : white : crimson : blue : orange.

ENGLISH CARPET (Lady Hulse). Dated 1614. 11 ft. 9 in. × 8 ft. 5 in. (See Plate 89 and p. 79.)
Warp : Hemp. 14 to 1 inch.
Weft : Hemp. One shoot after each row of knots.
Knots : Wool. Ghiordes. 9 to 1 inch. 60 to the square inch.
Colours : Many. Shades of green, yellow, red and blue : purple : white : black.

ENGLISH CARPET made at Exeter. Dated 1757. 14 ft. 9 in. × 12 ft. (See Plate 90 and p. 81.)
Warp : White wool. On two levels. 19 to 1 inch.
Weft : Wool of various colours. Two shoots after each row of knots.
Knots : Wool. Ghiordes. 8 to 1 inch. 80 to the square inch.
Colours : Many bright colours. The ground is blue.

ENGLISH CARPET at Syon House (The Duke of Northumberland). Dated 1769. 34 ft. 5 in. × 14 ft. 2 in. (See Plate 91 and p. 81.)
Warp : White wool. On two levels not much separated. 9 to 1 inch.
Weft : Black (some coloured) wool. Two shoots after each row of knots.
Knots : Wool. Ghiordes. 4 to 1 inch. 17 to the square inch.
Colours : Twenty or more.

(c) Materials

It may be stated that nearly every raw material that can be used for textile purposes has been employed in the manufacture of carpets, but many are so rarely met with that they can be left out of practical consideration. The important textile fibres—wool, cotton and silk, made into yarn—constitute the whole substance of most carpets, and if to these be added flax, hemp, jute, and metal thread, every other material can be neglected. Of the above substances, wool is by far the most important. It wears well, dyes easily and is pleasant in appearance, and as it can be used for warp, weft and pile, many carpets are made of it alone. The wool of both sheep and goats is used, and in practice a distinction need not be made between the kinds. The natural colour of wool ranges from white to black, and in substance it passes by imperceptible gradations from fine fibres, easily mistaken for silk, to long, coarse hair resembling that of the horse. The wool, or hair, as it is more often called, of the camel is also largely used, but it is not easy to dye and is mostly left in its natural colour. When wool is used for warp, that of a comparatively coarse staple is chosen, and it is usually spun into a rather hard-twisted two-ply yarn, which is sometimes dyed, though more often left white, or whatever its natural colour may be. On the other hand, a woollen weft is mostly dyed—red or brown being favourite colours—and is only slackly twisted, or perhaps may consist of two or more strands not twisted together at all. For the pile, wool stands pre-eminent, and it is here that the finest and most lustrous kinds are most esteemed. It is, of course, mostly dyed, and consists of yarn of two or more strands, not tightly spun.

After wool, cotton is the fibre most used. For the warp it is usually undyed and consists of several strands spun together. For the weft it is often dyed blue or pink and is loosely spun, an exception being that the very sinuous shoot between two straight ones (Fig. H) must be a fine and tightly-spun yarn. Although admirably suited for warp and weft, cotton is less satisfactory for the pile. It wears well, but is dead in appearance and tends to look dirty in course of time; and though it can be dyed without difficulty the colours fade and lose their beauty sooner than those on wool. For these reasons it is seldom used for the pile, though it is found in the rugs of Multan, and sometimes, in small quantities, in old Turkish rugs, where a pure white colour is required.

Silk is a material adaptable for all purposes, though it has not the wearing qualities of wool. Even in the East it is costly and can only be used in expensive carpets. Sometimes a rug made entirely of silk is seen, but more often, even when the pile is of silk, the warp and weft are of cotton, which in modern rugs is often mercerized. On the other hand, in many of the finest old Persian carpets a silken warp and weft is found associated with a woollen pile. For this there is a sound reason in the fact that a very fine yarn of reeled silk is stronger than a woollen one of similar size, whereas a coarser woollen yarn, even if not so strong as a silken one, has at least an ample margin of strength.

Of the less common materials, flax, or linen, is occasionally substituted for cotton in Eastern carpets, but its occurrence may be regarded as almost accidental. Coarse flax, or perhaps hemp, was the material used for the foundation of the earliest English knotted carpets. Jute is only used in very inferior hand-made carpets, though of wide employment in machine-made ones. The last material on the list—metal thread —stands on a different footing from the rest. It is sometimes used in parts of the surface of a carpet to give an unusually rich appearance. The thread consists, as a rule, of silk or other yarn covered over with a twisted strip of silvered or gilt metal. It is never used for the foundation of a carpet and is never knotted, but whether employed in a Kilim or in a pile-carpet it is inserted either by the tapestry method, as used for the weft of an ordinary Kilim, or else by a process very similar to that of Soumak weaving. Metal thread had the disadvantage of tarnishing badly and is almost unknown in modern pile-carpets.

(d) Dimensions and Shape

Even the size and shape of a carpet allow some conclusions to be drawn with regard to its provenance or classification. Very large carpets are certainly only made by non-nomadic peoples : whereas a want of regularity in shape, such as a difference between the widths of the ends or a tendency to lie unevenly, is evidence that the carpet in question was made by nomads. A carpet woven on a roughly-made loom, or one which had to be taken out of the loom and remounted several times, or rolled up for weeks on end, can scarcely be as regular in appearance as one made under more stable conditions with better appliances. The size of the tents used by nomadic people limits the dimensions of their carpets, as it is impossible for them to contain a tall or wide loom. Moreover, nomadic people have no need themselves for large and heavy carpets which are difficult of transport, and nomad carpets were, until quite recently, only manufactured for their own use. For this reason the size of their carpets is narrowly limited ; the width varying from 4 to $5\frac{1}{2}$ ft., and the length rarely exceeding two and a half to three times the width. But even the carpets of non-nomadic people, as long as only their own consumption was catered for, tended to have certain definite proportions. For instance, the rooms of Persian houses are for certain reasons generally oblong in shape, and a conventional arrangement of the floor-covering becomes customary (Fig. J). I is the show-piece (*khali*), the borders of which are covered by the other three carpets in order to preserve it, with the result that the long and narrow carpets II and III—known as *kanara*, or in English often as " runners "—are largely used in passing up and down the room. IV, the divan-cover (*sedjadeh*) is used most of all, for members of the household and visitors sit upon it.

As the European demand increased, and as the custom grew for buyers to commission carpets in Persia and Asia Minor, they naturally gave the local workers not only instructions as to the pattern but also as to the shape and size they required. Carpets so ordered were designed to correspond with European requirements, and to-day carpets of any proportions and dimensions may be obtained by any-one who orders them.

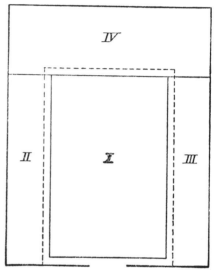

FIG. J.—PLAN OF PERSIAN ROOM.

Whereas rugs for use on the floor are generally rectangular in shape, other articles, such as bags, saddle-covers or tent-bands, are naturally of such shapes and sizes as their special use dictates. Even rugs for Oriental use are sometimes found with rounded corners, re-entrant angles or other peculiarities of shape, and were obviously made thus in order to fit into special positions. In the Victoria and Albert Museum there is a fragment of a Persian border which, running partly at an angle of forty-five degrees across the warp and weft and partly parallel to the weft, apparently came from the corner of a shaped carpet.

An average size for *kanara*, or runners, is about 3 × 15 ft. A very common size for rugs is about $4\frac{1}{2}$ × $6\frac{1}{2}$ ft., most prayer-rugs being of these dimensions. Larger than this, rugs can be found of all sizes up to about 15 × 20 ft., above which size specimens are rarer. That still larger carpets were made even centuries ago is witnessed by the great Ardabil carpet, which measures $17\frac{1}{2}$ × $34\frac{1}{2}$ ft., and the carpet made for the Palace of the Forty Columns at Ispahan, which, judging from the scale and pattern of the remaining fragments and the size of the hall where it was placed, must have been four times the size of the Ardabil carpet.

(e) Colour and Dyeing

The chief attraction of Oriental carpets is perhaps to be found in the charm of their colouring. This view is supported by a study of some of the Nomadic rugs, whose simple geometrical patterns, though inoffensive and even well-balanced, possess little artistic interest when seen in monochrome, but, when rendered in colour with Oriental skill, at once become endowed with a beauty at once satisfying and difficult to analyse. An incredible richness of colour and wealth of colour-combination is to be found in Oriental rugs. Between the dark Beluchistan, whose sombre character is all the more noticeable because of the white patches it contains, and the bright Ghiordes with its delicate prismatic hues, one may find in rugs every colour with which a kind Heaven has endowed the flowers of our fields. And as the flowers, however brilliant and varied their colours, always harmonize with each other, so the colouring of old Oriental rugs never strikes us as glaring, in spite of its many and powerful contrasts.

To say that the Oriental has an instinctive power of managing colour is not to give him more than his due, but it must be remembered that instinct is of little service when traditional methods are abandoned, and even when his instinct is admitted it goes a very short way towards explaining how his effects are produced.

One reason why harshness of contrast is avoided is that strongly contrasting colours are usually separated by a line of neutral tint, such as black or white, or of some intermediate colour ; but though this device may be effective against a close inspection, it can scarcely be sufficient when the carpet is viewed from a distance, as then the effect of such a line would be imperceptible.

A better explanation probably lies in the fact that the colours generally used are far darker in tone and much less vivid in hue than is realized by the eye. A knot removed from a carpet and viewed apart from it looks far greyer and darker than the patch of colour of which it formed part ; and if an attempt is made to match a colour in a rug by the eye alone, unaided by actual contact of the yarns, it is surprising what an error can be made. What looks a pure white in a carpet will often turn out to be, when contrasted with white paper, a half-tone of considerable depth. Manufacturers complain of the great difficulty they find in getting the whites of their carpets right, and this difficulty possibly is due to the fact that even experience shrinks from using yarn so much darker than the whites appear in the model which is being copied, or are wished to look in the new carpet. The extreme crudeness to be seen in many machine-made carpets will often be found on a critical examination to be due not so much to an incorrect disposition of the colours as to an excess of brilliancy in the tones of the dyes.

It is not, however, only by avoiding excessive contrasts that harmonious results are achieved. The colours must be in correct proportions and in patches of the right size, and in these respects the Oriental owes much to his willingness to follow tradition. He uses much the same dyes as his fathers, he reproduces the same paper designs, or copies successful rugs without materially altering the scale or proportions of their patterns; and though the small changes he makes may gradually lead to the evolution of new types, yet he is always ready to abandon any modification which does not result in improvement. The Oriental does not indulge in that wild striving for originality now so prevalent in the West, which, though sometimes leading to fresh beauty and inspiration, is too often rewarded only by disappointment. When all this is said, it still is likely that many old carpets were less pleasing when new than they are to-day. Time, bringing with it fading and wear, must have had much effect in adding softness and subtlety to many of the more brilliant carpets, but it certainly will not do to ascribe their delightful effect chiefly to time's mellowing influence.

There is no mystery about the nature of the dyestuffs used in the past, even if we do not know the exact details of their manipulation; and, of course, many of the tales told—for instance, that the wonderful colours were due to the grinding up of rubies and sapphires—will not bear serious consideration.

The blues are probably invariably derived from indigo, which, as is well known, is obtained by steeping the leaves of the indigo plant in water. The reds are produced by madder—the root of a plant— treated with various mordants; or by Kermes, which consists of the dried bodies of insects that live on the oak or on a species of cactus. In later times cochineal, the Mexican equivalent of Kermes, has been imported as a satisfactory substitute. No natural yellow dyestuff is quite as permanent as those for red and blue, but saffron, Persian berries and turmeric have all been used successfully. Catechu (or Cutch) gives a good brown colour, and black may be obtained by logwood in conjunction with an iron salt such as ferrous sulphate. This last dye has a somewhat corrosive effect upon wool, and in course of time may cause it to disappear completely. Natural black wool may be used instead, but like all undyed animal fibres will fade rather quickly.

The secondary colours are produced by dyeing successively with two of the primaries, but they never seem to last quite as well as the latter or to be quite so rich, and it is no doubt on this account that they are used in comparatively small proportions in old carpets.

Though the general nature of the dyestuffs used is fairly constant throughout the East, yet various districts specialize in the production of certain shades of colour, either from choice or because local peculiarities, such as the quality of the water or facilities for obtaining particular grades of dyestuffs, make the production of such shades easy. The brick-reds of Asia Minor, the rich crimsons of Persia, and the deep wine-reds of Central Asia are notable instances ; but there are many subtler colours which are highly characteristic of, and often peculiar to, certain districts, and accordingly most useful for purposes of identification.

European manufacturers assert, and not without justification, that the methods of dyeing in Europe are far superior to the primitive ones of the East. It is a fact that carpets are hardly ever found without differences of shade in colours which were intended to be the same throughout, and often the difference is so great that, if it did not occur in a way quite unconnected with the design, as for instance in the plain ground, it might be supposed that different hues were really intended.

The explanation of this phenomenon is that the primitive methods employed in dyeing are far too unscientific to ensure the same result on different occasions. It is difficult for nomadic tribes to carry supplies of wool sufficiently large to obviate the necessity for dyeing more before the carpet is finished, but even if they do so, their custom, forced upon them by necessity, of using small pots for vats, prevents them from mixing much of the dye at one time. These difficulties are still present, though in a lesser degree, with the sedentary weavers, so that the irregularities of dyeing are less noticeable in their work.

The differences of colour then, which can be seen like stripes running right across the carpet, are by no means intentional but are inseparable from the whole method of production. This element, which would be found annoying in a modern European carpet, gives an additional charm to the simple product of the East, just as we delight in the twisted streets and crooked roofs and corners of an old town, whereas the slightest irregularity or the smallest incline in the straight front of a new building would be intolerable to the eye.

Leaving out the unintentional variations of colour, it will be found that the number of different hues and shades in a single Oriental carpet is by no means large, ranging as it does from four to about twelve. A very large proportion of the area of a carpet is worked in three or four colours, and three or four others may be used in moderate quantity; but if still more are employed they are almost negligible in amount.

In spite of all their disadvantages it is generally admitted that the Oriental dyer of the past produced colours which for beauty and permanence have never been excelled; but unfortunately the superiority of the Oriental dyes does not exist now in the same degree as it did in bygone days. The later colours are often very glaring, and many of them will not stand washing or exposure to the sun. This deterioration is the result of Western influence, and its beginnings can be traced fairly accurately to the years 1865–70. During that period aniline dyes, which were invented in 1859, began to be used in the East. Their brilliancy, the ease with which they could be mixed, as well as their comparative cheapness, seduced the Oriental dyer just as they did his brother in the West. These brilliant colours, unfortunately, are often not permanent; it is probably safe to say that those first introduced never were. Many of them fade quickly in sunlight and come off when washed or even wetted. Naturally the employment of such colours in a carpet is simply disastrous, and the disadvantage has been recognized both in the West and the East. In 1910 an embargo was placed in Persia upon the import of chemical dyes either in solid or liquid form, but, nevertheless, these materials are still used considerably, largely on account of the ease with which they can be applied.

The worthlessness of the early aniline dyes for producing permanent colours led to a prejudice against all synthetic dyes, of which the aniline colours are but one small branch, a prejudice which is very slow to disappear. And yet the chemists have made immense strides since Dr. Perkin discovered mauve. The chemical nature of many of the vegetable dyestuffs (including indigo and madder) has been discovered; it is now possible to make them synthetically on a commercial scale, and the product is every bit as good as the original, except perhaps so far as impurities in the latter may give a pleasing irregularity. More important is the fact that new dyes are being discovered which surpass the older ones in point of resistance to light and other influences, and which supply the designer with fresh colours, even if the colours are not more beautiful than those already known. In spite of these facts—possibly in ignorance of them—it is very common still for writers to use the arguments levelled against the aniline dyes of more than forty years ago! It is so certain that the future lies with synthetic dyes that it seems a pity to entertain any prejudice on the subject or to do anything which is likely to retard their proper development. At the same time, unsound dyes, whether natural or chemical, should, of course, be discouraged in every way, and buyers can do much to abolish the cruelly wasteful system by which good materials and much labour are thrown away in producing an article which will not stand the test of time.

The vividness of some modern dyes, quite apart from the question of their soundness, and the consequent garishness of rugs in which they are employed, has led to the baneful practice of chemically washing the surface in order to tone down the colours and produce immediately a mellow effect. The processes are kept secret as far as possible, but they seem to consist of application of acids or of sea-water. The immediate effect is often pleasing, and no doubt some of the milder agents are not harmful; but, unfortunately, it happens that the wool is seriously damaged when the treatment has been severe. At its best the method produces an effect which is better left to the slower influence of time, and chemically washed rugs should be avoided if possible, though some classes of the best modern rugs are practically never left quite untouched.

It is rather consoling to reflect that even in older times many of the troubles of the present must still have been existent. The best-dyed rugs fade, and many magnificent old rugs may be seen in which some of the colours have completely changed. Also there seem to be few freshly dyed yarns which are quite unacted upon by water. Very fine and undoubtedly genuine silk rugs of the seventeenth century were recently sold in London, of which the colours came off easily on a damp cloth. It is probable that they had never been cleaned. The usual fate of a rug some centuries old is to be washed many times, and though at first the colours may have come off to a slight extent, eventually no such effect would be perceived, and the lightest colours would by that time have become so toned that the slight contamination would be invisible. It is not fair to condemn utterly a modern rug because its pure whites have become slightly tinged with the adjacent colours.

Chapter II

THE DESIGN OF CARPETS

A discussion of the design of carpets can well start with the consideration of the ways in which carpets are mostly used, for the proper treatment of the design must be based upon such a consideration. In the first place it should be remembered that a carpet is usually placed flat on the floor and that it is meant to be walked upon, that it is generally seen from some distance away and that it is liable to be looked at from all directions.

The first of these conditions points to the adoption of a design which will not be impaired by being fore-shortened, and the second indicates a conventional treatment as being the most suitable. A naturalistic treatment always gives a certain suggestion of relief to a design, and if the realism is carried to the extent of showing the shadows of the objects portrayed, then it is impossible to avoid the uncomfortable feeling that one has to walk on an uneven surface.

The third condition—that the carpet will often be seen from a distance—leads to the conclusion that the pattern must be fairly bold to be effective. It does not follow that the carpet will never be near the eye. As it is avowedly a work of art, it may at any time be examined closely, and, apart from this, in the East, at all events, it is customary to sit on the floor, in which case no great distance separates the carpet from the eye. There is accordingly no logical reason against having fine detail in the design as long as it is secondary to the general arrangement of the masses.

In the next place, as the carpet may be seen from all sides, it is advisable to avoid any important feature in the design which must, in order to be appreciated, be viewed from a particular direction. This rules out all pictorial subjects on a large scale from consideration as being suita le for inclusion. If small pictorial subjects, human figures, animals or trees are included, then they should be repeated several times in the composition with different orientations, so that some will be upright from any point of view. An exception may be made to this practice if the piece is intended to be seen only from one direction. The chief

123

instance of this is the prayer-rug, which is always deliberately planned so that its design is best seen when it is in use. Tent-bags or door-hangings would be other legitimate exceptions; but as it happens that these are mostly made by people who favour geometrical ornament, the liberty that might be claimed is rarely exercised. Exceptions are also found where they are perhaps not justified (see Plate 58), but in these cases the effect of the rug is displeasing when seen from the wrong point.

Another reason why deliberately pictorial subjects are unsuitable is that parts of a carpet are often hidden by furniture or other objects, and if part of the picture cannot be seen, the whole effect may be spoiled. On the other hand, repeating patterns and devices, symmetrical in themselves or symmetrically arranged, are especially suitable for decorating an object which may be partly concealed, for when such are employed the mind can follow the design even where it eludes the eye.

The above argument in favour of a conventional, bold and symmetrical treatment in the design of carpets may perhaps appear sufficient, but it is not necessary to rely upon theory alone, for the conclusion is amply borne out by the immemorial practice of the East.

The technique has also a certain influence upon design. It has already been explained how in KILIMS the change of colour in the weft causes vertical slits in the fabric, which are mostly avoided by the adoption of slanting or stepped outlines. This does not occur in pile carpets, but there are limitations of another nature. The surface of a pile-carpet is not, from the designer's point of view, capable of indefinite subdivision, but it may be regarded as atomic in structure, and the atom or unit of surface is a single knot. Every design must be interpreted in relation to this unit. The knots each occupy a small square, or more often a small oblong space, and they are arranged regularly in rows and columns. The narrowest line, therefore, that can be made is one con-sisting of a single line of knots; and curves can only be represented by a succession of straight lines, alternately vertical and horizontal, whose shortest length is the height or width of one knot. These considerations at once put a limit to the fineness of detail and the delicacy of drawing which is possible with a knotted surface. The size of each knot is dependent upon the fineness of the texture, so that the finer the texture the smaller are the details that can be rendered and the smoother are the curves.

This is no doubt the chief reason why the designs are more

conventional in the coarser carpets. A blossom that can be delicately rendered in a fine carpet may, in one of coarse texture, be so angular in outline as to become a mere geometrical rosette, so that in such circumstances there is considerable temptation to rely exclusively upon geometrical forms.

The colouring of carpets, no less than the design, tends to be conventional, and perhaps a correspondence can be traced between the degree of conventionalization in each. In the finer and more naturalistic carpets the blossoms and leaves usually have their proper colours ; in those rather more conventional there is a tendency to keep the colours, red, white, yellow and blue for the flowers, green or black for the leaves, and green, brown or black for the stems ; but in carpets with geometrically drawn floral forms, the colours will be found used indiscriminately and without any relation to the objects portrayed.

A most striking aspect of the designs of Eastern carpets—one not peculiar to them among works of art and yet developed perhaps to the greatest extent in their case—is the way in which the same patterns are repeated again and again in rugs of a given period, and even are handed down with slight modifications from age to age. It is not often that a rug is found which has no well-known feature in the design, and in fact the matter can be put more strongly, for it can be asserted that very few carpets are met with in which every detail of the pattern cannot be found with very little search in some other rug.

To illustrate this, it may be said that a collection of about 200 border-stripes may be made which will include at least 95 per cent. of all those to be found in Persian rugs, whether ancient or modern.

This persistence of pattern which runs throughout the art of the East is due to the inclination of the craftsman to let well alone. It might be thought at first that such a system would be unsatisfactory because giving a feeling of want of variety in design and poverty of invention in the weavers. Such a feeling, if it exists at all, is entirely outweighed by the pleasure of meeting with designs already known and in tracing the gradual changes that take place in them in the course of time. The familiar has as much charm as the novel, and a design sanctioned by custom can rarely be without merit. If all carpets were made with entirely different designs, the greatest interest of the carpet-collector would have vanished.

The adherence to type is, of course, most manifest in the rugs of the same district, or made by people of the same race, and so is of great value in the identification of carpets. It is rather the details of the design than the general character that give the most help in this problem, but one principle, which is of general application, is that geometrical designs are most favoured by the nomadic and, consequently, the least cultured people ; while a floral basis and especially a naturalistic treatment are usually associated with a sedentary population having superior technical appliances, and a greater incentive to the rendering of intelligible forms induced by their manner of life.

An analysis of the design of carpets, having regard to the general arrangement of the pattern as well as to the treatment of the details, is of great use in acquiring familiarity with patterns found in the various parts of the carpet-making world, and in learning the true principles upon which the most pleasing designs are based.

The general arrangement and massing of the pattern of a carpet may be considered quite apart from the nature and drawing of the details, and will be a useful preliminary to the review of the latter. A great majority of carpets are rectangular in shape, and the natural place first to put ornament in an empty rectangle is round the edge. Thus at once is the border introduced, and it will soon be noticed that nearly every carpet has a border separated off from the rest. In Oriental carpets the border goes round the whole carpet and is separated from the field by straight boundary lines. Generally it is divided into from two to about ten parallel bands, each of which contains a repeating pattern. These bands (which may be called " border-stripes ") run continuously round sides and ends of the carpet, and generally each has the same pattern throughout. The end borders have the same number of rows of knots in their width as the side borders have, but as the knots are mostly shorter in a vertical direction, it follows that the end borders are generally narrower than the side borders, and it may be remarked in passing that a quick comparison of the widths will usually indicate the proportions of each knot. It very rarely, if ever, happens in Eastern carpets that the ornament of either border or field encroaches across the hard line that separates them, though in Western carpets this is done very frequently. Sometimes there will be an extra and external border-stripe at one or both ends of the carpet, but it is not common and only occurs in rugs of Central Asia and very rarely in those of Turkey. An extra internal border-stripe is also found at the ends of some Asia Minor prayer-rugs.

The kinds of patterns found in the border-stripes may now be briefly reviewed. In the narrowest stripes, consisting of a few rows of knots or even a single row, there may be very simple geometrical patterns, such as squares of alternate colours, vandykes, barber's-poles and the like, all of which are found even in rugs of a naturalistic type.

In the wider stripes, three main systems of arrangement must be considered. In the first, the space is filled with a succession of detached devices, which may either be all alike, or of different kinds, mostly only of two occurring alternately (Plate 198 (3 and 5)). When these devices are in the nature of leaves or sprigs, they are often arranged in contrary diagonal directions so as to give the effect of a continuous organic line. (Plates 111A, and 196 (11)). In the second system there is a wavy stem running along the border, from which leaves, blossoms, buds or other devices depend (Plate 202 (1 to 7)). Such an arrangement is very common in Persian, less so in Caucasian, and comparatively rare in Turkish carpets.

The third system is less common than the first two. In it a succession of devices extends along the centre line of the border-stripe, each, as it were, growing out of the last one (Plate 193). These devices may appear quite geometrical, but probably are mostly derived from a floral origin.

Other patterns which might be included in the previous types are noticeable rather on account of the nature of the devices than upon their arrangement. Among these may be mentioned borders with inscriptions, which range from the legible verses and texts of many Persian specimens, to the debased Kufic letters found in old Turkish and later Caucasian carpets (Plates 14, 43B, 63). Many border patterns also are based upon the S-form, which takes very varied shapes (Plates 194 (22), 196 (5, 9), 198 (6)). Other borders have a succession of panels, often of two shapes, which themselves can be filled with ornament of various kinds (Plate 49). More rarely the space is covered with an all-over diaper pattern, as in some Kulas (Plate 100).

A somewhat different border-stripe is made by a line passing along the middle on such a course that the space on one side of it is not only the counterpart but is also of the same form as that on the other. The two sides are usually rendered in different colours and the pattern may be called " reciprocal " or " counterchanged " (Plates 199 (17) ; 202 (20)).

The field of a carpet—that is, the space left when the border has been subtracted—may be decorated in very many ways, the most obvious of which is to fill it with an all-over repeating pattern which may be held to include, as an extreme case, a perfectly plain surface. After a plain field, the simplest patterns include small spots or geometrical diapers, which from a short distance can hardly be distinguished from an undecorated ground. The spots may by degrees develop into floral or geometrical figures of more or less elaboration. Among such figures may be mentioned, as of very frequent occurrence, floral sprigs and cone-devices. Great variety may be given to these patterns by the arrangement of the colouring; for example, the devices in the same rows, whether vertical, diagonal or horizontal, may be coloured alike (to give a striped effect), or many other systems may be adopted.

Other repeating patterns are afforded by the large group of lattices; either constructed of simple lines or of elaborate scrolls, stems or leaves. The interspaces of such lattices are often occupied by detached devices of various sorts. Some rather elaborate patterns are so frequently used as to have acquired special names which are very useful for speedy reference.

One of these, known as the " Herati," consisting of an assemblage of rosettes, blossoms and small, curved, serrated leaves, based on a vague framework of stems, may be seen illustrated on Plates 147, 148 and 155. This is found only in Persian rugs or, in a debased form, in a few others based on the Persian. Another pattern of rosettes, blossoms and leaves, more formally arranged, is called the " Mina Khani " and is illustrated on Plates 149, 150 and 166. Still another is the " Guli Hinnai," consisting of small upright sprigs of flowers. The last two are equally Persian in character with the Herati. A somewhat similar pattern, found very often in Indian rugs, consists of a lattice with several different kinds of floral sprigs in the various compartments. A repeating pattern peculiar to early Turkish rugs is shown on Plate 43B. In this the arabesques always seem to be in yellow on a red ground.

There are other patterns which, while resembling those already mentioned, do not repeat regularly throughout the field. Among these is a very famous one, known as the " Shah Abbas," because it was so common in Persian rugs of his time. It consists of an assemblage of palmettes, blossoms, leaves and cloud-bands, arranged evenly, but without formal repetition, throughout the field (see Plate 28). Such a pattern is capable of infinite modifications, and may introduce among the other motives vases, animals, trees and many other devices.

Still more elaborate patterns of curving stems and flowers are very common in the early Persian silk carpets, and in the modern rugs of Tabriz and Kashan, though they rarely fill the whole field (see Plate 151).

A less common scheme than many mentioned above is the division of the field into narrow parallel bands, either vertical or diagonal, each of which contains a pattern of the same character as those of carpet borders (see Plate 164A).

Sometimes much more irregularly arranged patterns are found distributed fairly evenly over the field; but such usually occur only in the more barbaric rugs. In Caucasian carpets, for instance, it is quite common for the field to be filled with small geometrical or floral devices without any mutual connexion, scattered capriciously all over (see Plate 117).

When the ornament is not distributed regularly throughout the field, there must be part of the latter to which extra prominence is given, and the parts which naturally call for such treatment are, first of all, the middle of the rug, and, next, the four corners. Accordingly, it is often found that there is in the middle a panel or medallion, of more or less compact form, but with a tendency to be longer in the direction of the length of the rug. Medallions, as all such devices may be conveniently called, of many shapes occur; the commonest being circular, hexagonal, ogival or lobed. Sometimes there are two or more concentric medallions; and very frequently the medallion has small projecting pieces or panels at each end, when it is sometimes spoken of as a pole-medallion (see Plates 9, 169).

The corners of the field are often filled with shaped pieces resembling the quarter of a central medallion, and not infrequently these corner-pieces repeat the pattern contained in the central medallion of the same rug.

Corner-pieces may extend until they meet at the ends and even at the sides of the field, so as to form either a kind of arch at each end, or a shaped inner contour to the field. Such a shaped contour gives an effect approaching that of a central medallion, but can usually be distinguished on account of its being, as it were, obviously moulded from without and not from within.

That part of the field not occupied by the central medallion and corner-pieces may be left plain or filled with any of the repeating or irregular ground patterns already described; and the space within the medallion and corner-pieces is also sometimes filled with such patterns, but is more often occupied with less formal ornament having more relation to the space it fills.

In a KANARA or any carpet whose length is considerably more than the width, instead of a single central medallion, there often are two or more in a line, and these are not always detached but may be connected by a narrow neck (Plate 174).

The multiplication of medallions can be carried to a greater extent still, and they may occur in other parts of the field than on the centre-line. A very common pattern of the Turkish carpets of the sixteenth and seventeenth centuries was one which included one or more large medallions on the middle line and several incomplete medallions of another design against the boundaries of the field (see Plate 44).

The number of medallions may be increased until the resulting design merges into the class of repeating patterns. A good example of this is afforded by the rugs of Central Asia which so often have a pattern of repeated octagons, with diamond-shaped figures between them (see Plate 179).

In all the schemes of design already mentioned the field has been treated as a whole, but it can also be divided into several separate panels, each with a design of its own, though not necessarily different from the others. The most common plan is to divide the length of the field into three or more panels, as in Plates 110, 136, but it can also be divided into four panels by cross-lines, as in the "Katchli" rugs of Central Asia (Plate 182), and of course many other systems of subdivision are possible, though not often seen.

Allusion has already been made to the important type of design with an unsymmetrical field found in prayer-rugs. These are carried about by the devout Moslem and used by him when at prayer. At one end of the field there is an arch, which forms a niche-shaped space, occupying most of the field. When in use, the arched end of the rug is pointed in the direction of Mecca, the holy city, and the worshipper also faces that way. The ground of the niche is often left plain or lightly filled with ornament, but the spandrels above the arch are more richly decorated. The rugs of Asia Minor usually have a wide border, and, consequently, a field so long in proportion to its width that a niche occupying the whole of it would appear unduly attenuated. In the prayer-rugs it is therefore usual to reduce the length of the field by having one or more extra horizontal border-stripes, or panels, at the ends inside the real border (see Plate 101).

THE DESIGN OF CARPETS

The designs of the great majority of Oriental rugs will be found to be arranged in accordance with the methods described above; and though many other schemes of design are possible none of them will be met with at all frequently.

Most of the devices seen in carpet patterns require no explanation, as they are either simple geometrical forms or else based upon ordinary natural objects; but a few of them, either from the obscurity of their origin or on account of their known symbolical meaning, deserve some mention. First among these may be placed the cloud-band, which was derived from China, and was very largely used in the Persian carpets of the sixteenth century and onwards (see Plates 29, 205). This motive was repeated again and again, until it passed out of easy recognition, but probably still leaves its trace on many traditional patterns. It is possible that the widely used S-form is derived from it. The palmette (see Plates 18, 204) is very obviously a floral form. It may be derived from the palm, though its exact origin is uncertain. The name, however, is a useful one, as the motive is of such very widespread occurrence.

Another motive of great importance has no very satisfactory name, but is perhaps most commonly called the cone, or cone-device. The most plausible hypothesis is that it is derived from the inflorescence of the date-palm and symbolizes the principle of new birth. It is found in Persian and Indian art from very early times, but does not appear in carpets which can safely be ascribed to an earlier period than the eighteenth century. In Kashmir, where it is nearly always included in the far-famed shawls, it is called " Buta." In the West it has been variously known as the pear, river-loop, or crown jewel. This device is drawn in many ways. In its simplest form it is merely a comma-shaped blot, and from this it passes by many gradations through the plain angular form seen in Shirvan rugs (Plate 195 (12)), and the simple assemblage of florets of Sehnas and Sarabands (Plate 156), to the highly elaborated floral masses of Bakus (Plate 132B) and Shirazis. Two peculiar forms are the archaistic outlined one with a long bent neck, seen in some Karabaghs (Plate 142), and the compound ones of Khorassans (Plate 202 (13)).

Another device seen in Causcasian rugs would be quite impossible to interpret if it could not be traced from the debased Kufic inscriptions of some sixteenth-century Turkish rugs (Plates 136, 199 (16)). This in the most primitive form still remaining has been translated as signifying " Good Health."

HAND-WOVEN CARPETS

The lamp which is represented in many prayer-rugs confirms the theory that their design is derived from the gateway of, or arch in, a mosque, where a lamp would be a common object.

Another device often seen on prayer-rugs is the comb, which is a symbol of cleanliness—so important a virtue to the Moslem. Conventional hand-prints are seen in the spandrels—where the hands would naturally be placed—of the Beluchistan prayer-rug illustrated on Plate 192.

A symbol seen in some of the fine sixteenth-century Turkish carpets woven with the Sehna knot, consisting of three balls and two wavy lines, is discussed on page 51.

Much is often said about the symbolism in Oriental rugs, and it is quite certain that many of the devices have indeed a symbolic meaning; but it should not be supposed that whenever these devices are used, their symbolic aspect was at all prominent in the mind of the weaver. The significance attached to them in the first instance became gradually obscured with repetition until at last they are merely convenient ornamental motives. It has already been explained that fresh motives are rarely devised for rugs, but that existing ones are usually copied; so that the occurrence of symbolic devices in Oriental carpets has no more significance than that of roses, lions or fleurs-de-lys usually has in Western art.

Though many of the devices found in carpets have a wide range throughout the East, yet there are some that, either in their essence or in their particular rendering, are restricted to certain of the great geographical divisions.

In Plates 194 to 202 will be seen devices that are peculiar, or almost peculiar, to either the Turkish, Caucasian, Central Asiatic or Persian groups of carpets; and the comparison of the details of a specimen under examination with the devices contained in these plates will mostly allow the first step to be taken towards its correct classification.

Plates 203 to 205 contain motives found in early Persian carpets. On Plate 205, however, the "Badge of Tamerlane" in the upper right-hand corner and the somewhat similar device in the bottom row, are peculiar to the fine sixteenth-century Turkish carpets with the Sehna knot. The third device with black roundels—at the middle of the plate—is found in a Persian carpet and may be connected with the other two, but possibly the resemblance is merely accidental.

Chapter III

PRACTICAL CONSIDERATIONS

(a) Purchase

The properties of good and genuine carpets have been explained in some detail in the foregoing chapters, but it may still be useful to summarize the considerations to be borne in mind when purchasing them. Each of the many factors which, taken all together, make up a carpet should receive due and methodical attention. These factors may be stated to be: Design and colouring; manner of weaving; quality of materials; nature of dye stuffs; condition; genuineness. Though all these factors are important, they affect to different degrees a carpet according as it is new, obviously second-hand, or professedly antique. For example, if a carpet is new the question of its genuineness or condition hardly arises, but the nature of its dyestuffs is the most important question; if the carpet is more than fifty years old there need be no anxiety about the dyes employed, but its condition must be very carefully scrutinized; and, lastly, if it is claimed to be antique, then its genuineness is the most important consideration.

When a carpet is being examined it should first, in order to judge of its general effect, be placed flat on the ground and looked at in turn from all points of view. It is a favourite trick of dealers to throw a carpet which they wish to sell over tables or chairs so that it lies in beautiful folds, for not only does this show off the play of the colours to the best advantage, but it also makes it very easy to overlook faults in the weaving or other blemishes which are detected at once when the carpet is laid flat. Another plan is to cause an assistant to hold up one end and move it gently about; and still another—perhaps more legitimate—is to place it with a strong electric light falling on it at exactly the most advantageous angle. It may be remarked here in passing that a carpet does not look its best on a wall, and especially high up; a fact much to be regretted in connexion with museums, where it is generally impossible to exhibit them in any other way.

The merits of a carpet in respect of design and colouring cannot be usefully discussed here. The purchaser will naturally buy what pleases him, and whether his choice is a good one depends upon the soundness of his artistic judgment. Such help on this point as this book can give will be derived from a general perusal with perhaps special attention to the chapter on design.

Another aspect of a carpet's general effect calls, however, for notice ; that is its accuracy in respect of shape and flatness. Irregularities of shape or a disposition to lie unevenly on the floor are flaws indeed in a carpet, and to some extent have an influence on its value ; but the matter must be considered a little further. Anyone who is buying a big new Smyrna, Feraghan or Tabriz rug, will quite justly demand that it should lie perfectly smoothly, because such products are made in competition with European wares. On the other hand, it would not be fair to judge the unpretentious work of nomadic tribes by the same standard. In fact a perfectly rectangular and evenly lying nomad carpet is a very exceptional rarity. Anyone who makes a great demand in this direction merely betrays his ignorance about the origin and methods of production of such pieces.

The details of the weaving as described in Part II, Chapter I, should be examined as thoroughly as time will permit ; for it can hardly fail to help towards forming a sound judgment on the rug if such points as the material of warp, weft, and pile, the kind of knot used, the number and nature of the shoots of weft, and the finish of sides and ends are all carefully noted. One other point is of more importance than all these, and should be carefully observed, because it determines to a great extent the market value of the rug. That is the fineness of the knotting. It is by no means necessary to ascertain this very accurately : a measure can be held against the back of the rug parallel first to the warp and then to the weft, and the number of knots to one inch counted for each direction. These numbers multiplied together will give the number of knots to the square inch. So much it is advisable to do, because the eye alone cannot, without much practice, form a reliable idea of the fineness of the knotting.

It may be mentioned here that it is possible to some extent to remove folds, puckers, and general unevenness from a new carpet. The method is to nail the piece, stretched as tightly as possible, face downwards to a wooden floor, and then wet the back thoroughly with warm water. It is then left until it is quite dry, when it may be found to be considerably improved. In cases of extreme unevenness the treatment may be ineffective, but it is very useful when a carpet, originally fairly flat, has been stretched unequally by being tightly folded in transit, or from some similar cause.

A disposition to curl up at the edges only is mostly due to an imperfectly executed selvedge, and can often be remedied by fresh overcasting; but in some closely woven rugs curling of the edges will happen in damp weather though not at other times.

In a closely woven carpet it is not always easy to count the knots, specially those parallel to the weft, if they are in a patch of uniform colour, but it is always possible to find part of the pattern where the knots are separately visible.

With regard to the quality of the materials, the only thing that can be usefully observed in a superficial examination is the feel and appearance of the yarn constituting the pile.

And now comes the very difficult question of the soundness of the dyes. The first thing necessary for anyone who wishes to be able to form an opinion at all useful on this point is to study in soundly dyed carpets the principal colours, especially red, blue and crimson, but as many more as can be visually remembered.

If in a new or not very old carpet some of the colours appear to resemble those closely in tint and quality, they are probably dyed with the same materials and should be equally sound; but if there are brilliant hues of a different character they should be regarded as doubtful. Among the most suspicious colours are a bright orange-yellow, a glaring vermilion-red, and any very vivid purples or greens.

Each colour in the carpet should now be examined separately, in order to see whether there are signs of fading. The back should be compared with the front; also, after folding the carpet sharply, the pile near the knots, where it is protected from strong light, should be compared with the surface. Even in a new carpet this treatment may show that fading has already begun; while in a rather older one it may be found that parts of the pile, almost colourless, or of indefinite tint on the surface, are of a brilliant hue nearer to the knots. Such signs indicate that the colours concerned are not permanent, though there is a possibility that the superficial change of tint may be due to chemical washing.

The next test is to moisten a white cloth (the moisture of the mouth being slightly alkaline is very convenient for the purpose) and rub it vigorously on each colour in turn. Some will produce no effect; some will tint the cloth slightly; while it may be that others will stain it deeply.

Carpets with such colours as the last should be generally avoided. In the next place the whites should be inspected to see whether they have become contaminated with a stain from the adjoining colours. If they are, it may be due to the use of soluble dyes, or perhaps because the carpet, though soundly dyed, has been exposed to persistent damp. When the dyes have been shown not to be very soluble such a discoloration of the whites, if not unsightly, may be disregarded unless the threads themselves have deteriorated.

It should be remembered that if the purchaser rejects every carpet that has any suspicious dye in it he will have very few new carpets to choose from. It is so very usual for a carpet in the main quite good to have minute quantities of fugitive dyes—used probably on account of the extreme brilliancy not easily obtained with sound ones—that the purchaser may still wisely consider whether after all the carpet may not be a satisfactory acquisition. If he can picture to himself the carpet with the doubtful colours changed to a nondescript neutral tint, and decides that such a change would entail no real deterioration in the appearance of the carpet, then he need not fear to risk its purchase. After all, bad fading of unimportant colours has occurred in many real old carpets of the highest beauty, and if the effect of a modern carpet is due, as it often is, to large masses of good blue and red, very little harm may be done to the balance and tonality of the design by the weakening or disappearance of the minor colours. If, however, the main colours of a carpet are believed to be unsound, then it should be absolutely rejected without hesitation.

To judge the dyes of an old carpet is easy. They cannot be synthetic colours, and if they were originally fugitive they must already have faded so much that no further considerable change is likely. In short, the dyes can be judged on their present appearance.

The condition of a carpet determines in a high measure its value and utility and must be studied from every point of view by the purchaser. Luckily it is not very difficult to form an accurate opinion on the point when once it is known what alterations, due to time, wear and accident, are to be looked for. A new and unused carpet is naturally in good condition as a rule, but there is a possibility that it has been kept in the damp or exposed to sea-water in the course of transit, in which cases the foundation threads may have deteriorated badly without there being visible signs of the trouble, although it is more likely that there are stained parts and signs of the colours having run together. The strength of the warp- and weft-threads should be tested by absolute force. The carpet should be folded face inwards parallel to the warp and an attempt should be made as it were to pull the weft-threads asunder. There is no danger in applying this method to a sound carpet; but if the weft-threads actually break or loosen, or if a sound of cracking is heard, the foundation may be known to be rotten in that place. The warp-threads can be tested in a similar way, but the carpet must be very weak indeed for them actually to break. If the carpet is weak—excepting perhaps in a mere isolated spot—it should be rejected, for a new carpet with a rotten foundation is valueless.

The more obvious signs of wear, such as occur in a second-hand carpet, should now be taken into account. The ends and sides of a carpet, on account of their exposed positions, are the parts which first begin to wear away, and it should be noticed whether they are at all frayed, loosened or weak. Then the pile should be examined. If the carpet has seen service the pile must have worn down to some extent, at least in places, for such wear is seldom uniform. If the examination shows that the pile is worn away down to the knots, even in parts, it is almost certain that the carpet will not stand much more wear, and it will probably prove a bad investment. It may be obvious, but it is important to insist upon the fact that a much-worn carpet, however good it may have been and however beautiful it is in appearance, should not be bought by anyone who intends it for use on the floor.

More obvious blemishes, which are often very unsightly, such as holes, cuts, or localized stains, may be due to accidental causes and often are of little account, provided suitable allowance is made in the price. A skilful carpet-repairer can do wonders in such cases. Cuts can be sewn together by a process akin to weaving; holes can be re-knotted on freshly-inserted warps; and the knots of badly stained parts can be picked out and replaced by new ones. Such work is of course often done before the carpet is offered for sale, but by no means invariably.

It will aid the foregoing inspection if the carpet is held up with its face to a strong light and then looked at from the back. This will at once make visible small holes, slits, and thin, threadbare places, even if they were overlooked before. Sometimes, too, repairs will be visible by this means, but generally they are best detected by the sense of touch. If the fingers are passed over those parts of the carpet where are seen indefinite and vague dark lines, patches of slightly different colour, or unexpected breaks in the pattern, an extra thickness felt may show that the carpet has been joined together or repaired with stitching and new knots. Such repairs are not very detrimental if skilfully done and only of small extent.

Another defect of condition is that of extreme dirtiness of the surface. A dealer will rarely show such a carpet, for he knows what a wonderful change may be effected by cleaning; but it sometimes happens that a piece is met with casually, or perhaps at an auction sale, whose true quality is entirely obscured by the dirty condition. If in such a case any doubt is felt as to the improvement that cleaning will effect, a damp cloth rubbed on a small part will soon settle the point.

It is obvious that the whole of the examination outlined above cannot be carried out in some cases, such for instance as when carpets are put up for sale by auction, and may not be convenient even when they are seen in a dealer's shop. It is on this account that inexperienced buyers should be very cautious in making purchases at auctions, and should if possible in other cases have the carpet for a few days on approval before coming to a decision. Most dealers will agree readily to this, and indeed it rather tells against them if they are unwilling to do so. Even experienced buyers will be well advised to see a carpet at home before buying, because it may not suit its intended surroundings as well as was anticipated when it was seen in the shop, and also it is by no means uncommon for a carpet which appeals very strongly at first to the eye to seem more ordinary after a few days' familiarity.

By the genuineness of carpets is meant the correspondence between what they really are and what they appear to be, or are claimed to be by the man who wishes to sell them. Alas, a very great discrepancy is often to be found here. Many dealers describe their goods as being very old, especially if they suppose the purchaser sets store by age. In the East it is a general practice to add about a century to the age of a carpet, and this may be considered a practice of moderation in comparison with what is often said. A dealer who describes a carpet of fifty years old as a " genuine antique " must be regarded as being not very untruthful.

A carpet may be justly called antique if it is over a century old, and all such pieces, or even fragments, have a certain value unless the condition is exceptionally bad. As the age increases the value increases enormously, so that complete carpets of two or three centuries old in good condition command immense sums. It is not to be wondered at that sellers try to persuade customers that their carpets are of this class, and in some cases they no doubt believe the wares to be as they describe them. When, to quote an actual case, a modern Multan rug of indifferent quality and no artistic interest is offered as a seventh-century rug for the sum of £50,000, it is only fair to suppose that the owner is under a genuine misapprehension as to its real nature !

Mere errors of description are not perhaps very dangerous, because it is well known that the word of a vendor cannot always be relied upon ; and there are not many buyers who will give large prices for goods of whose value and nature they know little. A more insidious, if not quite such a common evil, is for carpets to be treated in various ways with the express intention of deceiving by making them appear to be different from what they really are. It may be useful to describe shortly a few of the operations of this sort which are commonly practised, and to give a few hints by which the deception may be exposed.

It is well in the first place to ask oneself whenever a carpet is seen for the first time : " Is this piece genuine ? " Of course, in the majority of cases an affirmative answer can be given immediately ; but the mere asking of the question, and still more an attempt to find evidence of deceit, will obviate the dangerous possibility of the purchaser being taken off his guard.

The commonest trick is that of chemical washing, which has been mentioned already. This is so widely done and is so well known that it cannot invariably be regarded as a deliberate deception. It has the effect of giving an appearance of age, but apart from that it is used to modify the crude and vivid colouring which is possessed by many modern carpets when new ; and it certainly does result in an immediate, if transitory and undesirable, improvement in the rug's appearance. It is practised to varying extents, from a sponging over with a mild acid, not very injurious, to a severe treatment with strong chemicals which alters the whole colouring and tonality of the design, and seriously impairs the wearing qualities of the wool. It is carried out in the East, probably often by the weavers of the carpets ; and to a still greater extent after they have reached the Western markets. In London there are firms who specialize in this business, and when it is said that the present cost of the process is about 9d. a square foot, it will be understood that the dealers are pretty sure that it adds to the attractiveness of their wares.

It is not easy to be certain whether a rug has been chemically washed. If, however, the whites are pure in colour and rather glaring it is certain that it has not been washed. If, on the other hand, the rug is in good condition and shows no signs of wear, and yet the whites are toned with a yellowish-grey, and all the colours are mellow and a little indefinite, then it is very probable that washing has been practised.

Another method of ageing carpets is more vicious if not more harmful. This is to expose a new carpet to bright sunlight, in a street where all the traffic will pass over it ; a service which the owner's neighbours will cordially assist in. After the rug is cleaned, it will have signs of wear which are not dissimilar to those obtained in genuine service. Thus a rug may look many years old when it is in reality quite new. There is perhaps no particular harm in this, though it is certainly a pity to reduce the life of a rug by artificial means. The chief protection to the buyer lies in the fact that this treatment is rarely accorded to really good rugs, but only to those whose merits are insufficient without the added glamour of age, to attract a purchaser. Anyone who is able to evaluate the quality of the rug apart from the signs of wear, is not likely to make a mistake here.

A fairly certain sign of genuine age is the unequal wearing of the different colours. It has already been explained that black-dyed wools generally wear away much faster than others, but nearly every dye has some effect upon the quality of the fibre as well as upon its colour. Some dyes actually seem to preserve the wool, but whether that is true or not it will generally be found that the pile of some colours is shorter, less bulky, or otherwise different from the rest. When it is seen that each separate colour is evenly worn throughout and that there are differences between the various colours, then it may be assumed with safety that the carpet is at least several, and probably as much as forty or fifty, years old.

A process has recently been devised for improving the appearance of the pile, by treating the carpet with glycerine and then passing it between hot rollers. A lustre is certainly given by this means, but it is different from the natural lustre of good wool, and it is almost certain that the effect cannot be permanent, even if it does not seriously injure the wool.

Other practices, perhaps more legitimate, have for their object the improvement of pieces whose condition is not good. One common artifice is to tint on the surface those parts of the pattern which are so threadbare as to show nothing but the foundation threads. This is permissible to a limited extent, in the case of old pieces kept for inspection only, as for example in Museums or other collections, when the judicious application of a little colour may prevent a few staring patches from entirely spoiling the intended effect of the carpet. For practical service such a method is of course useless, as the colour would not last. In such a case the correct remedy is re-knotting the injured parts; and, if this is not practicable, then the carpet is too far gone to be fit for use.

Old carpets which are badly worn, or much damaged in places, while the rest is fairly good, are often cut up and joined together again so as to make up a smaller piece of good appearance. Care is taken that the joins do not run across plain parts of the rug; but they are carried along lines such as the edge of a border or, when necessary, are made to follow more involved courses round the contour of the pattern. Carpets which have been mended cleverly may perfectly well be beautiful and valuable specimens in a collection, but if the purchaser does not detect the repairs, then he may unjustly have to pay the price of a perfectly preserved carpet, because only the best firms base their prices upon the real condition, as ascertained by experts.

A still more refined art is the deliberate manufacture of bogus antique carpets. A sketch of the process adopted by a certain factory will give an idea of the misapplied skill devoted to this fraud. A carpet with a good old design is made of the finest materials by the best available weavers. It is then taken to the sea and immersed long enough to soften and bleach the colours to the desired extent. Next it is rubbed down back and front with a pumice-stone; not evenly, but more in those parts where wear would be expected. After this it is, while damp, singed with a spirit-flame, so that the fluffiness and softness of the new wool shall be removed. Lastly, holes are burned in it with red-hot coals, and these holes are repaired so well as to be imperceptible without the closest examination.

Such productions will not often be dangerous to the ordinary buyer, because the cost of manufacture is so great that they can only be offered for very high sums. Experienced dealers have, however, bought such things under the impression that they were antiques of great rarity, which shows it is not easy to detect the imposture. A microscope, however, will show the burnt and slightly swollen ends of the woollen fibres.

Luckily, it seems almost impossible to imitate the pattern, colour, and materials of a real old carpet with perfect accuracy; so that there is nearly always something incongruous in the imitation to the trained eye. Very often the claim that a carpet is of a certain date, can be at once disproved by the fact that the design is one quite unknown until a much later period.

A close scrutiny of all the details which have been mentioned should give considerable help in arriving at a correct appraisement of any carpet whose purchase is contemplated ; but it must not be supposed that it will take the place of the experience which is derived from a long acquaintance and painstaking study of carpets. It is often hard, even when the facts are observed, to give them their due weight—neither more nor less—so that experts and dealers of long standing are sometimes mistaken in their conclusions. It is certain, however, that such methods of investigation as have been suggested will lead by degrees to the acquisition of the experience so much to be desired.

(b) Prices

The price of an Eastern rug depends upon so many indefinite factors that it is not easy to give much assistance on the point to a would-be purchaser, and nothing that is written can take the place of a practical acquaintance with the market. Although it is the hardest question upon which to give information, it is perhaps that upon which the student is most anxious to receive it, so that an attempt must be made to deal with it as well as may be.

Although carpets are mostly sold by the piece, it somewhat simplifies the question to consider the price per square foot, and, indeed, it is from this point of view that the dealer fixes his prices. Leaving aside the question of mere area, it is obvious that a piece which entails much work must be sold for a higher price than one which is more quickly made, and accordingly a finely-knotted rug is more costly than a coarse one. In comparison with the labour involved, the materials used do not account for a high proportion of the price, but a very heavy rug is usually more costly than the coarseness of its texture would imply. Other factors which increase the price out of proportion to the labour involved are beauty of design and colouring, rarity and age ; while, on the other hand, unsoundness of workmanship and—to an even greater extent—bad condition detract from the value.

In order to get a basis upon which to proceed it will be well to fix upon a kind of standard of quality and condition, and this standard should be one which is frequently met with. Let it be assumed then that the standard rug is well-woven, made of good materials and dyed with sound colours, and that it is either new or so little worn as not to have appreciably lost any of its wearing qualities, and that in point of design and beauty of colouring it is neither below nor above the average. When such rugs are examined it will be found that, provided they are of the same fineness, it matters little from what country they come or of what type they are, but that the price is pretty constant for them all; and further it will be found that if two rugs differ in texture then their prices are approximately proportional to the number of knots in a square inch, though there is a tendency, on account of the extra material required, for the coarse rugs, as already stated, to be rather more expensive than this proportion would indicate. Some types of rugs, even when everything otherwise is equal, are rather more and some are rather less expensive than the average, but generally the divergence is not considerable.

The following table gives the present average retail price (July, 1922) per square foot in London of different types of rugs of the standard quality as defined above.

Type.	Knots per square inch.		Price per square foot.		Price for each 50 knots per square inch.
Smyrna or Turkey . . .	16	..	4/5	..	13/6
Smyrna or Turkey ("Standard")	20	..	5/–	..	12/6
Sparta	40	..	10/–	..	12/6
Chinese (modern) . . .	45	..	10/–	..	11/1
Feraghan.	50	..	10/–	..	10/–
Shiraz	50	..	7/6	..	7/6
Muskabad	50	..	7/9	..	7/9
Beluchistan	55	..	7/9	..	7/–
Meshed	70	..	10/–	..	7/2
Caucasian	70	..	10/–	..	7/2
Kurdistan	80	..	14/5	..	9/–
Kirman	80	..	12/3	..	7/8
Tabriz	80	..	12/3	..	7/8
Yomud	150	..	14/5	..	4/10
Bokhara	200	..	17/9	..	4/5
Sehna	240	..	33/4	..	6/8
Kashan	250	..	33/4	..	6/8
Kashan (silk)	250	..	44/9	..	9/–
	Warps to 1 inch.				
Persian Kilims . . .	10	..	3/4	..	—
Other Kilims	10	..	2/9	..	—
Soumak	8	..	7/6	..	—

The last column, which gives the price per square foot for each 50 knots per square inch, shows the relative value of the various types of rugs when the fineness of knotting is taken into account. The first four types are heavily-made rugs in which the sheer weight of material increases the proportionate cost. The relative value of the rest, it will be seen, does not vary very greatly. This column shows that the most expensive rugs in proportion to their fineness are Feraghans, Kurdistans, and Kashans with a silk pile ; while the cheapest are Central Asiatic rugs, such as Bokharas and Yomuds. Other rugs not mentioned in the table range about the average value, which may be said to be about 7s. 6d. per square foot for each 50 knots to the square inch.

Exceptionally pleasing design in colouring, as already said, will lead to an increased price, though it is quite impossible to suggest any system upon which the increase can be evaluated. It may be said, however, that for standard rugs the prices should rarely be twice as great as those given. On the other hand, an inferior appearance may cause a reduction in price, but it will not on that account fall much below the quoted figures. Bad condition may reduce the price indefinitely, and perhaps a rough guide to the decrease may be afforded by an estimate of how much of the rug's useful life has been destroyed by wear or misuse.

Generally speaking, the value of a rug increases with its age, as soon as the latter becomes considerable. Here again accurate figures cannot be given, but quite roughly it may be suggested that, if the condition is reasonably good for the age, then each century that has passed about doubles the value.

In this connexion it may be of some interest, even if of little practical use, to work out on these lines the approximate value of the Ardabil carpet, which is probably the best known and most famous rug in the world. It has about 350 knots to the square inch, and contains 604 square ft. Viewed as a standard new rug, its value would be about $604 \times 7 \times 7/6$, or £1,585. As it is nearly four centuries old, this value must be multiplied by 16 ; and as its condition is much above the average for such an age, and its interest is quite exceptional, the resulting price may fairly be at least doubled again. This would lead to the sum of £50,720, a figure not inconsistent with various estimates which have been made.

Again, to take an antique carpet of fairly common type, it will be found that an early eighteenth-century Ghiordes prayer-rug in fair condition, and containing about 30 square ft. and having 70 knots to the square inch, will cost about £60, which agrees with the formula $7/6 \times 30 \times 4 \times 70/50$. A Kula rug of the same kind will usually be rather more coarsely woven and will probably be sold for from £45 to £50.

PRACTICAL CONSIDERATIONS

It will not be supposed from what has been said above that the general level of carpet prices is free from market fluctuations—and indeed such is far from being the case—but in ordinary circumstances the changes are not very great or very rapid. All the time, however, there is a certain movement going on, sometimes in one direction and sometimes in the other, though the general tendency is for prices to get higher year by year. Up till 1914 they had been slowly but steadily mounting, and then the war, which had such a profound effect upon all prices and values, caused a very rapid increase, and a level was reached such as had never been thought of before. In fact there are few commodities not necessary to life or to the supply of munitions of war which increased in price as much as carpets. The apex was reached about 1918 and 1919, but it is not easy to give a definite figure for the increase, as the various types of carpets were very differently affected. The really old and rare carpets whose prices were already very high suffered the least change, while some more ordinary kinds in special demand at the moment went up to at least five times their pre-war value. Perhaps it would be near the mark to say that the general level, taking one type with another, exceeded by 200 per cent. that existing before the war. Afterwards prices fell again even more rapidly than they had risen and very many carpets had to be sold by dealers at prices much lower than had been given for them. At present (July, 1922) the general level may be taken to be about 20 per cent. higher than it was in 1914, so that it is probable, taking the natural rise into account, that prices are not very different now from what they would have been if there had been no war.

As to the future, it is dangerous to speak, but it hardly seems possible that the present level will not soon be very much heightened. The tempting prices of the war caused the accumulated stores in private hands to be drawn away to the West; and the general disturbance in the East, to say nothing of the actual destruction of the weavers and their property, must, it would seem, inevitably reduce fresh production. It also seems likely that labour conditions will change so much, as profoundly to alter the cost of manufacture, so that it is quite possible that in a few years the prices of hand-made Eastern carpets may be such as to make the present ones seem insignificant.

(c) Treatment

A few hints may perhaps be usefully given as to how carpets ought to be treated.

HAND-WOVEN CARPETS

The first problem to be dealt with is that of the best way of cleaning them when dirty. A carpet, even when bought straight from a dealer, or in any case after it has been in use for a number of years, will generally be full of dust, and dirty on the surface, and it is essential to have it cleaned occasionally if its beauty and strength are to be retained.

If the carpet is fairly strong in structure it should have the dust removed by beating with a broad carpet-beater, while it rests face downwards on some level and slightly yielding surface; the use of a stick, whether it is supple or not, can in no circumstances be recommended. A suitable surface for resting the carpet on while it is beaten is a dry lawn, or in winter time on clean snow. It may also be placed on an ordinary floor covered with several layers of newspapers, but it is not advisable to hang a carpet on a line for beating. The use of vacuum cleaners, or of compressed air, is very suitable for new carpets or older ones whose condition is still good; but if these methods are employed on old carpets which are weak or have been much mended, the powerful suction or pressure of the air causes the loss of a great deal of wool, especially in the repaired places.

After this process of dry-cleaning, carpets ought to be washed, when, of course, it is essential that the colours are such as will not be spoiled by wetting. Washing, however, must not be left to the mercy of an ordinary laundry, because they would use very hot water and possibly alkalis, the result of which is that the carpet will return with dead and lustreless wool. The best way is to wash it with warm water and carpet or wool soap, which is a compound of ordinary good soap and ox-gall. The lather can be applied freely with a soft brush rubbed the way the pile lies. The soap must be well washed away by repeated soakings, or treatment with a hose-pipe, after which as much water as possible should be pressed out by stroking with a smooth stick in the direction of the pile.

This process gives softness and even an enhanced lustre to a carpet when once it is thoroughly dry.

Carpets are best preserved by washing every few years, and only beating occasionally and moderately in the meantime. They must, of course, be swept or brushed frequently. This should be done chiefly in the direction in which the pile lies. Brushing from side to side may be done gently, but never should it be against the pile. In respect of this, domestic servants are very obstinate, for they often allege that more dust is removed by brushing in the wrong direction. They are quite right in the statement, but the reason is that the pile is raised and separated, so that far more dust can accumulate in it. When the brush is used in the right direction its bristles gradually coax the dust to the surface, and the pile is left in the condition best fitted for resisting wear. Mechanical carpet-sweepers are inadvisable as they sweep in both directions.

If the owner of a carpet has a small river handy he cannot do better than immerse it in the flowing water after he has secured it tightly. He may also spread it back uppermost on clean grass or on a network of ropes when heavy rain is falling, or may drag it about with its face on a patch of clean snow.

It will be seen that some of these processes are not easy to apply to large rugs, and it may be necessary to send them for cleaning to a reliable firm who understand the work. One great difficulty is the final drying of the carpet, which must be done out of doors or in a very large room where the air is circulating freely. As the drying often takes several days, it may happen, especially in big towns, that a lot of fresh dirt may fall on the carpet while it is exposed.

Other methods of cleaning carpets are sometimes recommended but are of doubtful value. Treatment with wood-shavings soaked in petrol is expensive, dangerous and not effective. Rubbing them while damp with rough sea-salt is liable to injure the colours.

The worst enemy of the carpet collector is the common moth. Carpets which are walked on are much safer from its attacks than those which are used as door or wall-hangings or turned into upholstery, but the greatest danger is to rugs which are stored away. As moths have a liking for quiet, warm places it is advisable to disturb them by airing floor carpets and shaking hanging specimens as often as possible. Moths have a preference for certain colours, especially red, and for loose textures rather than for tightly-knotted ones. For this reason it is particularly desirable that pieces which have once been affected with moth should be examined with especial care.

A very useful way of keeping moth away from carpets is to place the wings of birds, such as hens, pigeons and crows, on the top of cupboards. Moths have quite a peculiar passion for feathers and will lay their eggs in them in preference to any other place. By leaving such temptation about and making examination from time to time it is comparatively easy to destroy these enemies.

If carpets must be put away for a time, it is well to pack them with naphthalene, camphor, or lavender oil, in tin-lined cases, or strong paper parcels into which the flying moth cannot penetrate. If, however, the eggs of the moth are packed up in the carpet they may hatch out, in spite of any strong-smelling substance, and do much damage. It is, accordingly, wise to make as sure as possible that the carpet is free from infection when put away, and as there is never complete certainty as to this, there is danger unless the carpets are examined from time to time.

A safe plan is to put the goods into cold storage, but this is expensive, and in many places not practicable. It is claimed that petrol poured over will destroy the eggs of the moth ; but it is not quite certain whether it is a fact. An ingenious method of destroying infection, and one which has been tried with success, is to place the carpets in a warm chamber, saturated with the vapour of chloroform. The warmth hatches out the eggs, but the grubs are immediately destroyed before they can do any damage.

It must be remembered that good carpets must be taken care of. For instance, heavy pieces of furniture with sharp edges should never be allowed to stand continuously on the same place of a carpet, or marks and holes will result according to the strength of the fabric. If a piece of linoleum, or, better still, a sheet of thick rubber is placed under the legs of tables and chests there will be little danger of damage

If it is necessary to put away, or pack a carpet, it is better not to fold it in both directions, especially if it is tightly-knotted or weak : folds in one direction only, do little damage unless the carpet is very stiff or very old. The best plan is to roll the carpet. Even this may injure a very stiff carpet, especially if it is subjected to pressure when rolled ; but the difficulty may be surmounted by rolling it round some cylindrical object like a strong tube of cardboard or another softer carpet. A small thin carpet may be protected by a stick in the middle, which will prevent the whole roll being bent.

It should be noted at times whether any attention is needed in the way of repairs. If the fringe gets ragged it should be trimmed evenly. If the ends or sides begin to unravel, they can be oversewn as a blanket is, or re-overcast, and perhaps the work will be stronger if a piece of webbing is sewn on at the back along the edge. Cuts and tears should be repaired as soon as possible, and holes or small threadbare places should be re-knotted. Old rugs that will not stand much wear but are still beautiful objects can be hung up instead of being left on the floor ; but it is often possible to find a place in the house where they can be placed flat and yet only occasionally be walked on.

CHAPTER IV

CARPETS IN THE MARKET—THEIR GROUPING AND IDENTIFICATION

(a) Turkish

Turkish carpets may be divided into two groups : (i) those produced in factories and (ii) those produced as a home industry.

(i) *Turkish Carpets made in Factories.*—The sedentary Turk is not a craftsman ; so that practically all carpet-making in the Turkish dominions is the work of other races, such as the Greeks and Armenians. The Greek element is strongly predominant along the coast of Asia Minor, and for this reason it has been possible to evolve a factory-system, which is now so highly developed and so ready to cater for the needs of the West that carpets of any design and colour, and of almost any size, may be ordered and finished within six or eight weeks. The factories are well-equipped and not lacking in capital, which accounts for one of the chief differences between their products and those made in the homes. The latter is carried on by the poorer people in their small living-rooms and, consequently, it is not practicable to have a loom measuring more than about 6 ft. wide. The rich factories on the other hand have large premises which permit of the erection of looms up to a width of perhaps 45 ft. For this reason Smyrna, and its back country, Kula, Ghiordes and Demirdji, are able to produce large carpets 6 × 9, 8 × 11, 9 × 12, 11 × 13, 12 × 15 ft. in size and even much larger ones, which are known under the collective name of SMYRNA carpets in Europe and America. They are exported in large numbers and are found all over the world, chiefly in use in public rooms, business offices, and dining-rooms.

These carpets may be regarded as the descendants of the large Ushak carpets which were made in Asia Minor from at least the sixteenth century. Though they are inferior in design and coarser in texture, they yet retain much the same colouring and many of the same technical peculiarities. Such carpets were brought into Europe freely in the eighteenth century, and ever since have been very largely used. So well-known has this type been, that the name " Turkey Carpet " was at one time applied to all Oriental rugs, just as it is now common for nearly all to be included by the term " Persian." The best known types of Smyrna carpets are very thick and durable, but among the coarsest-woven of all rugs, there being only from 13 to 20 knots to the square inch. They are made entirely of wool, and while the warp is usually white, the weft is almost invariably dyed red. Plates 93 to 97 show five common types of Smyrna carpets.

PLATE 93. Modern Smyrna carpet—also known as Ushak or Medallion Carpet. Carpets of this kind have from 10 to 16 knots to the square inch. They range in size from about 6 × 8 ft. to 20 × 40 ft., and they are made almost exclusively of three colours, red, green and blue. They are among the cheapest of Eastern carpets.

PLATE 94. Modern Smyrna carpet—also known as Ghiordes carpet. Carpets of this kind have from 13 to 18 knots to the square inch. They range in size from 6 × 9 ft. to 20 × 40 ft., and can be obtained in whatever colours are in favour in Europe at the time. They are also made with more elaborate designs as in the next Plate. They are the cheapest of the Smyrna carpets.

PLATE 95. Modern Smyrna carpet—also called Demirdji carpet. Carpets of this kind have from 16 to 22 knots to the square inch. They range in size from 6 × 9 ft. to 20 × 40 ft., and can be obtained in whatever colours are in favour in Europe at the time. They are also made with a central medallion on a plain ground as in the last Plate. They tend to be rather more expensive than the last type.

PLATE 96. Modern Smyrna carpet—also called after various towns of Asia Minor. Carpets of this kind have from 19 to 58 knots to the square inch. They range in size from 6 × 9 ft. to 20 × 40 ft., and may be purchased in any colours, and in a great variety of modern and old Persian designs. When of the same texture, they are about the same price per square foot as the last type.

PLATE 97. Modern Hereke carpet—also called Smyrna carpet. Carpets of the kind have from 45 to 64 knots to the square inch, and so are the finest-knotted of the Smyrna carpets. They are made in the factory of the Sultan at Hereke (close to the railway from Scutari to Angora). They are of various designs and in all sizes. The Plate shows one of the best types, but cheaper carpets are made with designs as in Plates 51 and 52. The price is higher than the other Smyrna carpets in proportion to the fineness of the texture.

A kind of carpet made of recent years in Smyrna is sold under the name of SPARTA. These are mostly of small or medium size and are knotted rather more closely than the ordinary Smyrna carpet. Their designs are very varied but are usually based upon Anatolian or Caucasian models and they may easily be mistaken for products of the latter region.

(ii) *Turkish Carpets of the home Industry.*—Carpets are woven in the homes about Smyrna and also in the less accessible parts inland, but especially in Anatolia where the full assistance is obtained of the Armenian element in the population.

The fact that Anatolia borders in the West on the region of the factories and that in the East it approaches the zone of Persian influence, has had considerable effect on the kinds of carpet made. Those of western Anatolia are reminiscent in quality, colour and pattern of the products of the coast, whereas those from the Eastern side compete in quality and beauty with the good Persian and Caucasian specimens.

Generally speaking, Turkish carpets are made entirely of wool, though in some of the finer ones, especially those from Ghiordes, cotton is sometimes found in the warp and weft. Other materials are so rare as to be quite exceptional. The warp is usually of white or at least undyed wool: in the more barbaric types it tends to be coarse and browner than in the others. The weft is mostly of red wool, though white, yellow and even blue are not uncommon colours. The usual plan is to have two shoots of weft after each row of knots, and in the coarser rugs when more shoots are found, the larger number is not constant throughout the carpet, but happens at occasional intervals.

A peculiarity often seen in the weft, but perhaps never in rugs of any other country, is that it does not invariably go right across from side to side, but goes backwards and forwards over sections of the carpet; each section being roughly triangular in shape. The diagonal lines, marking the juncture of the sections, are clearly seen at the back and are sufficient to identify the specimen with Anatolia. The convenience of this plan when several weavers are at work on a large rug is obvious, for each weaver can go on for a time independently of the others, and need not wait till all are ready to allow a shoot of weft right across the loom. The habit is still often retained in smaller rugs, and sometimes it is carried to the extent of using weft of different colours. It will be seen that the plain field of some prayer-rugs has a weft of the same colour as the pile, and this no doubt helps to give a superior effect to the colour of the ground. In some cases it may have induced the belief that the border was added recently to a rug of older date.

The pile consists of lustrous wool of good quality and is mostly of medium length. In the Yuruk rugs it is, however, rather long, and in the Ghiordes rugs it is notably short—in fact in these the collars of the knots are sometimes almost visible. The Turkish or Ghiordes knot is invariably used. The selvedge usually consists of a narrow web of several cords overcast with wool, and the ends are nearly always fringed.

The colours are bright and varied. No attempt is made to get a rich effect by means of deep colours of quiet tone, but prismatic hues are placed together in juxtaposition, rather in the manner of a mosaic. In the newer rugs this somewhat daring method often gives unpleasantly crude effects, but the older ones challenge comparison with those of Persia and other parts, although the colour-scheme is so different.

In point of design the first thing to notice is the great prevalence of prayer-rugs, which certainly outnumber all other kinds. The niche in such rugs more definitely suggests an archway than those of Persia. Often there are two columns supporting the arch, but even when these are not present, or when they are represented by a mere band running down the side of the field, there is often an indication at the springing of the arch of a flattened surface ready for receiving them. The arch is angular rather than curved in shape, though the straight lines are often softened by having a stepped contour. The exact form varies considerably in different districts, though nearly every district has a type almost peculiar to itself. Cross-panels (in reality short horizontal border-stripes) are mostly found, either above or below the niche or sometimes in both positions. The niche itself is plain more often than not, but it may be ornamented with floral forms projecting from the sides, or sparsely scattered, or hanging from the top. Ornament in the last position evidently takes the place of the lamp, which itself is sometimes present there, or in the spandrels above. The field is never covered with an all-over pattern (apart from a very small spot or diaper) but always, even when most ornate, gives the impression of a plain field with a little superimposed decoration. Prayer-rugs with several niches side by side are found in Anatolian work, and are often falsely supposed to come from Eastern Turkestan, where that form is much more common. The other rugs of Anatolia are of various sizes, but never very large. Runners are very uncommon.

The details of the design are mostly derived from floral forms highly conventionalized; and even when geometrical devices are seen it will often appear on closer study that they really have a floral origin. There is, however, a certain amount of purely geometrical design, and the rugs in which it occurs have a great resemblance to those of Caucasia and are often mistaken for them. Certain floral devices are almost peculiar to Anatolian patterns—the carnation on short stems, which in various stages of conventionalization often projects into the central panel ; little sprigs of three blossoms or three leaves ; sprays of hyacinths ; and tall tulips on upright stems, which last are often described as Rhodian lilies. Human figures and animals are very rarely found.

The border-stripes, unlike those in Persian and Caucasian rugs, rarely have continuous wavy stems, but are usually filled with detached sprays, leaves, blossoms, or S-forms, though these are often so closely arranged as to give the effect of a continuous pattern. Some of the borders still in frequent use are derived with very little alteration from forms found in carpets of the sixteenth century and onwards. Many of the more elaborate border patterns are almost peculiar to certain types of rugs and, accordingly, assist greatly in the problem of identification. Plate 194 shows devices found almost exclusively in Turkish carpets. The majority of these are freely used throughout the group, but some are almost peculiar to certain types. For examples Figs. 1 and 14 in the plate are characteristic of Ladiks ; Fig. 3 of Mujurs ; and Figs. 5 and 11 of Ghiordes rugs. Fig. 21 shows the lamp so often found in Turkish prayer-rugs, and it is a simplification of this device that may result in the small figure of the diaper referred to on p. 157.

It must be stated here that the quite modern Anatolian rugs are in every way inferior to the older ones. The patterns have perhaps altered least, but the texture is coarser and looser, and the colours are very crude and often unsound. In fact, apart from the Kilims, the modern Anatolian rugs are, as a whole, the worst of any produced in the East. The importance of the group lies with those of moderate or greater age, and nearly all that follows should be regarded as applying to those only.

The general characteristics of Anatolian rugs as described above are naturally somewhat varied in certain districts, but these variations when of consequence will be mentioned in the short description which follows of the recognized types of rugs.

As it is scarcely possible to give any system of classification of these types—apart from the broad distinction between the rough nomadic and the more refined rugs—it will suffice to take them without any methodical order.

GHIORDES RUGS, which get their name from the town on the site of the ancient Gordium, are perhaps the best known and most prized of the Anatolian group. They are fairly finely woven and the pile is so short that the wool never looks lustrous. The warp, and weft, and, less often, the white part of the pile are sometimes of cotton. In some pieces there is an added silk fringe at the corners. The colours are chiefly red, blue and white, which apart from the niche are never in large masses. In the later specimens the red inclines towards crimson. The niche usually has a plain blue or red field, and a high pointed arch, often supported by columns. There are mostly two cross-panels. The borders and spandrels are filled with fine floral detail. The other rugs usually have a hexagonal central panel fringed with projecting floral sprays, but are otherwise like the prayer-rugs though mostly larger. A special kind of prayer-carpet—known as the Ghiordes-Marpudjle—has narrow stripes running across the whole carpet.

KULA RUGS are rather similar to the last, but are usually coarser in texture. The colours are chiefly red, yellow, and blue. In most of the older rugs the red (why, is not known) has faded to a brownish yellow ; so that such rugs have a characteristic blue and yellow appearance. The arch of the prayer-rugs is pointed but flat, and there is only one cross-panel as a rule. The spandrels, and even the field sometimes, are filled with a diaper of repeated floral forms. The borders are peculiar, as they often consist of a large number of narrow stripes, each filled with small detached blossoms or buds. A type, known as " Cemetery Carpets," has one or more pieces of land with a tomb and cypress trees. The other carpets are mostly like double-ended prayer-rugs.

LADIK RUGS (named from Laodicea) often have the warp and weft dyed the predominant colour of the pile. The ends have a fairly wide red web, often striped with other colours, ending in fringes. The colours are chiefly red and blue, but with fairly large quantities of other hues, and they are used in larger masses than in Ghiordes rugs. They are mostly bright, but sometimes a rich but quieter colour-effect is found. The arch of prayer-rugs has three points, and there is a wide cross-panel above or below the niche, containing tall, upright tulips. A typical border-stripe is one with large rosettes alternating with sprays of three blossoms. The other rugs, which are not common, have various patterns, in which long hexagonal panels and stars are favourite devices.

MUJUR RUGS often have a red or brown weft. They are rather coarsely knotted and have a fairly long pile. The ends have coloured webs and fringes. The colours are bright and numerous—red, green, blue, yellow, and violet mostly being plentiful. The prayer-rugs have a steep, pointed, stepped arch, which opens out into a small lobe at the point. There is one cross-panel above the niche. The main border-stripe has a characteristic row of rosettes made into a square form by the addition of corner ornaments, and one of the smaller stripes usually has a succession of touching lozenges.

KIR-SHEHR RUGS resemble those of Mujur in weave and colour, though green is more plentiful. The arch of prayer-rugs is also similar to the last, but mostly has a larger number of narrow bands to form its contour. There is one cross-panel, either above or below the niche. A characteristic of the border is the occurrence of several narrow stripes like those of a Kula, but alternate ones are usually bright red in colour.

NIGDE and TUZLA RUGS resemble the last two, but are not important types.

BERGAMA RUGS (from the ancient Pergamum) have always a dyed warp and weft and a long silky pile. The ends have a wide web crossed by coloured stripes, and a tasselled fringe. These ends often have small rosettes on them, or shells and other small objects attached to them for the purpose of averting the evil eye. The colours are rich and dark and consist chiefly of red and blue. The rugs are nearly square in shape, and prayer-rugs are exceptional. When they do occur they have arches of various forms, including the peculiar one shown in Plate 108A. The designs are very varied and hard to describe, but they are mostly bold in proportion to the size of the rug and floral forms are highly conventionalized.

ANATOLIAN is the name given in the trade to a nondescript lot of rugs made throughout Anatolia. They are mostly small in size, and are coarsely-woven with long, shaggy, soft wool. The colouring is rather crude and the designs are very varied, but often copy features from the better defined classes. Any small rug that does not conform to one of the well-known types can with justice and convenience be called Anatolian.

MELAS RUGS (named from Melassa) form an ill-defined group characterized chiefly by the form of the prayer arch, which is narrow and furnished with a diamond-shaped lobe at the point (Plate 113).

KONIA RUGS (named from Iconium) are similar to the last group, but have a pointed arch with a small triangular projection at its springing (Plate 113).

MAKRI RUGS are sometimes called Rhodian, but are not made in that island. They are divided into a number of arched niches and are often compared to a cathedral window.

YURUK RUGS, unlike the last few classes, form a well-defined group. They are made by the Kurdish mountaineers of the West and have much in common with the Nomadic rugs of the Caucasus. The wool is long and shaggy and the colours are dark and characteristic, consisting of brown, red and blue, with a little deep-toned white. The pattern consists mostly of concentric diamonds, heavily fringed with latch hooks. They are often mistaken for Caucasian products ; but should be distinguished by their colour-scheme.

The Plates 98 to 114 show specimens of all the principal types described above, and should be sufficient for identifying any fairly characteristic specimen. Pieces which do not follow these types may be difficult or impossible to associate with any definite district, but those who have had many through their hands can often, by paying attention to their subtler features, group them with certain well-known types even if they differ from them in many particulars.

PLATE 98. GHIORDES PRAYER-CARPET.

Carpets of this kind have from 65 to 110 knots to the square inch. The size is generally about 3½ ft. × 6½ ft. They are somewhat rough to the touch, and have a short and lustreless pile. The chief colours are red, blue and white. The ground of the niche is usually blue or red, the former being perhaps the more common ; a white ground is very rare. The main border-stripe of this specimen has a pattern which has come down almost unchanged from the sixteenth century ; in it may be seen sprays of the hyacinth, which was so much used in early Turkish art. Ghiordes prayer-rugs more often have no columns and a steeper arch than this one, and one of the two cross-panels is generally below the niche. Ghiordes rugs command rather higher prices than similar rugs in equal condition. A good specimen is considered to show the best work done in Anatolia during recent centuries.

PLATE 99. KIS (i.e., Maiden)-GHIORDES CARPET.

These are given as presents to brides, or according to another account are woven by a bride as a sample of her skill in carpet-making. They have from 60 to 90 knots to the square inch. The size is generally about 3½ ft. × 6 ft. They are rough to the touch, and have a short and lustreless pile. The chief colours are white, blue and red. The arrangement of the field, both with regard to the medallion and the shape of the corners, follows a type of rug common in the sixteenth century. The main border-stripe, which is a corruption of an early pattern, is peculiar to Kis-Ghiordes rugs. The small objects forming the diaper of field and border may possibly be conventionalized lamps.

PLATE 100. KULA PRAYER-CARPET.

Carpets of this kind are known in the trade very generally, but erroneously, as Ghiordes. They have from 60 to 90 knots to the square inch. The size is about 4 ft. × 6 ft. They are fairly hard to the touch. The pile is short and differs from that of most of the Anatolian prayer-rugs in being without any lustre. The chief colours are blue, red and yellow. This example has the typical Kula colouring, the red being fairly well preserved. It has not the usual repeated narrow stripes in the border, but the arrangement of leaves in the principal stripe produces much the same effect. Antique pieces, probably owing to the short pile and rather loose weave, are generally in very bad condition. Kula prayer-carpets with a purple ground are not much prized.

PLATE 101. KULA PRAYER-CARPET.

Carpets of this kind are called " Cemetery Carpets," and in the trade are also, erroneously, known as Ghiordes. They have from 60 to 90 knots to the square inch. The usual size is about 3½ ft. to 6 ft. They are somewhat rough to the touch and have a short and lustreless pile. The chief colours are blue, red and yellow. The repeated designs in the field represent a tomb with a cypress and another tree ; from which, of course, the name " Cemetery Carpet " is derived.

PLATE 102. LADIK PRAYER-CARPET.

Carpets of this kind are known in the trade also as Ghiordes or Kula. They have from 65 to 110 knots to the square inch. The size varies from 3 ft. × 4 ft. to 4 ft. × 6 ft. They have a lustrous pile of medium length. The principal colours are red, blue, green, and yellow.

PLATE 103. LADIK PRAYER-CARPET (Dated A.H. 1211 = A.D. 1797).

Carpets of this kind are also known in the trade as Ghiordes or Kula. They have from 65 to 90 knots to the square inch. The size is generally from 3 ft. × 4½ ft. to 4½ ft. × 6 ft. They are soft and flexible and have a lustrous pile of medium length. The chief colours are red, blue, green, and yellow. The main border-stripe is almost peculiar to Ladiks.

HAND-WOVEN CARPETS

PLATE 104. LADIK CARPET.

Carpets of this kind have 50 to 70 knots to the square inch. The size is about 3 ft. × 4½ ft. They are soft and pliable, with a lustrous pile of medium length. The chief colours are light red, blue, and green. This design would not often be found ; but the Plate serves as an example of the kind of pattern seen in Ladiks that are not prayer-rugs.

PLATE 105. LADIK CARPET.

Carpets of this kind have about 70 knots to the square inch. The size is 3½ ft. × 7 ft. They are soft and pliable with a lustrous pile of medium length. This specimen is not characteristic of the type, and clearly has been affected by nomadic influences, as can be seen by the small conventional animals and other detached devices. A study of the illustration without an examination of the actual carpet would be insufficient to connect this with certainty with the typical Ladiks. It shows well, however, the kind of variation from type that may be met with.

PLATE 106. MUJUR PRAYER-CARPET.

Carpets of this kind are known in the trade also as Anatolian or Sultan carpets. They have from 45 to 65 knots to the square inch. The usual size is 3½ ft. × 5 ft. They are soft and pliable and have a fairly short and lustrous pile. The chief colours are red, green, blue, yellow and violet. The two largest border-stripes are characteristic. It should be noted that the cross-panel is an abbreviated form of that commonly seen in Ladiks. These rugs have a very sparkling appearance. They are made in the town of Mujur on the river Kisil-Irmak.

PLATE 107A. KIR-SHEHR PRAYER-CARPET.

Carpets of this kind are known in the trade also as Sultan or Anatolian carpets. They have from 45 to 65 knots to the square inch. The usual size is about 3½ ft × 4½ ft. They are soft and pliable and have a lustrous pile of medium length. The chief colours are red, green, white, and blue. The narrow stripes in the border are more clearly marked in most specimens. The multiple bands forming the arch may be contrasted with those in Plate 57. They are made in the town of Kir-Shehr on the river Kisil-Irmak.

PLATE 107B. ANATOLIAN SAPH (OR FAMILY) PRAYER-RUG.

Carpets of this kind have about 50 to 70 knots to the square inch.

The size is usually about 3½ ft. × 11½ ft. They are soft and pliable and have a lustrous pile of medium length. Each carpet is equivalent to several single prayer-rugs joined together and it is from this that their name is derived. The niches are variously coloured in the same carpet. These carpets are sometimes erroneously supposed to come from Chinese Turkestan. Some, however, are found with patterns so close to other Anatolian rugs, such as Mujurs, that no mistake can be made in their case.

PLATE 108A. JAKSHIBEHDIR (i.e., charcoal-burner) PRAYER-CARPET.

Carpets of this kind constitute a subdivision of Bergama carpets and are often called by that name. They have from 50 to 65 knots to the square inch. The size is generally about 2½ ft. × 3½ ft. They are soft and pliable and have a long and often very close pile. The chief colours are dark blue and dark red; and the whole colour-scheme is sombre, whence is derived the name.

PLATE 108B. BERGAMA CARPET.

Carpets of this kind have from 50 to 80 knots to the square inch. The size ranges from 2½ ft. × 3½ ft. to 4 ft. × 5 ft. They are soft and pliable, and have a fairly long and lustrous pile. The chief colours are dark cherry-red, dark blue, dark brown, and that of natural camel-hair. The pattern is often picked out with yellow and white.

PLATE 109. ANATOLIAN KILIM PRAYER-CARPET.

Carpets of this kind are tapestry-woven and have about twelve warp-threads to the linear inch. They are soft and thin. The size is about 3½ ft. × 5½ ft. The colours are very bright but the effect, even in the modern specimens, is rarely displeasing. Large numbers are made by the mountain-tribes from the region of Erzerum; but the manufacture is fairly widespread. It is quite common to find metal thread woven in with the wool. Kilims, other than prayer-rugs, are made in still greater numbers. Many of the largest are in two strips sewn together down the middle. The patterns are often reminiscent of those of the well-known types of pile-rugs, though the technique does not allow a very close adherence. They are extremely useful for hangings and covers of all sorts, and are comparatively inexpensive.

PLATE 110. ANATOLIAN CARPET.

Carpets of this kind are also known in the trade as Mosul, Yuruk, Kurd, or Montagnard. They have from 40 to 60 knots to the square inch. The size is usually about 3½ ft. × 7½ ft. They are generally made in the mountainous regions and are pliable and have a long, rough and lustrous pile. The shape is almost invariably irregular. The colours are chiefly cinnamon-red, dark blue, and yellow. They are closely akin to the Yuruk carpets.

PLATE 111A. MAKRI CARPETS.

Carpets of this kind are also called Rhodian Carpets. They have from 45 to 65 knots to the square inch. The size is about 3½ ft. × 6½ ft. They are rather stiff, and have a lustrous pile of medium length. The chief colours are blue, yellow and red. The sparkling patches of colour, together with the arrangement of the field, give an effect which has been aptly compared to that of a stained-glass window.

PLATE 111B. ANATOLIAN CARPET.

Carpets of this kind are also known in the trade as Sultan carpets. They have from 45 to 65 knots to the square inch and range in size from 2½ ft. × 3 ft. to 3½ ft. × 4½ ft. They are soft and pliable, and have a long and lustrous pile. The chief colours are red, yellow, blue and brown.

PLATE 112A. ANATOLIAN CARPET.

Carpets of this kind are also known in the trade, on account of their light background, as Akterai (i.e., White Castle). They have from 40 to 60 knots to the square inch, and are usually small and almost square in shape. They are soft and pliable and have a fairly short and lustrous pile. The colour of the ground is white or yellow, and the pattern is dark in tone, often with brown-black predominating. The likeness to Caucasian design, which is so commonly noticed in Anatolian carpets, is very marked here.

PLATE 112B. MELAS CARPET.

Carpets of this kind have from 60 to 80 knots to the square inch. They are soft and pliable, and have a very lustrous pile of medium length. Older pieces, which are now getting very scarce, are generally striped as in the illustration and are very bright in colour.

PLATE 113. MELAS PRAYER-CARPET.

Carpets of this kind are known in the trade also as Anatolian. They have from 60 to 80 knots to the square inch. The size is generally about 2½ ft. × 4 ft. They are made in the town of Melassa and its environs near to the south-west coast of Asia Minor, and are soft and pliable and have a fairly short but very lustrous pile. The chief colour is strawberry-red, but there is often a good deal of yellow in the border. This example has the characteristic Melas prayer-arch.

PLATE 114. YURUK CARPET.

Carpets of this kind are sometimes erroneously known in the trade as Daghestan or Kasak. They have from 50 to 70 knots to the square inch. The usual sizes are 2½ ft. × 3½ ft., 3½ ft. × 5½ ft. and 3 ft. × 7 ft. They are soft and pliable and have a long, lustrous pile. The chief colours are dark red, brown, dark blue, and white. The border of this specimen is characteristic of the type.

(b) Caucasian

Although the production of carpets in the Caucasus does not, as far as is known, go back much beyond the eighteenth century, and although the proximity of both Turkey and Persia—two such great carpet-weaving countries—has naturally had much influence, yet the Caucasian carpets are a more independent and well-marked group than might be expected. On the whole the influence of Turkey has been greater than that of Persia, especially with regard to technique.

Caucasian carpets are made almost entirely of wool, though, as will be seen later, a little cotton occurs in the foundation of some of the rugs. The warp is mostly undyed and ranges in colour from pure white to a deep brown. Wools of different colour are often mixed before spinning, but even when the colour of each strand is uniform, it is often found that differently-coloured yarns are twisted together to make a thread. The weft also is commonly undyed. The normal plan is to have two shoots of weft after each row of knots, but a feature in some of the nomadic rugs is the occurrence of three or more shoots at irregular intervals. The Ghiordes knot is exclusively employed in the pile-carpets. The pile is invariably of wool which is mostly of good quality and lustrous in appearance. In the nomadic rugs the pile is long and in the others of medium length, or short, but never very short. The sides are usually finished with an overcast woollen selvedge of several cords, though the Persian method of employing a single-cord selvedge is not unknown. The ends are very simply treated, there being a short plain web and a simple fringe, after perhaps a few rows of knots formed by tying small groups of warp-threads together.

HAND-WOVEN CARPETS

In the design of Caucasian rugs, naturalistic drawing is not found, and floral forms, though perhaps not more conventionalized than in Turkish rugs, are not used to so great an extent. Geometrical design, which does not differ in its general aspect from that in Turkish rugs, is very much used, but though the general aspect is similar, in the details of the drawing it is easy to notice a difference between Caucasian and Turkish designs. The same borders and field devices are found over and over again in the two countries, but the treatment of the Caucasian version is always distinct from that of the Turkish (cf. Plate 196, No. 8, with Plate 194, No. 22), though it is not easy to give a general description of the kind of change that is found. Perhaps it may be said that the Caucasian rendering shows greater angularity and more quaintness.

Many patterns have also been borrowed from Persia. Borders with wavy floral stems, so rarely found in Turkey, are quite common, though the treatment is decidedly more angular and the blossoms have usually degenerated to almost geometrical rosettes. Lattice field-diapers, which are met with in a few types of rugs, have also a Persian origin. Caucasian carpets have, in addition, numerous field and border patterns quite peculiar to themselves. Generally the masses of colour are greater in Caucasian than in Turkish or Persian rugs, and fine detail is not common. The popularity of the latch-hook is very probably due to its utility in softening the outline of a large mass of colour. Central medallions, which are so common in Persian rugs, are almost unknown ; while scattered devices such as stars, octagons, rosettes, quite unrelated to each other, are much employed. It might be said that the rugs of Persia are designed from the centre and those of the Caucasus from the ends.

Among other features commonly seen in the field may be mentioned rectangular panels ; large irregular forms of radiating contour, sometimes known as " sunbursts " ; and small conventional renderings of animals, birds, and human figures.

Plates 195 to 199 contain motives for the most part peculiar to Caucasian carpets. Counterchanged border patterns are shown in Plate 196 (1, 2 and 6), and Plate 199 (17) ; and various renderings of S-forms are seen in Plate 196 (5, 8 and 9) ; Plate 198 (6, 11 and 15), and Plate 199 (7). It is probable that Plate 196 (3, 4 and 10), and Plate 199 (12 and 16) are all debased forms of early borders with Kufic lettering. Plate 196 (19) is the " Crab " pattern, almost peculiar to Kazaks, and Plate 196 (22) is the " Leaf and Wine-cup " border very often seen in Shirvans.

Plate 198 (18) is the so-called " Georgian " pattern; and Plate 198 (19) is the border characteristic of Chichi rugs.

The colouring is usually bright and vigorous but rarely unpleasing; even the modern rugs being as a rule satisfactory in this respect. The dyes of the latest rugs are not on the whole inferior to those of other countries, though a certain—and too large—amount of crude and unsound colours is met with.

The classification of Caucasian carpets into definite types, depending upon the place of their manufacture, is a very difficult problem even for the experienced connoisseur. The attempt of many writers to do more than is possible in this respect has led to much confusion, and to the bewilderment of amateurs, who cannot understand the distinction between the types as defined in the text-books, and despair of reconciling the description given by dealers with these definitions. Only a very simple classification will be attempted here, though the various trade names will be mentioned with as much, or as little, information as can be given about their significance.

The various Caucasian carpets may be divided into two main groups, according as they are produced north or south of the great mountain range which crosses the country from north-west to south-east. To the north of the mountains lies the province of DAGHESTAN, which has given its name to some of the best Caucasian carpets produced. They are fine in texture and have frequently a cotton warp and weft. Lattice-diapers in the field, and a diagonal arrangement of small devices, are common. The drawing is refined and the detail finer than in most of the Caucasian products. There is a tendency towards a mosaic effect in the design. The weaving, as seen from the back, is very regular.

KABISTAN is a name given to some Daghestan rugs. It is not claimed that the difference is great but they are said to be slightly inferior. As the word Kabistan is a corruption of Kubistan, which is derived from the town of Kuba, and as the name Kuba is assigned to another alleged type, it will be seen at once that the geographical distinction is negligible.

DERBEND, or Derbent, the main town of Daghestan and the distributing centre of its rugs, is the name given to a somewhat coarser variety of rug with a woollen foundation.

If a Daghestan rug has a rather floral pattern, or exhibits large " sunbursts," it is called a KUBA, from an important town towards the south.

LESGHIAN is a name applied to nomadic rugs of the province, but no serious attempt has been made to distinguish them from Trans-Caucasian nomadic rugs, though they are said to have a selvedge of several cords rather than of one.

To the south of the mountains lies the district of SHIRVAN, which produces many rugs, and the name is applied to all Caucasian carpets that do not appear to belong to one of the other types. They are similar to the products of Daghestan, but tend to be coarser and to have larger and less refined patterns and colouring. Cotton is more rarely used. So great is the variety of design found in Shirvan rugs that it is almost impossible to give an adequate idea of it. A few types of field design, however, are so common that they must be mentioned. One of these is a succession of diamond-shaped panels, each the full width of the field, and touching the next one at the angle. The diamonds are mostly fringed with latch-hooks. Often the diamonds are so deeply stepped as to appear rather octagonal or cross-shaped in form. Another plan is to have a succession of large rectangular panels, separated only by a narrow space. A modification of this arrangement is to have the field itself contracted at intervals, so that virtually a succession of rectangles connected by wide necks is formed. This last design is characteristic of Shirvans. Nearly all the border-stripes found in Shirvan rugs are also used in other Caucasian types, but one much favoured is known as the " leaf and wine-cup " border. A wavy line of serrated leaves has in the interspaces devices resembling wine-cups on stems, but probably really conventionalized floral buds.

A group of Shirvans with a border peculiar to itself (see Plate 198 (19)) are known as CHICHI, TCHETCEN, or TZITZI from the name of the tribe that makes them.

The city of BAKU gives its name to rugs with dull, faded-looking colours and a pattern of large, elaborately-drawn cones of peculiar form in the field.

An important group of rugs made by wandering tribes and having the usual characteristics of nomadic weavings, is called by the name KAZAK, which is a form of the word Cossack. The pile is long and lustrous and the weft often crosses three or more times at intervals. The sides are finished with a selvedge of several cords, overcast with wool of different colours, which extends for various distances along the side. These changes of colour in the selvedge seem to be quite capricious but are highly characteristic of the type. The ends have fairly wide coloured webs and knotted fringes. The patterns of Kazak rugs are very varied and are not dissimilar to the more geometrical of the Shirvans. There is usually only one wide border-stripe, which often has patterns peculiar to the type (e.g. Plate 196 (19)). The dyes are mostly sound and the colouring, though bold and bright, is almost invariably very pleasing. Though not of very fine texture, these rugs are among the most satisfactory to be had nowadays.

The towns TIFLIS and KUTAIS give their names to unimportant or indefinite types of rugs, resembling Kazaks, but differing from them in having cone-patterns and tree-forms in the design.

TCHERKESS (or Circassian) rugs are Kazaks of a tawny colour, and with heavy, braided ends.

There is a flourishing carpet industry in the southern province of KARABAGH. The ordinary specimens bear the name of the district and the better ones are called after the town of SHUSHA. The latter tend to be broader in proportion. Both kinds are rather loosely woven and have a pile of medium length. The weft is often dyed red, and the selvedge is usually in lengths of different colours like in the Kazaks. The designs have a tendency to resemble Persian models. The colouring of Karabagh carpets is characteristic, as it nearly always includes an amount of bright purple and light blue. Shusha carpets have a rich colour scheme, consisting chiefly of dark blue, dark red and brown.

Rugs called after the town of GENGHA in the same province are very much like the Kazaks. They have, however, an unusually large number—up to six or eight—shoots of weft at frequent intervals; and white is a prominent colour in the design.

Kilims are woven throughout the Caucasian region. They are sometimes not easy to distinguish from the similar rugs of Turkey, but often there is so much resemblance in their patterns to exclusively Caucasian designs as to put their origin beyond doubt.

Thin and soft Kilims made in the neighbourhood of Shusha are known in the trade by the name of VERNÉ.

Another variety of Kilim, called SILÉ, is distinguished by its type of design.

The woven carpets known as SOUMAKS are said to get their name from the Caucasian town of Shemakha. The chief centre of their production is, however, Derbend. Soumaks as usually met with range in size from about 5 ft. × 7 ft. to 7 ft. × 10 ft.; though there is in the Victoria and Albert Museum an exceptionally finely-woven one measuring only 3 ft. 6 in. × 7 ft. A very usual field pattern consists of three or more flattened octagons; but the variety in design is considerable. The older Soumaks have a deep and rich colouring, but the modern ones are cruder and often have unsound dyes.

On the whole the Caucasian region may be said to produce most desirable carpets. Their prices are not high, and it is at least as easy to find among them, as anywhere else, soundly-woven rugs of good colour and design.

Plates 115 to 146 show most of the commoner types of these carpets.

PLATE 115. DAGHESTAN CARPET.

Carpets of this kind are known in the trade also as Karabagh, Kazak, Kenguerlu, or simply as Persian. They have from 50 to 80 knots to the square inch. The usual sizes are about $2\frac{1}{2}$ ft. × $3\frac{1}{2}$ ft. and 4 ft. × $6\frac{1}{2}$ ft. They have a soft and lustrous pile of medium length. The chief colours are red, blue and white; the first two alternating with the third in the field.

PLATE 116. DAGHESTAN PRAYER-CARPET (Victoria and Albert Museum).
  Dated A.H. 1287 (= A.D. 1870). 3 ft. 10 in. × 3 ft. 2 in.
  Warp: Three-ply white wool. On one level. 21 to 1 inch.
  Weft: White cotton. Two shoots after each row of knots.
  Knots: Wool. Ghiordes. 10 to 1 inch. 105 to the square inch.
  Colours: Nine. White (field and spandrels): red (2nd border):
    dark blue (3rd border): blue: black (1st border): ochre:
    light green: brown: dark red.

PLATES 117 AND 118A. DAGHESTAN CARPETS.

Carpets of this kind are known in the trade also as Kazak, Gengha, Karabagh, or simply as Persian. They have from 50 to 80 knots to the square inch. The usual sizes are about $2\frac{1}{2}$ ft. × $3\frac{1}{2}$ ft., 4 ft. × 9 ft. and $4\frac{1}{2}$ ft. × $6\frac{1}{2}$ ft. They have a soft and lustrous pile of medium length. The chief colours are red and blue, with some white and grey; the main border-stripe usually being white.

PLATE 118B. CAUCASIAN KILIM. 9 ft. 4 in. × 5 ft. 6 in.
  Warp: Brown and white wool. 15 to 1 inch.
  Weft: Wool. About 55 shoots to 1 inch.
  Colours: Ten. Crimson (field): white: green-blue: black (border):
    blue: dark red: red: yellow: ochre: light red. The pattern
    of this carpet is a rendering, as close as a somewhat coarse
    tapestry texture will allow, of the well-known "sunburst"
    device.

CARPETS IN THE MARKET : GROUPING—IDENTIFICATION

PLATE 119. DERBEND CARPET.

Carpets of this kind are known in the trade also as Persian. They have from 45 to 60 knots to the square inch. The usual size is 5 ft. × 10½ ft. They are soft and pliable and they have a long and very lustrous pile. The chief colours are blue and red, with some white. The pattern of the illustrated specimen with its curious bracket-like forms is typical of Derbend rugs. The main border-stripe is adapted from a common Ghiordes pattern. Old rugs of this type are rare, and modern pieces fetch rather higher prices than other Caucasian carpets of similar quality.

PLATE 120A. DAGHESTAN CARPET.

Carpets of this kind are known in the trade also as Karabagh, Gengha, Mosul, or simply as Persian. They have from 50 to 100 knots to the square inch. The usual sizes are 3 ft. × 4½ ft. and 4 ft. × 9 ft. They have a lustrous pile of medium length. The chief colours are blue, red and white ; the darker stripes in the field being often alternately blue and red. Such a diagonal arrangement of the field is common in Daghestans.

PLATE 120B. SHIRVAN CARPET.

Carpets of this kind are known in the trade also as Moghan, Talish, Daghestan, and also simply as Persian. They have from 60 to 85 knots to the square inch. The size is about 3½ ft. × 7½ ft. They are fairly hard to the touch and have a short and not very lustrous pile. The chief colours are dark blue, red and white. The large-tailed birds in the field should be noticed.

PLATE 121. SHIRVAN CARPET.

Carpets of this kind are known in the trade as Kuba, Kabistan, Talish, Gengha, and also simply as Persian. They have from 60 to 100 knots to the square inch. The size is about 3½ ft. × 9 ft. They are fairly hard to the touch and have a short and not very lustrous pile. The colours are chiefly red and blue with lesser quantities of white and yellow. This specimen has the field contracted at intervals, which arrangement is peculiar to Shirvans ; and in the border are two stripes with a small repeating pattern of carnations, which is found in various types of Caucasian carpets.

PLATE 122A. SHIRVAN CARPET.

Carpets of this kind are known in the trade also as Kuba, Kabistan, Talish, Gengha, and also simply as Persian. They have from 60 to 100 knots to the square inch. The size is about 3½ ft. × 9 ft. They are fairly hard to the touch, and have a short and very lustrous pile. The chief colours are red and blue with a smaller quantity of white. This specimen shows the cross-panels and the " leaf and wine-cup " border which are so common in Shirvans.

PLATE 122B. SHIRVAN CARPET.

Carpets of this kind are also known in the trade as Kuba, Kabistan, Talish, Gengha, and also simply as Persian. They have from 60 to 85 knots to the square inch. The size is about 3½ ft. × 9 ft. They are fairly hard to the touch and have a short and not very lustrous pile. The chief colours are red, blue, and lesser quantities of white and yellow. This carpet with its rayed medallions is of the kind mostly called Kuba. The peculiar pattern in the widest border-stripe is usually known as the " Georgian " border, after the district of Georgia. Its origin is not clear, though there is little doubt that it is derived from some floral form. It is quite peculiar to Caucasian carpets.

PLATE 123. SHIRVAN CARPET.

Carpets of this kind are known in the trade also as Daghestan or simply Persian carpets. They have from 60 to 85 knots to the square inch. The size is about 3½ ft. × 5 ft. They are fairly hard to the touch and have a short and not very lustrous pile. The chief colours are dark blue, red and white. The main border-stripe has the " leaf and wine-cup " pattern.

PLATE 124. SHIRVAN CARPETS.

Carpets of this kind are known in the trade also as Daghestan, Kasak, or simply as Persian. They have from 50 to 75 knots to the square inch. The size is about 2½ ft. × 5 ft. They are rather hard to the touch and have a short and not very lustrous pile. The chief colours are dark blue and red, with little or no white.

PLATE 125. SHIRVAN CARPET.

Carpets of this kind are known in the trade also as Daghestan, Mecca, or simply as Persian. They have from 65 to 100 knots to the square inch. The size is about 3½ ft. × 6½ ft. They are rather hard to the touch, and have a short and not very lustrous pile. The chief colours are dark blue with lesser quantities of red and white. The pattern of the field in this specimen is a comparatively rare one.

PLATE 126. SHIRVAN CARPET.

Carpets of this kind are also known in the trade as Kuba, Kabistan, Talish, Gengha, or simply as Persian. They have from 60 to 85 knots to the square inch. The size is about 3½ ft. × 9 ft. They are fairly hard to the touch and have a short and not very lustrous pile. The chief colours are red and blue with lesser quantities of white and yellow. The main border-stripe with two kinds of angular S-forms is based on a common Turkish pattern (see Plate 194, No. 22), though this rendering is typically Caucasian.

PLATE 127. SHIRVAN OR CHICHI CARPET.

Carpets of this kind are known in the trade also as Daghestan, Mecca, or simply as Persian. They have from 50 to 85 knots to the square inch. The size is about 3½ ft. × 6½ ft. They are fairly hard to the touch and have a short and not very lustrous pile. The chief colours are dark blue, with lesser quantities of red and white. The main border-pattern, consisting of rosettes separated by diagonal ribbon-like bands, is that associated with the name " Chichi."

PLATE 128. SHIRVAN OR BAKU CARPET.

Carpets of this kind are known in the trade also as Mecca, Daghestan, Koltuk, Kuba, or simply as Persian. They have from 50 to 85 knots to the square inch. The size is about 3½ ft. × 5 ft. or 4½ ft. × 9 ft. They are rough to the touch and have a short and not very lustrous pile. The chief colours are blue, red and purple, often rather faded.

PLATE 129. SHIRVAN OR BAKU CARPET.

Carpets of this kind are known in the trade also as Daghestan, Mecca, and simply as Persian. They have from 60 to 90 knots to the square inch. The usual sizes are 3½ ft. × 5½ ft. and 5 ft. × 9 ft. They are rough to the touch and have a short and not very lustrous pile. The chief colours are blue and red with a lesser amount of white. The conventional birds seen in this specimen are very common in Baku rugs.

PLATE 130. SHIRVAN CARPET.

Carpets of this kind are known in the trade also as Derbend, Kuba, or simply as Persian. They have from 60 to 90 knots to the square inch. The usual sizes are 3½ ft. × 5 ft. and 5 ft. × 9 ft. They are rough to the touch and have a short and not very lustrous pile. The chief colours are blue and red, with a lesser amount of white. The pattern of this specimen is not so common as those of the other Shirvans illustrated.

PLATE 131. SHIRVAN CARPET.

Carpets of this kind are known in the trade also as Mecca, or simply as Persian. They have from 60 to 90 knots to the square inch. The usual size is about 4 ft. × 9 ft. They are rough to the touch and have a short and not very lustrous pile. The chief colours are blue and red, with a lesser quantity of white. The dotted stripes of several colours in the border and the angular S-forms are typically Caucasian, though a border somewhat like the former is found in the Persian rugs of Shiraz. It may be mentioned here that Shirvan and Shiraz rugs, though coming from such distant places, are often confused, and the name " Mecca " is erroneously given to both classes. A close study of the technique will soon show the difference between the two, even when they are superficially alike in pattern.

PLATES 132A AND 133. KAZAK CARPETS.

Carpets of this kind are known in the trade also as Daghestan, Gengha, or simply as Persian. They have from 50 to 80 knots to the square inch. The usual sizes are about $2\frac{1}{2}$ ft. × 4 ft., 4 ft. × 9 ft. and $4\frac{1}{2}$ ft. × $6\frac{1}{2}$ ft. They have a thick, long and lustrous pile. The chief colours are red and blue, with a lesser amount of white, the ground of the main border-stripe usually being white. The border-pattern, which is seen in two degrees of conventionalization, is derived from the motive of four leaves springing from a rosette; but from the resulting form is often known as the " Crab " pattern.

PLATE 132B. SHIRVAN OR BAKU CARPET.

Carpets of this kind are known in the trade also as Daghestan, or simply as Persian. They have from 50 to 85 knots to the square inch. The size is about 3 ft. × 5 ft. or $4\frac{1}{2}$ ft. × 9 ft. They are rather hard to the touch and have a short and not very lustrous pile. The chief colours are blue, red, and some purple, but they are often faded to a dull brownish appearance. This specimen has the typical pattern of elaborately drawn cones, which is associated with the name " Baku."

PLATE 134. KAZAK CARPET.

Carpets of this kind are known in the trade also as Gengha, Karabagh, or simply as Persian. They have from 50 to 80 knots to the square inch.

The usual sizes are 2½ ft. × 4 ft., 4 ft. × 9 ft. and 4½ ft. × 6½ ft. They have a long, thick and very lustrous pile. The chief colours are red, blue and white.

PLATE 135. KAZAK CARPET.

Carpets of this kind are known in the trade also as Daghestan, Gengha, or simply as Persian. They have from 50 to 80 knots to the square inch. The usual size is about 5 ft. × 6½ ft. They have a thick, long and very lustrous pile. The chief colours are red and blue, with some white and green, the ground of the main border-stripe being commonly white.

PLATES 136 AND 137. KAZAK CARPETS.

Carpets of this kind are known in the trade also as Daghestan, Gengha, Derbend, or simply as Persian. They have from 50 to 80 knots to the square inch. The usual sizes are 2½ ft. × 4 ft., 4 ft. × 9 ft. and 4½ ft. × 6½ ft. They have a thick, long and very lustrous pile. The chief colours are red and blue, with some white and green, the border usually having a fair amount of white.

PLATE 138. KAZAK PRAYER-CARPET.

Carpets of this kind are known also in the trade as Daghestan, Gengha, Derbend, or simply as Persian. They have from 50 to 80 knots to the square inch. The usual sizes are 2½ ft. × 4 ft., 4 ft. × 9 ft. and 4½ ft. × 6½ ft. They have a thick, long and very lustrous pile. The chief colours are red and blue, with some white and green, the border usually having a fair amount of white. The small angular arch at the top of the field, and the oblong recess at the bottom, constitute the usual arrangement of Kazak prayer-rugs.

PLATES 139, 140 AND 141. KAZAK CARPETS.

Carpets of this kind are known in the trade also as Daghestan, Shirvan, Gengha, or simply as Persian. They have from 50 to 80 knots to the square inch. The usual sizes are 2½ ft. × 4 ft., 4 ft. × 9 ft. and 4½ ft. × 6½ ft. They have a thick, long and very lustrous pile. The chief colours are red and blue, with some white and green, the border usually having a fair amount of white.

PLATE 142. KARABAGH CARPET (Victoria and Albert Museum).
8 ft. 9 in. × 4 ft. 10 in.
Warp: White wool. On one level. 16 to 1 inch.
Weft: White wool. Two shoots after each row of knots.

Knots : Wool. Ghiordes. 6 to 1 inch. 50 to the square inch.
Colours : Ten. Purple (field and 2nd border) : light blue (1st
 border) : dark blue (panels in field) : white : yellow : black :
 light red : brown : red : green.

PLATES 143 AND 144. VERNÉ CARPETS.

These are made by the ordinary Kilim process, and are thin, soft
and almost alike on both sides. The usual size is about 4 ft. × 5½ ft.
The chief colours are Indian red, white and yellow. They are mostly
used for covers.

PLATE 145. SILÉ CARPET.

Carpets of this type are woven by the ordinary Kilim process. They
often consist of two pieces sewn together and are thin, soft, and almost
alike on both sides. Their principal use is for covering tables and for
similar purposes. The usual size is 4 ft. × 5½ ft. The chief colours
are Indian red, white and yellow.

PLATE 146. SOUMAK CARPET.

Carpets of this kind are known in the trade also as Persian. They
are woven by the special Soumak method, and have from 8 to 25 warp-
threads to the inch. The usual sizes are about 5½ ft. × 6½ ft., 6½ ft. ×
10 ft. and, more rarely, 8 ft. × 11½ ft. The chief colour is dark Indian
red, with the pattern picked out in yellow. The flattened octagons in
this specimen are typical of the group.

(c) Persian

Of all the great classes into which the carpets of the East are divided,
the carpets of Persia have the highest reputation, and on the whole this
reputation is deserved. It must not be supposed for a moment that
Persian carpets of medium or of good quality are better than the best
from other parts, but the finest Persian specimens, either of the past
or the present, do certainly surpass all others in refinement of drawing,
in subtlety and harmony of colour, and in perfection of weaving. There
is so much variety to be found in the carpets that come from different
parts of this vast region that it is somewhat difficult to give a general
description of them, and in order to make the subject manageable it is
almost necessary to divide them into geographical groups before discussing
the separate types ; but as far as it is possible to treat the whole class
together, it will be advisable to do so.

CARPETS IN THE MARKET: GROUPING—IDENTIFICATION

Even in Persia wool is by far the commonest material used; but cotton, which is rare in Turkey and Caucasia, is employed to a very large extent in the foundation of carpets; and silk, which is quite exceptional in those countries, is here found fairly often. For the warp, wool and cotton are used about equally, and both are as a rule undyed. The arrangement of the warp on two levels, one set being right behind the other, is very common in Persia, but scarcely ever seen in other countries. The weft is usually of the same material as the warp. A woollen weft is commonly undyed, but in a few types is coloured red or brown. When the weft is of cotton, it is frequently dyed, blue and red being the favourite colours. Two shoots of weft is the usual number, but in a few types only one shoot is employed, and in many of the older carpets, and a few of the recent ones, three shoots are found.

For the pile, both the Sehna and the Ghiordes knot are largely used, whereas the former is unknown in modern Turkish and Caucasian carpets. The texture, on the average, tends to be fine, for while the coarser carpets are about the same as those of Turkey and Caucasia the finer ones are two, three or several times more closely knotted than any from those countries. With certain exceptions the ends of Persian carpets are finished in a very simple way, there being a short web either terminating at the loops of the warp, or furnished with a plain fringe. The sides nearly always have a selvedge of one cord only, overcast with fine wool or silk.

There is a tendency for Persian carpets to fall into two groups according to the general nature of their technique, and these groups may be said quite roughly to have separate geographical ranges. Towards the north-west there is mostly found a woollen warp on one level, associated with a coarse texture, a long pile and the Ghiordes knot. Towards the south-east the warp is usually of cotton arranged on two levels; the texture is fine, the pile is short and the Sehna knot is used. There are exceptions to this rule, but the general tendency cannot be overlooked.

Persian carpets have a soft, rich and deep colouring rather than a brilliant and decided one. The softness is to a great extent due to the use of several shades of each colour and to the fact that the various colours rarely occur in large masses.

In point of design, Persian carpets are far more naturalistic than any other kind, though even with them the naturalism is not really carried far. Nearly all the ornament is based on floral forms and, if a few unimportant border-stripes be excepted, purely geometrical patterns are very rare. The general character of Persian design can be best understood by the study of such examples as are illustrated in the second volume of this work; but a few features often met with may be briefly mentioned.

First, attention may be drawn to the prevalence of central medallions of all sorts often associated with corner-pieces which soften the rectangularity of the field. Secondly, the field, or that part of them not occupied with medallion or corner-pieces, is very often covered with comparatively small repeating patterns, such as diapers or lattices; or with an intricate arrangement of scrolling stems interspersed with leaves and blossoms. Thirdly, a great majority of the borders are filled with wavy floral stems, rather than a succession of detached devices which is so common in Turkish and Caucasian carpets.

Devices and patterns peculiar to Persian rugs are illustrated on Plate 202.

For the purpose of discussing in more detail the various recognized types of Persian carpets, it is convenient to divide them into six large groups, according to the provinces in which they are made.

(i) *Azerbaijan.* In KARADAGH, a district bordering in the north on Caucasia, carpets are produced which resemble closely in quality and pattern the carpets of Karabagh. They have a woollen warp and weft and a long, lustrous and fairly coarse pile, tied with the Ghiordes knot. A peculiar and characteristic red colour is much used, and the ground is often of undyed camel-hair. The field is mostly covered with a floral diaper, or the Herati or Mina Khani pattern, and the border is more geometrical than that of most Persian rugs.

Near the town of TABRIZ, a type of carpet has been made lately which is considered one of the best-knotted and most beautiful of Persian rugs. The warp is of cotton on two levels, and the weft is also of cotton frequently dyed pink. The Ghiordes knot is used; the pile is short and harsh to the touch, and the texture is fine. There is mostly a two-cord selvedge, and the rugs are stiff and tend to curl at the edges. The designs are of the elaborate floral type, and are perhaps somewhat too formally and accurately balanced, which is due no doubt to the strong European influence under which they are manufactured.

In the district of GOREVAN (or Yoraghan), not very far from Tabriz, new carpets are made also under European influence. The warp and weft are of cotton, which in the case of the latter is mostly dyed blue or brown. They have the Ghiordes knot and are coarsely woven. The colour-scheme is unusual, consisting of copper-red, dark blue and buff, distributed in rather conspicuous masses. The design nearly always includes concentric hexagonal medallions; and the drawing is peculiarly bold and angular.

HEREZ, SERAPI and BAKSHI are names given to carpets which do not differ in important particulars from Gorevans. SUJ-BULAK, a village in the province, gives its name to carpets resembling those of Kurdistan.

(ii) *Irak-Ajemi*. One of the most famous types of Persian carpets is made in this province and is called after the elevated plain of FERAGHAN. These carpets have both warp and weft made of cotton, the weft sometimes being dyed blue or pink. The warp is on one level. In the older pieces the Sehna knot is used, but in later specimens the Ghiordes knot is also common. The pile is fairly short and of good wool. A large number of different colours generally occur in the rugs, and as usual red and blue predominate, though there is also a notable amount of green. The colours are not used in large masses unless for a plain ground, and generally when viewed from a distance no part of the rug differs much in tone from the rest. The field is mostly covered with a repeating pattern such as the Herati, Guli Hinnai or some other floral diaper, the first-named being the most common. A feature almost peculiar to the type is the cutting off of the corners of the field by straight serrated lines. Occasionally a pole-medallion on a light-coloured ground is seen, but this is not very common. The border is narrow in proportion to the size of the rug, and a favourite pattern in the main stripe, which often has a green ground, is that sometimes known as the " turtle " (Plate 155). Feraghans were largely made at one time, but new ones of good quality are rather rare. They are very satisfactory for their wearing qualities.

Another type of rug similar in technique to the Feraghan is known as the SARABAND (from Sarawan, a mountainous district). The weft is nearly always blue, and the knot is the Sehna, though sometimes a small proportion of Ghiordes knots are mixed with them—a very unusual thing in other types. It is in their designs that these rugs chiefly differ from the Feraghans. They have neither central medallions nor corner-pieces, but the field is covered with a repeating pattern of detached cone-devices. The main border-stripe usually has a white ground, and contains a wavy stem with a cone depending from each bend. They are often of the Kanara shape, and are very strong and serviceable.

A well-marked group of carpets are called HAMADAN, after the town of that name on the site of the ancient Ecbatana. They have a white cotton warp, and a weft of cotton, wool or camel-hair. The weft only crosses once after each row of knots. The Ghiordes knot is used and the pile is of medium length. The most striking thing about the colouring is the large amount of natural camel-hair that is used. The other colours are soft and harmonious. There is usually a pole-medallion in the field, or more than one if the rug is a long one; and the corners of the field are frequently shaped. The ground is much lighter in tone than the medallions and corner-pieces, and is sometimes covered with a delicate diaper. The border-stripes have no characteristic patterns, but a peculiarity connected with the border is that there is a wide, plain band of camel-hair all round the edge of the rug. This band, which often has small devices upon it arranged quite capriciously, is very characteristic and enables an unmutilated specimen to be recognized at a glance. A good many Kanara are found among Hamadans, but they are often skilfully cut down so as to appear like rugs of the commoner type.

The town and district of JUSHAGHAN has been noted for its carpets for a long time (see p. 37). The warp and weft are of cotton, or sometimes of wool, which in the case of the weft is mostly dyed red or brown. There are sometimes three shoots of weft after the knots. The Ghiordes knot is used and the pile is thick, soft and lustrous. The colouring is very rich and mellow. The field does not have a medallion but is covered all over with an irregular floral diaper on rather a large scale, and there is often an impression of an incomplete lattice running through it. The border has no characteristic patterns.

The city of KASHAN gives its name to a type of rugs which are considered to be the best that Persia produces nowadays. The warp is of cotton and lies on two levels; the weft is of fine blue cotton. The Sehna knot is used and the pile, which is very closely knotted, is fairly short but lustrous and very soft and velvety. The colours are deep, rich and mellow; and, unfortunately, to get this effect the modern rugs are nearly all slightly washed, though not to an injurious extent. The design is rather like that of Tabriz rugs but is less formal. There are usually medallions in the field, and the whole of the rug including the border is filled with gracefully drawn floral patterns tending towards the naturalistic. It is not probable that many rugs of this group are actually made in Kashan, but the type is a fairly definite one, though on account of its high reputation it has become customary to call any good rug a Kashan.

Most of the silk rugs made in Persia during the last half-century can be associated with the Kashan group. They are mostly very fine in texture and rarely have fewer than 200 knots to the square inch. The warp is either of silk or cotton, and the weft usually of cotton. The designs are sometimes based upon the early Persian traditions, but more often follow, though not very closely, the modern woollen rugs of Persia. In the East they are not usually placed upon the floor, for which position they are indeed unsuited; but are used for covering seats and for similar purposes by the wealthier people. None of the later silk rugs appear to go back farther than the middle of the nineteenth century, and there is no evidence that such rugs were made in Persia during the century or more preceding that date.

The name SARUK (not to be confused with Sarakhs) is given to rugs similar to Kashans but not of quite such good quality. They sometimes have a rendering of the early palmette pattern, which is known as the " Shah Abbas."

In the neighbourhood of MUSKABAD are made rugs rather like the Kashans and Saruks but considerably coarser. The warp lies on two levels not widely separated, and the Ghiordes knot is sometimes used instead of the Sehna. The colouring is quiet and harmonious, and the designs are similar to those of the Feraghans.

The town of SULTANABAD is a centre of the European-controlled carpet industry, and as Muskabads are marketed there, they are often called by its name.

MAHAL and SAVALAN are other trade names given to some Muskabads.

(iii) *Ardelan*. In this province is the town of Sehna, which has given its name to the knot largely used in Persia, and also to one of the most esteemed types of Persian carpets. The SEHNA carpet has a warp and weft of white cotton, the former being on one level. The weft generally crosses only once after each row of knots, but in some pieces it crosses twice. The Sehna knot is used and the texture is as fine as in any type of carpet, there being occasionally more than four hundred knots to the square inch. The pile is very short and stands so nearly upright that the surface feels rough and like a file in whichever direction the hand is passed over it. The wool is good and lustrous, though the lustre is not very apparent owing to the shortness of the pile. The colours are numerous and rather bright; but they are only used in small masses, so that the general effect is soft rather than vigorous. The designs resemble those of Feraghans and Sarabands. There are often concentric pole-medallions and corner-pieces, and the rest of the ground is either plain or covered with the Herati pattern or some other floral diaper, or else filled with repeated cone-devices. The whole field may be covered with such patterns to the exclusion of medallions and corner-pieces. The border is rather narrow and has no patterns peculiar to the type. The rugs are thin, yet rather stiff, and are not suited for hard wear. The edges, as often in the case with tightly-woven rugs, have a tendency to curl up.

From the town of BIJAR come rugs very different from the Sehnas. The warp is of thick wool, and lies on two levels. The weft is also of wool, which is often dyed red. The pile is of heavy lustrous wool of medium length, tied with the Ghiordes knot. The colours are rich and bright—red, blue, white and natural camel-hair colour predominating. The designs are very various, but generally combine the features found in such rugs as Sehnas with those of the truly Kurdish rugs made in the neighbourhood. A peculiarity often noticed is for the pattern to be quite irregular and suddenly change in the middle or at one end of the rug. Bijar rugs are sometimes called by the names SARAKHS and LULE.

Throughout the province the Kurds make rugs which are given specifically the name KURDISTAN. They have a coarse woollen warp lying on two levels only slightly separated, and a woollen weft. The Ghiordes knot is used and the pile is very long and thick. The rugs are so stoutly woven that frequently they can hardly be bent. The ends are often treated very elaborately, and have coloured threads running through or woven patterns on the webs. The loose ends of the warp are looped and braided, or interwoven with each other in a great number of intricate ways. The colours are rich and fairly numerous, with red, blue, and white predominating. Quite a feature is the want of uniformity in each colour, which often consists of several different shades. As a consequence of this, the grounds are frequently streaked in a very noticeable way. Patches of colour varying from blue to green are very characteristic and very pleasing. The designs are various, but lattice patterns are much favoured, and the floral diaper called the Mina Khani is very common. The border is not conspicuous. Kurdistan rugs, though coarse, are mostly soundly made and harmonious in appearance, and are consequently a very useful kind.

The city of MOSUL gives its name to a large number of rugs which are marketed there. They are practically Kurdistans from the country both West and East of Mosul, and they cannot be distinguished by any rigid criterion from the Kurdistan rugs as described above. In specimens called by the trade Mosul, it will usually be found that the warp lies on one level, and that the rugs are softer and more flexible than other Kurdistans. The more definite patterns are not as a rule found, but the design tends towards small diapers.

Another name, restricted to a group of Kurdistans made near Hamadan, is KARAJE. These are distinguished chiefly by the fact that the weft only crosses once after each row of knots, though the one shoot may consist at irregular intervals of two or more untwisted strands.

The city of KERMANSHAH in this province gives its name to a group marketed there but made near Tabriz or Sultanabad. They have the general characteristics of the rugs of the districts where they are made, but have a tendency to resemble in colour and design the rugs of Kirman.

(iv) *Khorassan*. Of the various kinds of carpets made in this province, one kind is called specifically KHORASSAN. These have a cotton warp on two levels; and a cotton weft which is usually dyed blue. The Sehna knot is used and the pile is long, lustrous and often unevenly cut. A peculiarity of the knotting that is frequently seen is for the knots to be tied on four warp threads instead of two, at intervals throughout the rug. This causes a line across the back, which appears at first sight to be due to a difference in the manner of inserting the weft, rather than, as it actually is, to a change in the knotting. The colours are numerous and bright. Rose-red, dark blue, white and purple are mostly included, and the general effect is rather purple in character. A deep vermilion and a red-purple which fades easily are often found and are rather characteristic. In the design a very common motive peculiar to the type is a compound cone-device consisting of two or more small cones springing from a larger one (see Plate 202 (13)); these devices are found in both field and border, detached, or forming a diaper. Central medallions and corner-pieces are common; or the Herati pattern is used. Sometimes the field is divided into a number of narrow vertical bands, each resembling a border. A common border-pattern is shown on Plate 202 (2). Khorassan rugs are usually large in size, and one peculiarity is that there are often short ends of thread hanging loose at the back.

A group of Khorassan carpets is called MESHED, after the chief town of the province. They are generally finer and more firmly woven, with a shorter and more even pile. The colouring tends to be more delicate, with less of the purple character. The designs are mostly of the central medallion type, and do not include the peculiar Khorassan border, and not so often the compound cone-device. Mesheds and Khorassans, however, may be regarded as the two halves of a graduated series of rugs, so that some specimens cannot be certainly classified.

A quite different type of rug, and one much more closely resembling the rugs of North-West Persia, is called after the town of HERAT. The warp and weft may be either of wool or cotton, and the warp lies on two levels, though they are not always very widely separated. The Ghiordes knot is mostly used and the pile is soft and of medium length. The chief colours are dark blue, red, white, green and yellow; but there is mostly a faint tinge of purple in the colouring. The field is covered all over with a floral diaper, mostly the Herati (which of course gets its name from the same city), but sometimes the Mina Khani or some other pattern. The border is mostly conspicuous; a favourite pattern being that shown on Plate 202 (1).

(v) *Kirman.* The carpets made in this province have been practically free from Western influence, and though considerable variation of pattern is seen in them, they are all called KIRMANS. The warp is of cotton and lies on two levels; the weft is of blue cotton or sometimes of fine wool. The Sehna knot is used, and the pile is soft and silky, of medium length and very closely woven. The colours are light in tone and soft and delicate; those most frequently occurring being white, grey, rose, pale brown and pale blue. The design is generally more naturalistic than in any other kind of carpet. Many sorts of flowers, especially roses, are nearly always included in the design. Besides these, there often are trees such as the cypress, vases, animals, birds and even human figures. Inscriptions, stating the name of the maker, are perhaps more common in these rugs than in any others. There may be a medallion or other arrangement of the ornament, but it is the naturalistic detail that is so characteristic.

In quite recent years it has become a custom to make rugs of an extraordinarily fine texture, with as many as a thousand knots to the square inch. Though, of course, these are very costly to produce, the result unfortunately is not equivalent to the expenditure, for the knotting is too fine to give either a pleasing or a durable fabric. The designs too of these very fine rugs are rarely satisfactory. They depart entirely from tradition and exhibit perhaps symbolical or narrative subjects with lengthy inscriptions; or there may be crowds of historical personages, or a spiritless copy of a European picture. In fact, the designs are not suitable for carpets, and the subjects would be much better rendered in some other medium. The originality of the Kirman weaver is shown in other ways too, among which may be mentioned the production of carpets with a plain-woven, unknotted ground, and a pattern knotted in the usual way. In some of these rugs a gold-coloured or grey weft is used, probably with the idea of giving the effect of the gold and silver backgrounds of some of the antique Persian rugs.

(vi) *Farsistan* or *Kashkai*. All the carpets made in this province have marked characteristics of technique which make them easy to recognize, though there is considerable variety of design. Different types are described by writers, but the difference between them is so slight that they cannot always be distinguished. The most important type is known as SHIRAZ, after the town of that name. These have a white woollen warp on one level, and a red woollen weft that crosses twice after each row of knots. The Sehna knot is the most common, but the Ghiordes is also used. The pile is fairly long and is very soft and lustrous, and the wool gives, perhaps, richer and more transparent colours than any other grown in Persia. There is a single-cord selvedge, which is overcast in short lengths of different colours, mostly red and blue, and there are often tassels depending from the selvedge at intervals. There are broad webs at each end woven in horizontal coloured stripes, again mostly red and blue; and these webs are often embroidered slightly with coloured wool. The colours are deep and rich. Blue and red predominate, but there are usually small areas of white which stand out very conspicuously. Another favourite colour is a peculiar grey-green, which is not often seen in other rugs. The design is more geometrical than that of most other Persian carpets, and as free use is made of latch-hooks and small conventional animals and birds, Shiraz rugs are often mistaken for Caucasian products. The most common field-design is a long hexagonal panel, or a succession of hexagonal panels linked together. The field is often shaped in various forms outlined with straight lines. The ground outside the panel is often filled with parallel bands, each of which has a small pattern. The whole field is frequently covered with a succession of small angular cones, which may have different colourings but are often arranged so that those in diagonal lines are coloured alike. When none of these schemes are used, the field is usually filled with a variety of detached geometrical or conventional floral devices, among which will mostly be found small birds and animals. The border often consists of a large number of stripes, some of which are filled with the common Persian motive of blossoms depending from a wavy stem. Another favourite border-stripe is the barber's-pole, the successive bands of which usually show all the colours of the rug. Shiraz rugs are, as a rule, very pleasing and desirable pieces, but they nearly always have the slight disadvantage of not lying quite flat on the floor. A good many saddle-bags come from Shiraz, and some of them are exquisitely woven. In the Victoria and Albert Museum there is a small saddle-bag with the cone pattern on a yellow ground, so finely knotted that there are over six hundred knots to the square inch.

A very similar group of rugs coming from the east of Shiraz is called NIRIS (the name of a salt-lake in the district) or alternatively LARISTAN. They have the Ghiordes knot and a warp on two levels more or less distinct. They favour the all-over cone pattern rather than the central panel, and the cones are often elaborately drawn and large rather than small and angular. Sometimes the field has a small lattice pattern, or a diaper of small devices arranged so as to have a pronounced striped effect.

SHIRAZ and NIRIS rugs are frequently called MECCA, for the reason, so it is said, that large numbers of them are taken to and left at Mecca by pilgrims.

Illustrations of the principal types of Persian rugs will be found on Plates 147 to 175.

PLATES 147 AND 148. KARADAGH CARPETS.
Carpets of this kind are known in the trade also as Feraghan, Karabagh, Shiraz, and simply as Persian. They have from 50 to 100 knots to the square inch. The usual sizes are 2½ ft. × 5 ft., 4½ ft. × 6½ ft. and 5 ft. × 10 ft. They are pliable and soft to the touch, and have a short and not very lustrous pile. The chief colours are wine-red and black.

PLATE 149. KARADAGH CARPET.
Carpets of this kind are known in the trade also as Feraghan, Karabagh, Shiraz, or simply as Persian. They have from 50 to 100 knots to the square inch. The usual sizes are 2½ ft. × 5 ft., 4 ft. × 6½ ft. and 5 ft. × 10 ft. They are pliable and soft to the touch, and have a short but lustrous pile. The chief colours are blue, red and white.

PLATE 150. KARADAGH CARPET.
Carpets of this kind are known in the trade also as Feraghan, Karabagh, Shiraz, and simply as Persian. They have from 80 to 100 knots to the

square inch. The usual sizes are 2½ ft. × 5 ft., 4½ ft. × 6½ ft. and 5 ft. × 10 ft. They are pliable and soft to the touch, and have a short and not very lustrous pile. The chief colours are blue, red and green.

PLATE 151. TABRIZ CARPET.

Carpets of this kind are known in the trade also simply as Persian. They have from 200 to 260 knots to the square inch. The usual sizes are 8 ft. × 11½ ft., 10 ft. × 13 ft. and 11½ ft. × 15 ft. The chief colours are red, blue and green, and the general scheme of colour is soft and harmonious. They are among the most perfectly made of modern carpets. The complicated mass of floral scrolls is typical.

PLATE 152. GOREVAN OR YORAGHAN CARPET.

Carpets of this kind are also known in the trade simply as Persian. They have from 30 to 40 knots to the square inch. The usual size is about 10½ ft. × 15 ft. They are very harsh to the touch and have a thick, long and dull-looking pile. The chief colours are chocolate-red, blue and white. The characteristic angular drawing of the detail, as well as the heavy massing of the colour, are well shown in the illustration.

PLATE 153. HAMADAN CARPET.

Carpets of this kind are known in the trade also as Camel-hair, or simply as Persian carpets. They have from 30 to 40 knots to the square inch. The usual size is 4½ ft. × 15 ft. They are harsh to the touch and have a very thick and long pile. The chief colours are the brown of camel-hair, red and blue.

PLATE 154. HAMADAN CARPET.

Carpets of this kind are also known in the trade as Kirman, or simply as Persian. They have from 30 to 40 knots to the square inch. The usual sizes are 4 ft. × 11½ ft. and 6½ ft. × 16½ ft. They are somewhat harsh to the touch and have a fairly long and lustrous pile. The chief colours are the brown of camel-hair, red and blue. The ground of this specimen has a more elaborate pattern than usual, and there is little doubt that the rug had once an outer edging of camel-hair.

PLATE 155. FERAGHAN CARPET.

Carpets of this kind are known in the trade also simply as Persian. They have from 65 to 130 knots to the square inch. The usual sizes are 8 ft. × 11½ ft., 10 ft. × 13 ft. and 11½ ft. × 15 ft. Antique pieces are generally about 4 ft. × 10 ft. The more recent pieces have a fairly short, but the older ones a long pile. The illustration shows a typical Feraghan with the usual Herati pattern.

PLATES 156 AND 157. SARABAND CARPETS.

Carpets of this kind are known in the trade also as Feraghan, Shiraz, Mecca, or simply as Persian. They have from 100 to 160 knots to the square inch. The usual sizes are $2\frac{1}{2}$ ft. $\times$ 4 ft., 4 ft. $\times$ $8\frac{1}{2}$ ft. and $5\frac{1}{2}$ ft. $\times$ $6\frac{1}{2}$ ft. They have a fairly short and rather lustrous pile. The chief colours are dark blue, red and green. The first specimen illustrated has a pattern much like a Feraghan with the cone-diaper substituted for the Herati or similar pattern. Neither shows the most typical Saraband border-stripe of cone-devices depending from every bend of a wavy stem.

PLATE 158. JUSHAGHAN CARPET.

Carpets of this kind are also known in the trade as Ispahan, Shah-Abbas, or simply as Persian. They have from 100 to 160 knots to the square inch. The usual size is about $6\frac{1}{2}$ ft. $\times$ 13 ft. They have a soft and lustrous pile of medium length. The chief colours are dark blue, red and yellow. The pattern, which is typical of Jushaghans, is obviously descended from the well-known design of palmettes, blossoms and cloud-bands which is seen so often in Persian rugs of the sixteenth and seventeenth centuries.

PLATE 159. SARUK OR KASHAN CARPET.

Carpets of this kind are also known in the trade simply as Persian. They have from 160 to 225 knots to the square inch. The usual sizes are 6 ft. $\times$ 10 ft., 10 ft. $\times$ 13 ft. and $11\frac{1}{2}$ ft. $\times$ 18 ft. They have a short, close and very lustrous pile. The chief colours are copper-red, blue and green.

PLATE 160. PERSIAN SILK CARPET (Victoria and Albert Museum). 6 ft. 5 in. $\times$ 4 ft. 5 in.

Warp : White silk. On two levels. 29 to 1 inch.
Weft : Blue cotton. Two shoots after each row of knots.
Knots : Silk. Sehna. 21 to 1 inch. 300 to the square inch.
Colours : Eight. White (field) : light green (border) : purple : black : blue : yellow : red : magenta.

PLATES 161 AND 162. MUSKABAD CARPETS.

Carpets of this kind are also known in the trade simply as Persian. They have from 40 to 45 knots to the square inch. The usual sizes are

10 ft. × 13 ft. and 11½ ft. × 15 ft. They have a rather lustrous pile of medium length. The chief colours are dark blue, red and white.

PLATES 163, 164A, B, 165, 167B. SEHNA CARPETS.

Carpets of this kind are also known in the trade as Kirman, or simply as Persian. They have about 200 knots to the square inch. The size is nearly always about 5½ ft. × 8 ft. They are very thin and have a close pile, rather rough to the touch. The chief colours are blue, red and white. There are no better carpets than these in point of technique and delicacy of drawing, and their price is high, but not when allowance is made for the very close knotting.

PLATE 166. KURDISTAN CARPET.

Carpets of this kind are known in the trade also as Iran, Mosul, Hamadan, and simply as Persian. They have from 40 to 65 knots to the square inch. The usual sizes are 3½ ft. × 8 ft. and 5½ ft. × 13 ft. The chief colours are red, blue and white. They are very thick and have a coarse pile, which is lustrous in the older specimens but less so in the modern ones.

PLATES 167A AND 168. KHORASSAN CARPETS.

Carpets of this kind are known in the trade also simply as Persian. They have from 90 to 110 knots to the square inch. The usual sizes are 10 ft. × 13 ft., 11 ft. × 18 ft. and 14 ft. × 20 ft. Smaller carpets are rare. They are soft to the touch, and have a lustrous pile of medium length. The chief colours are rose-red, blue, white and green.

PLATES 169, 170, 171, 172. KIRMAN CARPETS.

Carpets of this kind are also known in the trade as Tabriz, or simply as Persian. They have from 200 to 260 knots to the square inch. The usual sizes are 8 ft. × 11½ ft., 10 ft. × 13 ft., 11½ ft. × 15 ft., 11 ft. × 21 ft. and even larger. They are thin and have a short and not very lustrous pile. The chief colours are red, blue-green and white.

PLATES 173, 174, 175B. SHIRAZ CARPETS.

Carpets of this kind are also known in the trade as Mecca, or simply as Persian. They have from 45 to 100 knots to the square inch. The usual sizes are 4½ ft. × 6½ ft. and 5½ ft. × 11½ ft. They have a rather loose texture and are soft to the touch. The pile is very lustrous and of medium length. The chief colours are dark blue, red and white. No. 174 has the triple medallion and shaped field that is so common in Shirazis, and No. 175B has the other characteristic pattern of small angularly drawn cones.

PLATE 176.   PERSIAN KILIM (Victoria and Albert Museum).   6 ft. ×
    4 ft. 6 in.
Warp : Three-ply white wool.   17 to 1 inch.
Weft : Two-ply wool.   About 96 shoots to 1 inch.
Colours : Eight.   Dark blue (field):   white (central medallion):
    red: light blue (1st and 3rd borders):   light red: green:
    yellow (2nd border):   brown.

(d) Central Asiatic

The vast and wild region which lies between Persia and China is sparsely inhabited by fierce and uncultured nomadic tribes, and yet it produces carpets which are beautifully made and of great artistic interest.   A great part of this region falls within the Russian political sphere, and as a consequence most of the first rugs to leave were exported by way of Russia.   The carpets made in the eastern part of the region under consideration show strong Chinese influence, but all the others have a resemblance to each other that is very remarkable when it is considered how many different and antagonistic tribes are engaged in their production and what great distances separate the boundaries of the region.

The carpets of Western Turkestan are made almost entirely of wool which is of very good quality.   Both warp and weft are commonly white, or at least not dyed, and the weft crosses twice after each row of knots. The Sehna knot is generally used, though there are a few exceptions. The knotting is never very coarse and often is remarkably fine, and the counting of the knots in making the pattern is done at least as carefully as anywhere else.   It is true that the style of pattern adopted almost necessitates careful weaving, for any serious miscalculation would be very apparent; but even then it is remarkable that nomadic people on the most primitive looms should produce such very accurate work.

Another peculiarity of the texture is that the knots are considerably smaller in the direction of the warp than in the direction of the weft. In fact the small rectangle occupied by each knot is about twice as wide as it is high.

The most characteristic feature of these rugs is their colouring, which is quite unlike that of any other class.   The colours are almost invariably deep and sombre, and when bright colours are used they occur only in very minute quantities. Red is by far the commonest colour, but it is never brighter than a deep brick tint, and is more often a deep wine-red or a brown- or purple-red. Dark blue is the next most common colour, and there is a fair amount of white, which is often rather conspicuous. Black, green, blue and brown are sometimes used in smaller quantities, while very little of other colours is seen.

The designs are on the whole more geometrical even than those of Caucasian rugs. Floral devices do occur, but, with a few exceptions, they are so highly conventionalized as to be almost unrecognizable. Two types of design are so widely spread through the different groups of rugs that they must be mentioned here. In one type the field is covered with a repeating pattern of octagons, regularly arranged in rows and columns; the octagons are considerably flattened, on account of the unusual proportions of each knot in the texture. In the other type the field is divided by two crossing bands into four panels approximately equal and square. These latter pieces are really portières.

There are many borders and smaller details of the designs which are exclusively found in Central Asiatic carpets, and several of these will be seen illustrated on Plates 200 and 201.

Central Asiatic carpets are very rarely of large dimensions, and only a small proportion of them are rugs. The majority of pieces are saddle-bags, tent-bags, mats or tent-bands, and even some of the larger pieces, which look like rugs, were really intended for hanging across the doorway of a tent. As all carpets of this class were meant for use rather than show, and, what is more, for the use of nomads, it is not remarkable that very old pieces are quite unknown. A certain number may be found going back to the eighteenth century, but it is very doubtful whether any pieces of an earlier date still exist. Carpets of a moderate age are invariably sound in colour and weaving, and even modern ones are nearly always well woven, though they have suffered in common with most new carpets from unsound dyes. Almost without exception they wear well, and if the dyes are sound they are very desirable carpets.

Most of the rugs made in Western Turkestan are called BOKHARA, though very few are made there. It is best as far as practicable to classify the rugs according to the tribe that made them, though there are great difficulties in the way of a strict nomenclature and much confusion on the subject. The rugs made by the Salor tribes (known frequently as ROYAL BOKHARA) have a pattern of repeated octagons of the kind illustrated on Plate 175A. In the interspaces between the octagons there are various figures which are roughly diamond-shaped in contour. Salor rugs are not woven now and have become very rare, but their patterns have been adopted by other tribes.

The majority of Turcoman rugs are made by the TEKKE tribes whose pieces are generally coarser than those already mentioned. The warp, which is of medium wool or goat-hair, lies on two levels slightly separated. There is mostly a three-cord selvedge and the ends have a long, coloured web and a long fringe. The border shown on Plate 201 (27) is almost invariably found. The chief colour is red, which ranges from a brick-red to a purple-red.

The rugs of the PINDÉ tribes are darker in tone than the last. The ground is of a deep brown-red or purple-red, sometimes approaching a purple-black, and the pattern stands out rather strongly in white lines.

All Katchli pattern rugs are often erroneously called prayer-rugs.

In the neighbourhood of KHIVA rugs are made which much resemble those called Bokhara, but tend to be coarser and generally more barbaric in appearance. Animals and geometrical forms rather like the Caucasian are introduced.

The rugs woven by the YOMUD tribes form a group more easy to recognize than many of the others. They have a rather coarse warp which tends to lie on two levels. The Ghiordes knot is commoner than the Sehna, whereas the latter is almost invariably found in other Central Asiatic rugs. They have not the flattened octagons, but mostly have patterns constructed with diamond-shaped latch-hooked figures often of two types or at least coloured in two ways. Some of their border-stripes are characteristic (Plate 201 (1, 7, 13, 18, 22, 23)). The Yomud tent-bags are not as a rule rectangular, but are pointed at the top and are mostly furnished with long fringes and cords at the corners. The colour-scheme mostly includes a purple-brown and a rich red as well as a fair amount of rather conspicuous white. A great peculiarity of knotting is seen in some Yomud carpets, but perhaps in no other kind. Its nature and the reason for it will require a little explanation. The simplest diagonal contour that can occur in a knotted pattern is formed by carrying one of the two colours concerned one knot farther in each successive row, and if the knots are approximately square this makes an angle of about 45 degrees. In Central Asiatic carpets the knots are much wider than they are high, so a diagonal line formed as above will be much less steep. If an angle of 45 degrees is wanted it can be obtained by carrying one colour one knot further in every *second* row, but the line will not be a smooth one. The Yomuds get out of the difficulty by breaking up the pairs of warps on which most of the knots are tied and by tying in the new row midway between those of the previous row. The knots are thus arranged like the bricks in a half-brick wall, and a fairly smooth diagonal line of about 45 degrees will result. This is only done where necessary in the pattern, and the usual arrangement is restored by tying a knot on three warps at each end of a row of abnormally-placed knots.

Rugs called AFGHAN are made by wandering tribes partly in Afghanistan but also outside its boundaries. They are coarsely-woven and have broad webs at each end divided into several coloured bands, and usually long fringes. The pattern mostly consists of large repeated octagons which almost touch each other in the vertical direction, and these octagons mostly contain trifoliate forms (Plate 201 (20)). The colours are chiefly dark red and brown, and the rugs have a reddish-tawny appearance.

The rugs called BESHIRE, from a district to the west of Khiva, have a coarse or medium texture, and usually have wide striped webs at the ends, and fringes. The colours are mostly red and brown with a fair amount of blue. The patterns are more floral than those of other Central Asiatic rugs, and often are reminiscent of Persian designs. Trellis patterns are not uncommon, and sometimes a curious pattern consisting of repeated scrolls having a vermiculated appearance are seen (Plate 189). The prayer-rugs have a simple pointed arch occupying nearly the whole of the rug (Plate 190). Beshire rugs have only been exported in fairly recent times.

A well-marked type of rugs akin to the Turcoman is called BELUCHISTAN or BELUCHI, and some may actually be made there by wandering tribes ; but probably the majority are made by similar tribes further to the north. The rugs are very dark and sombre, the prevalent colours being dark blue, dark red and black ; invariably, however, there are small areas of white which are very conspicuous, and sometimes there is a good deal of natural camel-hair. On account of the blue, which is unusual in Central Asiatic rugs, they are sometimes called BLUE BOKHARA. The designs are different from the Turcoman rugs. They are to some extent geometrical, but they also have conventional tree-forms of a peculiar kind, and also copy some of the simpler floral patterns of

Persia. The prayer-rugs of this group are fairly numerous and have a simple rectangular arch. The rugs are thick and well woven, and the pile is rather long and mostly very lustrous. They wear well, and in spite of their dark colour are very attractive.

Quite different from the Central Asiatic rugs already described are those from Eastern or Chinese Turkestan. They have usually a cotton warp on two levels and a cotton weft. The Sehna knot is used, and the texture is coarse and rather loose with from about 40 to 65 knots to the square inch. These rugs usually have a rich yellow and brown appearance, and are so closely connected with the Chinese carpets in point of design that they are most conveniently classed with them. A further description will be found in Part I, Chapter VI (b).

Plates 175A, and 177 to 193 illustrate the principal types of Central Asiatic rugs apart from those of Eastern Turkestan.

PLATE 175A. TURCOMAN CARPET.

Carpets of this kind are also known in the trade as Bokhara. They have from 130 to 200 knots to the square inch. The usual sizes are 5½ ft. × 10 ft., 5 ft. × 8 ft., as well as 1 × 2 ft., and 2 × 4 ft., in which case they are sometimes known as YASTIK. They are closely knotted and have a short and lustrous pile. The chief colours are red-brown with smaller quantities of dark blue and white.

PLATES 177. TURCOMAN STRIPS or TENT-BANDS.

Carpets of this kind are also known in the trade as Bokhara or Khiva. These border-like pieces are used as decorations, chiefly round the walls of tents where the sides join the roof. The ground is of plain weaving and the pattern is knotted in the usual way. The usual size is 6 ins. × 10 ft., though some are much larger. The ground is white, or the natural colour of the wool, and the pattern is chiefly in dark purple, blue and white.

PLATES 178 and 179. TURCOMAN CARPETS.

Carpets of this kind are known in the trade also as Bokhara. They have from 130 to 200 knots to the square inch. The usual size is 2½ ft. × 5 ft. They are closely knotted and have a short and lustrous pile. The chief colours are red-brown, dark blue, and white.

PLATES 180, 181, and 182. TURCOMAN CARPETS.

Carpets of this kind are known in the trade also as Bokhara, Khiva, Tekke, and Kisiliyak. They have from 105 to 106 knots to the square inch. The usual size is 3½ ft. × 5½ ft. They are closely knotted and have a short and lustrous pile. The chief colours are dark red-brown, dark blue, white and yellow; the white sometimes being of cotton.

PLATES 183, 184, 185. TURCOMAN YOMUD CARPETS.

Carpets of this kind are also known in the trade as Bokhara. They have from 130 to 200 knots to the square inch. The usual size is 5 ft. × 10 ft. They are closely knotted and have a short but frequently very lustrous pile. The chief colours are dark purple, blue and white.

PLATES 186A, AND 187. AFGHAN CARPETS.

Carpets of this kind are known in the trade also as Bokhara. They have from 45 to 70 knots to the square inch. The usual sizes are 4½ ft. × 7 ft. and 6 ft. × 9 ft. They usually have a long pile which is very lustrous in the better pieces. The chief colours are dark red-brown, dark blue, white and yellow.

PLATE 186B. TURCOMAN CAMEL BAG (Victoria and Albert Museum).
2 ft. × 4 ft. 4 ins.

Warp : White wool. On one level. 19 to 1 inch.
Weft : Red wool. Two shoots after each row of knots.
Knots : Wool. Sehna. 20 to 1 inch. 200 to the square inch.
Colours : Seven. Purple-red (field, 3rd border and edging) : red (2nd and 4th borders) : white : dark blue : green-blue : brown : yellow.

PLATES 188 AND 189. BESHIRE CARPETS.

Carpets of this kind have from 50 to 100 knots to the square inch. The usual sizes are 5 ft. × 11½ ft. and 6½ ft. × 16½ ft. The pile is very long and very lustrous. The chief colours are red-brown and dark blue, with a little white and yellow. These carpets have only been exported for twenty years or so, and are still not well known.

PLATE 190. BESHIRE PRAYER-CARPET.

Carpets of this kind have from 50 to 100 knots to the square inch. The size is about 3½ ft. × 6 ft. They have a long and lustrous pile. The chief colours are red, brown, white and dark blue.

PLATES 191, 192A, B, 193. BELUCHISTAN CARPETS.

Carpets of this kind are also known in the trade as Afghan and Bokhara. They have from 50 to 65 knots to the square inch. The usual size is about 5 ft. × 8 ft.; large pieces being very rare. They have a long and very lustrous pile. The chief colours are dark blue, brown, and an intense white.

PLATE 192C. BELUCHISTAN PRAYER-CARPET. 5 ft. 3 ins. × 2 ft. 7 ins.
Warp : White wool. On one level. 15 to 1 inch.
Weft : Black wool. Two shoots after each row of knots.
Knots : Wool. Sehna. 11 to 1 inch. 80 to the square inch.
Colours : Six. Camel-hair (field) : crimson-red : black (border) :
    red : dark blue : white.

BIBLIOGRAPHY

BODE, Wilhelm von.—Vorderasiastische Knüpfteppiche aus älterer Zeit. 92 (1 *chromo*) *process illus.* (10 × 7.) Leipzig : H. Seemann Nachfolger. 1901.

BOGOLOUBOV, Andreya Andreevich.—Tapis de l'Asie centrale, faisant partie de la collection réunie par A.B. (Text also in Russian.) 52 pp. 36 *chromo-lithogr.*, 7 *phototype plates and 2 maps.* (28 × 20.) St. Pétersbourg. 1908.

DUMONTHIER, Ernest.—Recueil de dessins de tapis et de tapisseries d'ameublement du mobilier de la Couronne. 8 pp. 48 (*some col.*) *phototype plates.* (25 × 18.) Paris : Librairie générale de l'Architecture et des Arts décoratifs. 1912.

GROTE-HASENBALG, Werner.—Der Orientteppich, seine Geschichte und seine Kultur. *Process illus. incl,* 137 *chromo, and map.* 3 vols. (10 × 10.) Berlin : Scarabaeus-Verlag. 1922.

HACKMACK, Adolf. Der Chinesische Teppich. 44 pp. *Process illus. incl.* 25 (1 chromo) plates, and map. (9 × 6.) L. Friederichsen and Co. Hamburg. 1921. (Eng. trans. reprinted by Dover)

HAWLEY, Walter A.—Oriental rugs, antique and modern. *Process illus., some chromo and maps.* (11 × 8.) New York : John Lane Co. 1913. (Dover)

HENDLEY, Thomas Holbein, Col.—Asian carpets : 16th and 17th century designs from the Jaipur palaces. 22 pp. 146 (138 *chromo*) *lithogr., incl. frontispiece and 1 phototype.* (20 × 14.) London : W. Griggs. 1905.

HOLT, Rosa Belle.—Rugs, Oriental and Occidental, antique and modern. A handbook for ready reference. 31 (12 *chromo*) *process illus.* (11 × 8.) Chicago : A. C. McClurg and Co. 1901.

KRYGOWSKI, T.—Polenteppiche (Polnische Knüpfteppiche). 23 pp. 11 *process illus.* (In " Orientalisches Archiv," II, 70, 106.) 1911–12.

LESSING, J.—Orientalische Teppiche. 12 pp. 13 (12 *chromo*) *plates and* 1 *text illus.* (19 × 13.) Berlin : E. Wasmuth. 1891.

LESSING, Julius.—Alt-Orientalische Teppichmuster, nach Bildern und Originalen des XV–XVI Jahrhunderts. Herausgegeben mit Unterstützung des Königl. Preussischen Ministeriums für Handel, Gewerbe und offentliche Arbeiten. 30 *chromo-lithogr.* (20 × 14.) Berlin : E. Wasmuth. 1877.

English translation. Ancient Oriental carpets, etc. 28 pp. 30 *chromo-lithogr.* (20 × 14.) London : H. Sotheran. 1879.

LEWIS, G. Griffin.—The practical book of Oriental rugs. 2nd edition. *Process illus., some chromo and map* (9 × 7.) Philadelphia : J. B. Lippincott Co. 1913.

BIBLIOGRAPHY

VICTORIA AND ALBERT MUSEUM. Guide to the Collection of Carpets. 49 *process illus.* (10 × 6.) London : H.M. Stationery Office. 1920.

VICTORIA AND ALBERT MUSEUM. Notes on Carpet Knotting and Weaving. 13 *process illus.* (8 × 5.) London : H.M. Stationery Office. 1920.

MARTIN, F. R.—A history of Oriental carpets before 1800. *Plates and illustrations in the text, many chromo.* (26 × 20.) Vienna : I. R. Court and State Printing Office. 1908.

MUMFORD, John Kimberly.—Oriental rugs. 33 (16 *chromo*) *plates, 2 maps, and illustrations in the text.* (11 × 8.) London : Sampson Low, Marston, and Co. 1901.

MUMFORD, John Kimberly.—The Yerkes collection of Oriental carpets. 62 pp. 27 *chromo process illus.* (22 × 14.) London : B. T. Batsford. 1910.

NEUGEBAUER, Rudolf, and ORENDI, Julius.—Handbuch der orientalischen Teppich-kunde. Mit einer Einführung von Richard Graul. *Process illus., many chromo.* (9 × 6.) Leipzig : K. W. Hiersemann. 1909.

INVENTAIRE GÉNÉRAL DES RICHESSES D'ART DE LA FRANCE. Vol. IV. Tapis en Savonnerie. P. 173 foll. Paris. 1913.

RIEGL, Alois.—Altorientalische Teppiche. 36 *process illus.* (9 × 6.) Leipzig : T. O. Weigel Nachfolger. 1891.

ROBINSON, Vincent J.—Eastern Carpets : twelve early examples. With descriptive notices by V. J. R., and a preface by Sir G. Birdwood. 44 pp. 12 *chromo-photo-lithogr.* (20 × 15.) London : H. Sotheran. 1882.

SARRE, Friedrich, and MARTIN, F. R.—Die Ausstellung von Meisterwerken muham-medanischer Kunst in München 1910. Vol. I. Miniaturen und Buchkunst : die Teppiche. 1 *chromo-photo-lithogr.*, and 46 *phototype plates.* (10 × 15.) München : F. Bruckmann. 1912.

STEBBING, Edward.—The Holy Carpet of the Mosque at Ardebil. 18 pp. 7 (6 *col.*) *photo-lithogr.* (25 × 21.) London : Robson. 1893.

VAN DE PUT, Albert.—Some 15th century Spanish carpets. 8 pp. *Process illus. incl.* 1 *chromo.* (In *Burlington Magazine*, XIX, 344 ; XX, 124.) 1911.

VIENNA.—K. K. Oesterr. Handelsmuseum. Katalog der Ausstellung orientalischer Teppiche im . . . Museum, 1891. (Preface by A. von Scala.) Cuts and 2 plans. (10 × 7.) Wien : Verlag des K. K. Oesterr. Handelsmuseum. 1891.

VIENNA.—K. K. Oesterr. Handelsmuseum. Oriental carpets. Published by Order of the Imperial and Royal Ministries of Commerce, Worship and Education. English edition edited by C. Purdon Clarke. *Chromo-photo-lithogr. and photo-types.* (26 × 20.) Vienna. 1892–96.

VIENNA.—K. K. Oesterr. Museum für Kunst und Industrie. Ancient Oriental carpets. . . . With preface by A. von Scala ; introduction by W. Bode ; text by F. Sarre. 16 pp. 25 *chromo-lithogr.* (27 × 20.) Leipzig : K. W. Hierse-mann. 1906–08.

PLATES

Plate 2. Persian garden-carpet, 17th century. (See page 12.) *The Hon. H. D. McLaren, C.B.E., M.P.*

Plate 3. Persian garden-carpet, 16th–17th century. (See pages 12, 103.)
Wagner Collection.

Plate 4. Persian garden-carpet, 17th century. (See page 12.) *Orendi
Collection.*

Plate 5A *(left).* Armenian carpet, 17th century. (See pages 8, 13.) Plate
5B *(right).* Armenian carpet, 17th–18th century. (See pages 16, 104.)
Victoria and Albert Museum.

Plate 6. Armenian carpet, 17th century. (See page 15.)

Plate 7. Armenian carpet, made in 1679. (See page 15.)

Plate 8. Armenian carpet, probably 17th century. (See pages 16, 104.)
Victoria and Albert Museum.

Plate 9. Persian carpet, 16th century. (See pages 16, 104.) *Victoria and Albert Museum.*

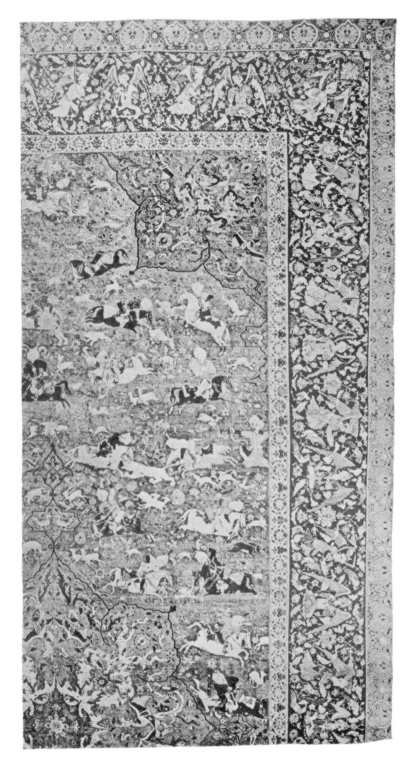

Plate 10. The Imperial Austrian hunting-carpet, 16th century. (See page 16.)

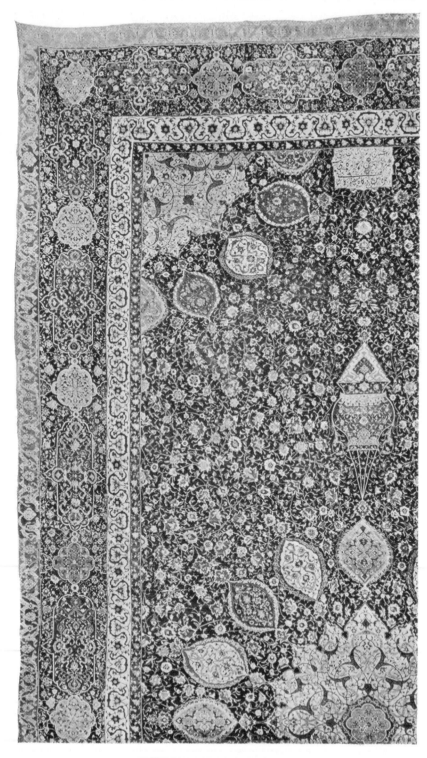

Plate 11. The Ardabil carpet, made in 1540. (See pages 17, 104.) *Victoria and Albert Museum.*

Plate 1. Persian carpet, 15th–16th century. (See pages 19, 103.)
Victoria and Albert Museum.

Plate 14. Persian carpet, probably 17th century. (See pages 9, 21, 105.) *Victoria and Albert Museum.*

Plate 53 *(left)*. Ghiordes prayer-carpet, late 17th century. (See page 54.)

Plate 67 *(right)*. Chinese carpet. (See page 64.)

Plate 82. Spanish(?) carpet, 17th century. (See page 71.)

Plate 89. English carpet, dated 1614. (See pages 79, 114.) *The Hon. Lady Hulse.*

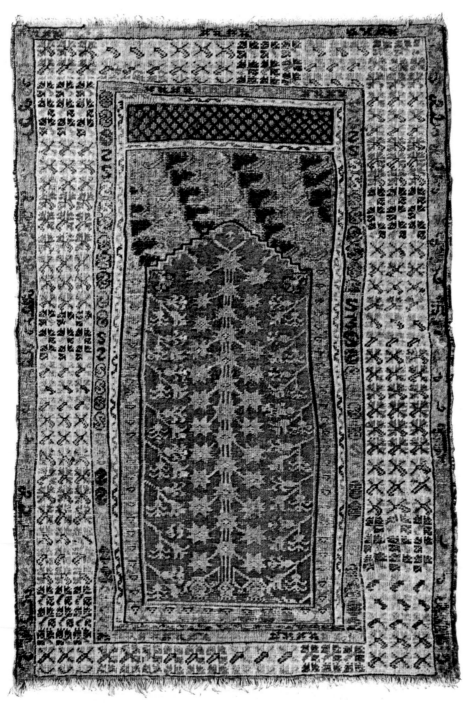

Plate 100. Kula prayer-carpet. (See page 157.)

Plate 102. Ladik prayer-carpet. (See page 157.)

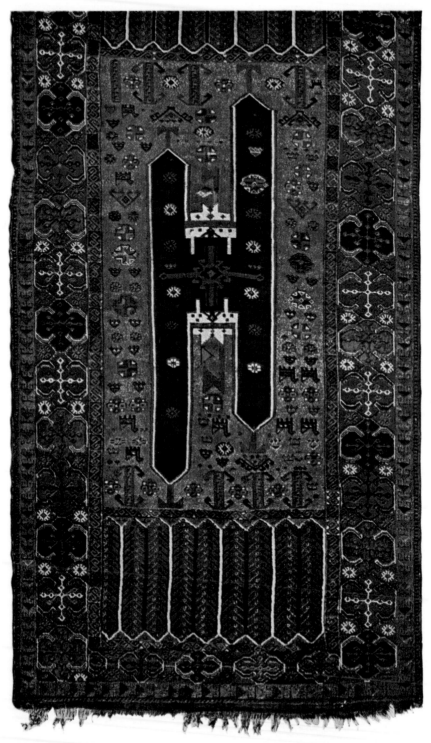

Plate 105. Ladik carpet. (See page 158.)

Plate 110. Anatolian carpet. (See page 159.)

Plate 121. Shirvan carpet. (See page 167.)

Plate 126. Shirvan carpet. (See page 169.)

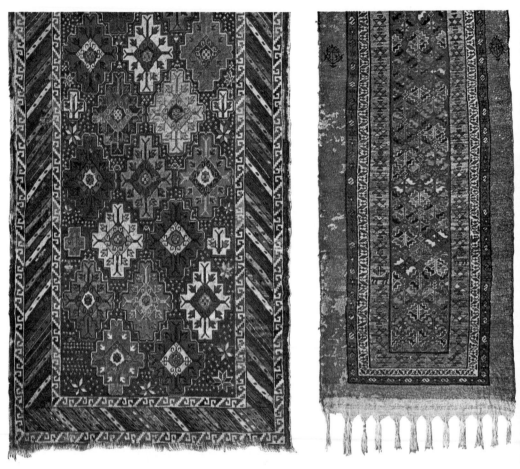

Plate 131 *(left)*. Shirvan carpet. (See page 170.)
Plate 153 *(right)*. Hamadan carpet. (See page 183.)

Plate 158. Jushaghan carpet. (See page 184.)

Plate 162. Muskabad carpet. (See page 184.)

Plate 166. Kurdistan carpet. (See page 185.)

Plate 178 *(left)*. Turcoman carpet. Pindé. (See page 190.)
Plate 193 *(right)*. Beluchistan carpet. (See page 191.)

Plate 12. Persian carpet, 16th–17th century. (See pages 20, 104.) *The Earl of Ilchester.*

Plate 13. Persian carpet, 17th century. (See page 20.) *Gobelins Museum, Paris.*

Plate 15. Persian metalwork. (See page 22.)

Plate 16. Persian miniature painting, 17th century. (See page 23.)

Plate 17. Indo-Persian miniature painting. (See page 24.)

Plate 18. Persian carpet, 17th century. (See page 24.) *Museum of Art and Industry, Vienna.*

Plate 19. Persian carpet, 17th century. (See pages 24, 105.) *Victoria and Albert Museum.*

Plate 20A *(left)*. Armenian carpet, 17th–18th century. (See pages 35, 59.) Plate 20B *(right)*. Persian carpet, 17th century. (See pages 25, 105.)
Victoria and Albert Museum.

Plate 21. Persian carpet, late 16th century. (See pages 26, 106.) *Portions in the Victoria and Albert Museum.*

Plate 22. Persian carpet, 16th–17th century. (See page 27.) *The Duke of Buccleuch, K.T.*

Plate 23. Persian carpet, 16th century. (See page 28.) *Musée des Arts décoratifs, Paris.*

Plate 24. Persian silk carpet, 17th century. (See page 32.) *Royal Collection of Saxony.*

Plate 25. Persian silk carpet, 17th century. (See page 33.) *The Gobelins Museum, Paris.*

Plate 26. Persian tapestry-carpet, 17th century. (See page 33.) *The Louvre Museum, Paris.*

Plate 27A *(top)*. Persian carpet, 17th century. (See page 35.) Plate 27B
(bottom). Persian carpet, 18th century. (See pages 35, 59.)

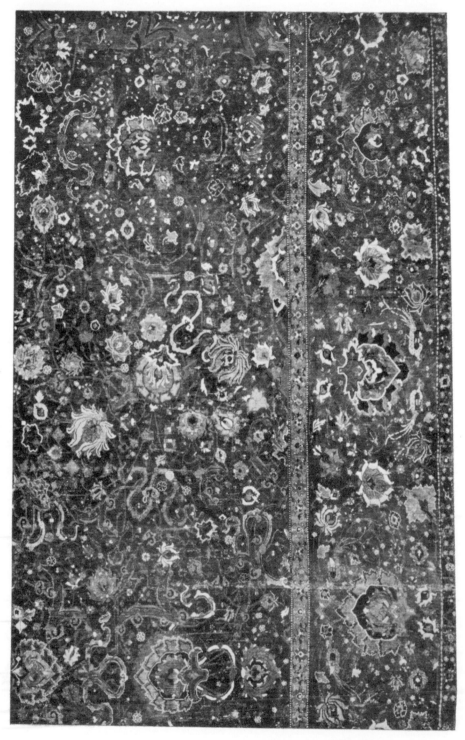

Plate 28. Persian carpet, 17th century. (See page 35.)

Plate 29. Persian carpet, 17th century. (See page 35.)

Plate 30A *(left)*. Jushagan carpet, 18th century. (See pages 36, 106.)
Mr. George Mounsey. Plate 30B *(right)*. Persian prayer-carpet, 17th
century. (See page 35.)

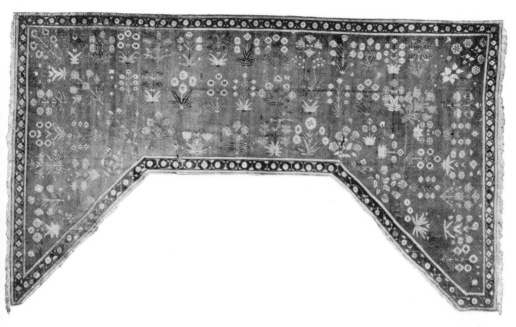

Plate 31. Indian carpets, made for the Palace at Amber; early 17th century. (See pages 39, 106.) *Mr. Lionel Harris.*

Plate 32. Indo-Persian carpet, early 17th century. (See pages 39, 106.)
Victoria and Albert Museum.

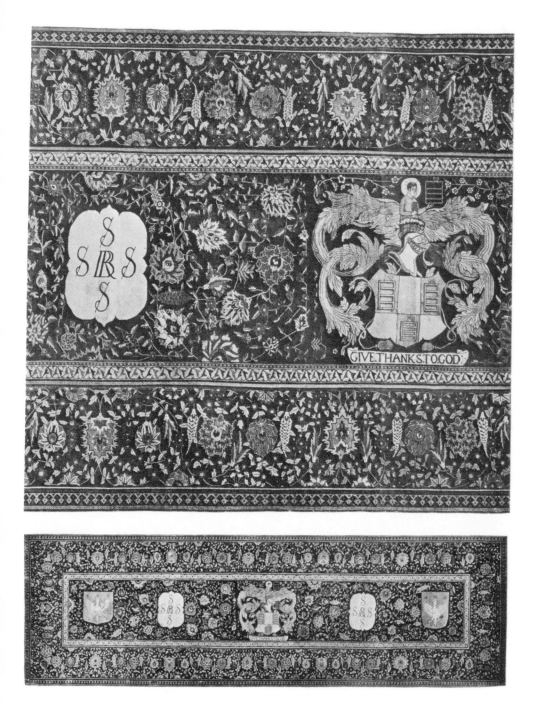

Plate 33. The Girdler's carpet, presented in 1634. (See pages 40, 106.)
The Girdlers' Company, London.

Plate 34. Indian carpet, early 17th century. (See page 40.)

Plate 35. Indian (Tanjore) carpet, early 19th century. (See page 41.)
Victoria and Albert Museum.

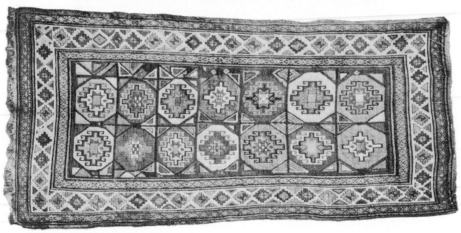

Plate 36A *(top)*. The Virgin and Child, by Hans Memlinc. (See page 45.) *Austrian Imperial Collection*. Plate 36B *(bottom)*. Caucasian carpet, probably 19th century. (See page 45.)

Plate 37A *(top).* Asia Minor carpet. (See pages 13, 46.) *Kaiser-Friedrich Museum, Berlin.* Plate 37B *(bottom).* Asia Minor carpet, 16th century. (See pages 48, 107.) *Victoria and Albert Museum.*

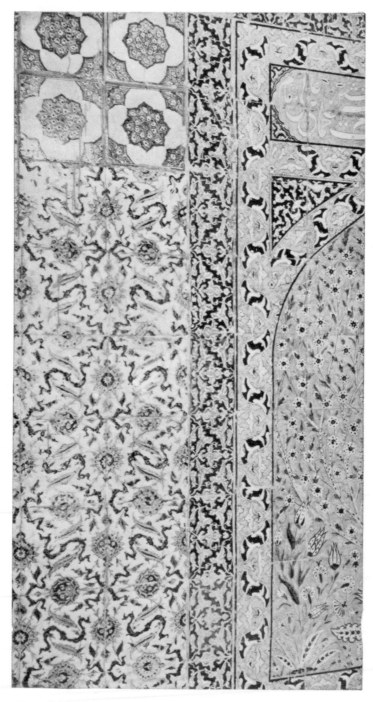

Plate 38. Panel of tilework from Constantinople. (See page 46.)

Plate 39. Asia Minor carpet, 16th century. (See pages 47, 107.) *Victoria and Albert Museum.*

Plate 40. Asia Minor carpet, 16th century. (See pages 47, 107.) *Victoria and Albert Museum.*

Plate 41. Asia Minor carpets, 16th–17th century. (See page 47.) *Dr. Wilhelm von Bode.*

Plate 42. Asia Minor carpet, 16th century. (See pages 48, 107.) *Mr. George Mounsey.*

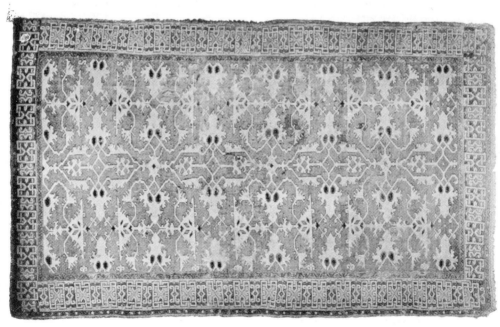

Plate 43A *(top)*. Ushak carpet, 16th–17th century. (See page 48.) Plate
43B *(bottom)*. Asia Minor carpet, 16th century. (See pages 49, 108.)
Victoria and Albert Museum.

Plate 44. Ushak carpet, 16th–17th century. (See pages 49, 108.) *Victoria and Albert Museum.*

Plate 45. Asia Minor carpet, 16th–17th century. (See page 50.) *Probst Collection*.

Plate 46A *(left).* Asia Minor carpet, 16th–17th century. (See page 50.)
Prince Adolf Schwarzenberg. Plate 46B *(right).* Asia Minor mat, 17th
century. (See pages 55, 108.) *Mr. George Mounsey.*

Plate 47. Oriental carpet, 16th century. (See pages 51, 108.) *Mr. George
Mounsey.*

Plate 48. Oriental carpet, 16th century. (See pages 51, 109.) *Mr. George Mounsey.*

Plate 49. Asia Minor carpet, 17th century. (See page 52.)

Plate 50. Asia Minor carpet, 17th–18th century. (See page 52.)

Plate 51. Asia Minor carpet, 17th–18th century. (See page 53.)

Plate 52. Asia Minor carpet. (See page 54.) *Kaiser-Friedrich Museum, Berlin.*

Plate 54. Asia Minor prayer-carpet, 18th century. (See page 55.)

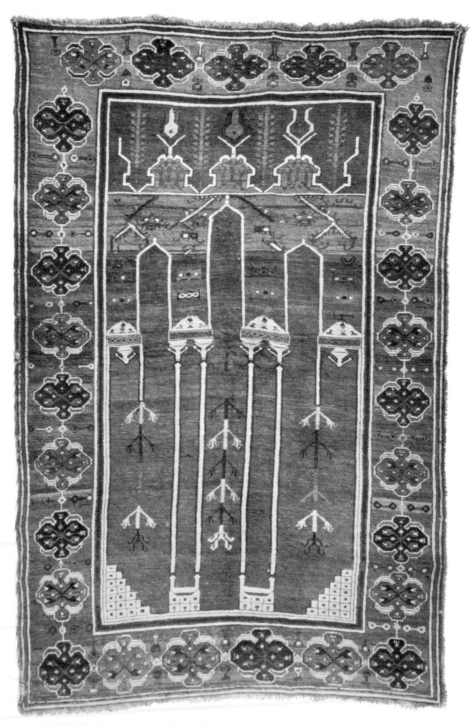

Plate 55. Asia Minor carpet, 18th century. (See pages 54, 56.)

Plate 56. Asia Minor prayer-carpet, late 17th century. (See pages 55, 109.) *Mr. George Mounsey.*

Plate 57. Asia Minor carpet, 18th century. (See page 56.)

Plate 58. Asia Minor carpet, 18th century. (See pages 56, 109.) *Mr. George Mounsey.*

Plate 59. Asia Minor carpet, 18th–19th century. (See page 57.)

Plate 60. Caucasian (?) carpet, 19th century. (See page 57.)

Plate 61. Caucasian carpet, probably 18th century. (See page 59.)

Plate 62. Caucasian carpet, 18th century. (See page 59.)

Plate 63. Caucasian carpet, 18th–19th century. (See page 60.)

Plate 64. Caucasian carpet, 18th–19th century. (See page 60.)

Plate 65. Chinese carpet in silk and gold. (See page 63.)

Plate 66A *(top)*. Chinese carpet in silk and gold. (See pages 64, 109.)
Lady Cunliffe. Plate 66B *(bottom)*. Chinese silk carpet. (See pages 66,
110.) *Lieut.-Col. G. B. Croft-Lyons, F.S.A.*

Plate 68. Chinese carpet, 18th century. (See pages 64, 110.) *Victoria and Albert Museum.*

Plate 69. Chinese carpet, 18th century. (See pages 64, 110.) *Victoria and Albert Museum.*

Plate 70A *(left).* Chinese chair-cover, 18th–19th century. (See pages 65, 110.) *Victoria and Albert Museum.* Plate 70B *(right).* Chinese carpet, 18th century. (See pages 64, 111.) *Victoria and Albert Museum.*

Plate 71. Chinese carpet, probably 18th century. (See pages 65, 111.)
Victoria and Albert Museum.

Plate 72. Chinese pillar-carpet, 18th century. (See pages 65, 111.)
Victoria and Albert Museum.

Plate 73. Chinese pillar-carpet, 18th century. (See pages 65, 111.)
Victoria and Albert Museum.

Plate 74. Eastern-Turkestan carpet, 18th century. (See page 65.)

Plate 75A *(top).* Eastern-Turkestan mat, 18th–19th century. (See page 65.) *Victoria and Albert Museum.* Plate 75B *(bottom).* Chinese mat, 18th–19th century. (See pages 66, 112.) *Victoria and Albert Museum.*

Plate 76. Spanish heraldic carpet, 15th century. (See page 69.) *Formerly in the possession of Mr. Lionel Harris.*

Plate 77A *(top)*. Spanish carpet, 15th century. (See page 69.) *Kaiser-Friedrich Museum, Berlin*. Plate 77B *(bottom)*. Spanish carpet, 16th century. (See pages 70, 112.) *Victoria and Albert Museum*.

Plate 78. Spanish carpet, 15th century. (See pages 69, 112.) *Victoria and Albert Museum.*

Plate 79. Spanish carpet, late 15th century. (See pages 71, 112.) *Victoria and Albert Museum.*

Plate 80. Spanish carpet, late 15th century. (See pages 71, 112.) *The Hon. H. D. McLaren, C.B.E., M.P.*

Plate 81. Spanish carpet, 16th century. (See pages 71, 113.) *Victoria and Albert Museum.*

Plate 83. Polish carpet, late 17th century. (See page 72.) *Professor
Friedrich Sarre.*

Plate 84. Finnish carpet, dated 1799. (See pages 73, 113.) *Victoria and Albert Museum.*

Plate 85. Savonnerie carpet, late 17th century. (See pages 74, 113.)
Mobilier National, Paris.

Plate 86. Savonnerie carpet, late 17th century. (See pages 74, 113.)
Mobilier National, Paris.

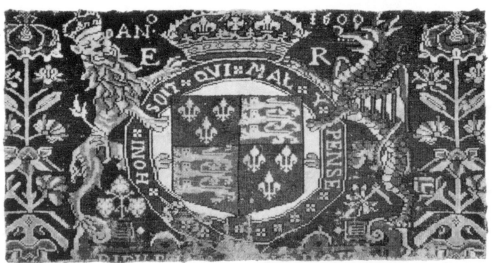

Plate 87A *(top)*. "Queen Elizabeth's Carpet," English, dated 1570. (See page 78.) *The Earl of Verulam.* Plate 87B *(bottom)*. English carpet, dated 1600. (See pages 79, 113.) *Victoria and Albert Museum.*

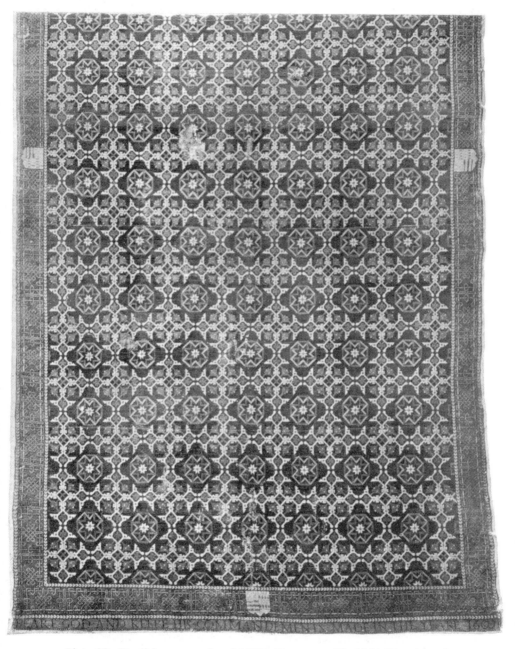

Plate 88. English carpet, dated 1603. (See pages 78, 114.) *Victoria and Albert Museum.*

Plate 90. English carpet, made at Exeter in 1757. (See pages 81, 114.)
Mr. Lionel Harris.

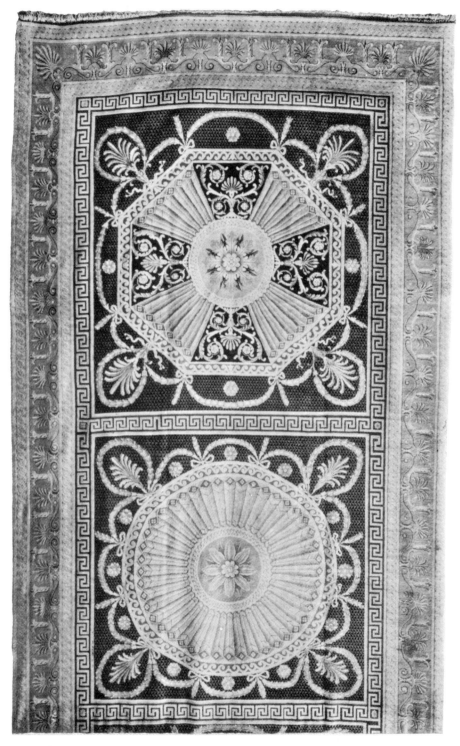

Plate 91. English carpet, made in 1769. (See pages 81, 114.) *The Duke of Northumberland, M.V.O.*

Plate 92A *(top).* Persian carpet-loom. (See page 89.) Plate 92B *(bottom).*
Turkish carpet-loom. (See page 89.)

Plate 93. Modern Smyrna carpet. (See page 150.)

Plate 94. Modern Smyrna carpet. (See page 150.)

Plate 95. Modern Smyrna carpet. (See page 150.)

Plate 96. Modern Smyrna carpet. (See page 150.)

Plate 97. Modern Hereke carpet. (See page 150.)

Plate 98. Ghiordes prayer-carpet. (See page 156.)

Plate 99. Kis-Ghiordes carpet. (See page 156.)

Plate 101. Kula prayer-carpet. (See page 157.)

Plate 103. Ladik prayer-carpet. (See page 157.)

Plate 104. Ladik prayer-carpet. (See page 158.)

Plate 106. Mujur prayer-carpet. (See page 158.)

Plate 107A *(top)*. Kir-Shehr prayer-carpet. (See page 158.) Plate 107B *(bottom)*. Saph or family prayer-carpet. (See page 158.)

Plate 108A *(top)*. Jakshibehdir prayer-carpet. (See page 159.) Plate
108B *(bottom)*. Bergama carpet. (See page 159.)

Plate 109. Anatolian Kilim prayer-carpet. (See page 159.)

Plate 111A *(top)*. Makri carpet. (See page 160.) Plate 111B *(bottom)*.
Anatolian carpet. (See page 160.)

Plate 112A *(top).* Anatolian carpet. (See page 160.) Plate 112B *(bottom).*
Melas carpet. (See page 160.)

Plate 113. Melas prayer-carpet. (See page 160.)

Plate 114. Yuruk carpet. (See page 161.)

Plate 115. Daghestan carpet. (See page 166.)

Plate 116. Daghestan prayer-carpet. (See page 166.)

Plate 117. Daghestan carpet. (See page 166.)

Plate 118A *(left).* Daghestan carpet. (See page 166.) Plate 118B *(right).* Caucasian Kilim. (See page 166.)

Plate 119. Derbend carpet. (See page 167.)

Plate 120A *(left).* Daghestan carpet. (See page 167.) Plate 120B
(right). Shirvan carpet. (See page 167.)

Plate 122A *(left)*. Shirvan carpet. (See page 167.) Plate 122B *(right)*.
Shirvan carpet. (See page 168.)

Plate 123. Shirvan carpet. (See page 168.)

Plate 124. Shirvan carpet. (See page 168.)

Plate 125. Shirvan carpet. (See page 168.)

Plate 127. Chichi or Shirvan carpet. (See page 169.)

Plate 128. Shirvan or Baku carpet. (See page 169.)

Plate 129. Baku or Shirvan carpet. (See page 169.)

Plate 130. Shirvan carpet. (See page 169.)

Plate 132A *(top).* Kazak carpet. (See page 170.) Plate 132B *(bottom).* Baku or Shirvan carpet. (See page 170.)

Plate 133. Kazak carpet. (See page 170.)

Plate 134. Kazak carpet. (See page 170.)

Plate 135. Kazak carpet. (See page 171.)

Plate 136. Kazak carpet. (See page 171.)

Plate 137. Kazak carpet. (See page 171.)

Plate 138. Kazak prayer-carpet. (See page 171.)

Plate 139. Kazak carpet. (See page 171.)

Plate 140. Kazak carpet. (See page 171.)

Plate 141. Kazak carpet. (See page 171.)

Plate 142. Karabagh carpet. (See page 171.)

Plate 143. Verné Kilim carpet. (See page 172.)

Plate 144. Verné Kilim carpet. (See page 172.)

Plate 145. Silé Kilim carpet. (See page 172.)

Plate 146. Soumak carpet. (See page 172.)

Plate 147. Karadagh carpet. (See page 182.)

Plate 148. Karadagh carpet. (See page 182.)

Plate 149. Karadagh carpet. (See page 182.)

Plate 150. Karadagh carpet. (See page 182.)

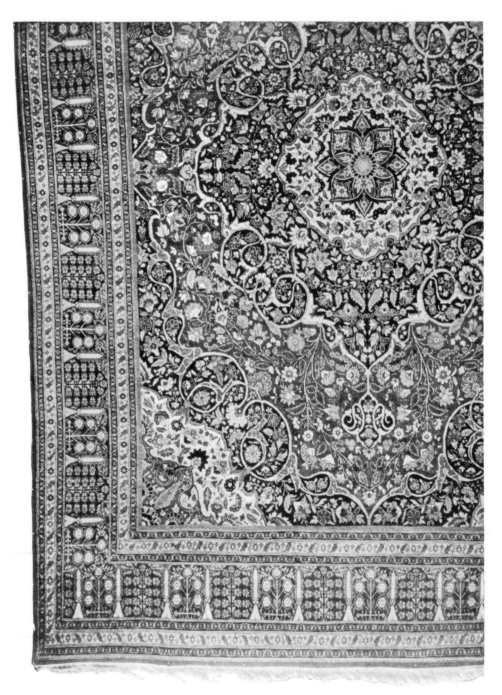

Plate 151. Tabriz carpet. (See page 183.)

Plate 152. Gorevan carpet. (See page 183.)

Plate 154. Hamadan carpet. (See page 183.)

Plate 155. Feraghan carpet. (See page 183.)

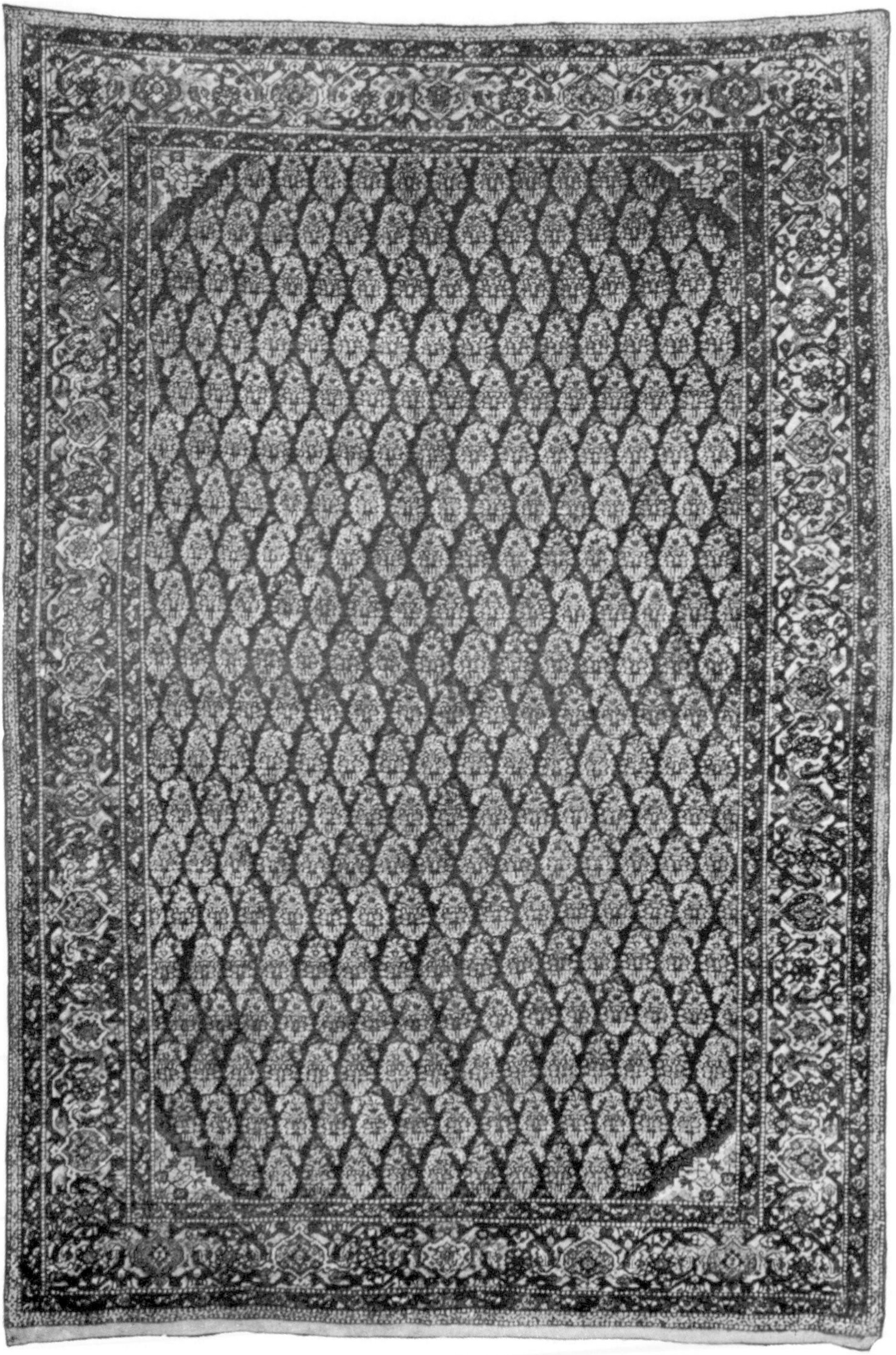

Plate 156. Saraband carpet. (See page 184.)

Plate 157. Saraband carpet. (See page 184.)

Plate 159. Saruk or Kashan carpet. (See page 184.)

Plate 160. Persian silk carpet. (See page 184.)

Plate 161. Muskabad carpet. (See page 184.)

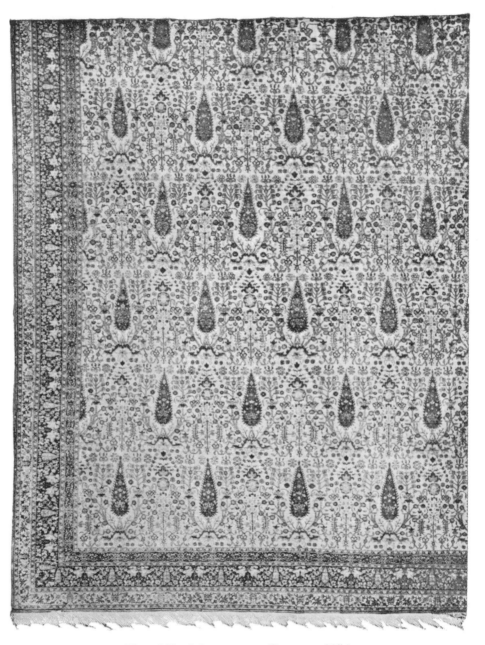

Plate 163. Sehna carpet. (See page 185.)

Plate 164A *(top)*. Sehna carpet. (See page 185.) Plate 164B *(bottom)*. Sehna carpet. (See page 185.)

Plate 165. Sehna carpet. (See page 185.)

Plate 167A *(top).* Khorassan carpet. (See page 185.) Plate 167B *(bottom).*
Sehna carpet. (See page 185.)

Plate 168. Khorassan carpet. (See page 185.)

Plate 169. Kirman carpet. (See page 185.)

Plate 170. Kirman carpet. (See page 185.)

Plate 171. Kirman carpet. (See page 185.)

Plate 172. Kirman carpet. (See page 185.)

Plate 173. Shiraz carpet. (See page 185.)

Plate 174. Shiraz carpet. (See page 185.)

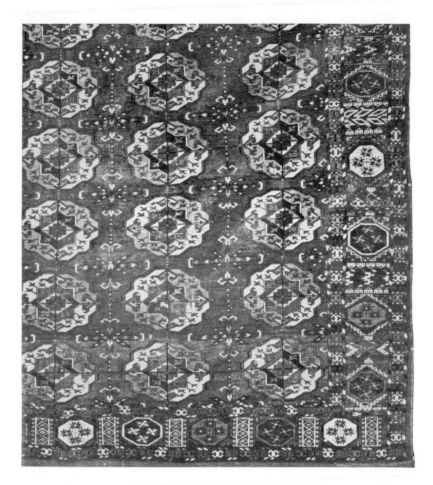

Plate 175A *(top)*. Turcoman carpet. Tekke. (See page 190.) Plate 175B *(bottom)*, Shiraz carpet. (See page 185.)

Plate 176. Persian Kilim. (See page 186.)

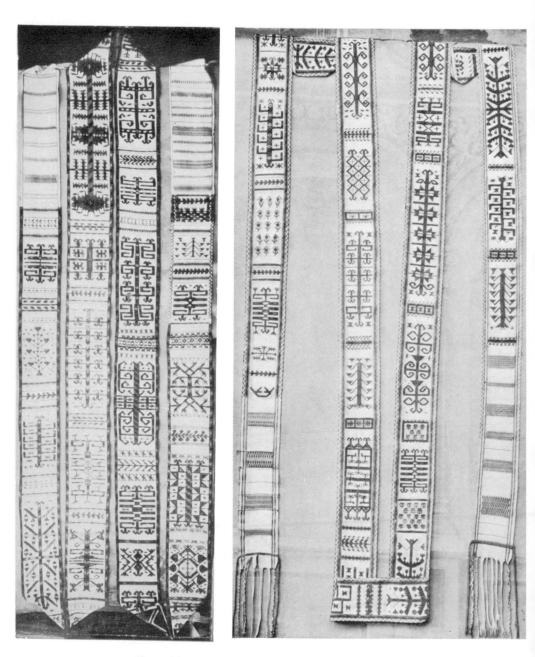

Plate 177. Turcoman tent-bands. (See page 190.)

Plate 179. Turcoman camel-bag. Salor pattern. (See page 190.)

Plate 180. Turcoman Katchli carpet. Pindé. (See page 190.)

Plate 181. Turcoman carpet. Pindé. (See page 190.)

Plate 182. Turcoman carpet. Tekke. (See page 190.)

Plate 183. Turcoman Yomud carpet. (See page 191.)

Plate 184. Turcoman Yomud carpet. (See page 191.)

Plate 185. Turcoman Yomud carpet. (See page 191.)

Plate 186A *(top)*. Afghan carpet. (See page 191.) Plate 186B *(bottom)*.
Turcoman camel-bag. Tekke. (See page 191.)

Plate 187. Afghan carpet. (See page 191.)

Plate 188. Beshire carpet. (See page 191.)

Plate 189. Beshire carpet. (See page 191.)

Plate 190. Beshire prayer-carpet. (See page 191.)

Plate 191. Beluchistan carpet. (See page 191.)

Plate 192A *(top)*. Beluchistan carpet. (See page 191.) Plate 192B *(bottom left)*. Beluchistan carpet. (See page 191.) Plate 192C *(bottom right)*. Beluchistan prayer-carpet. (See page 192.)

Plate 194. Motives found in Turkish carpets. (See page 153.)

Plate 195. Motives found in Caucasian carpets. (See page 162.)

Plate 196. Motives found in Caucasian carpets. (See page 162.)

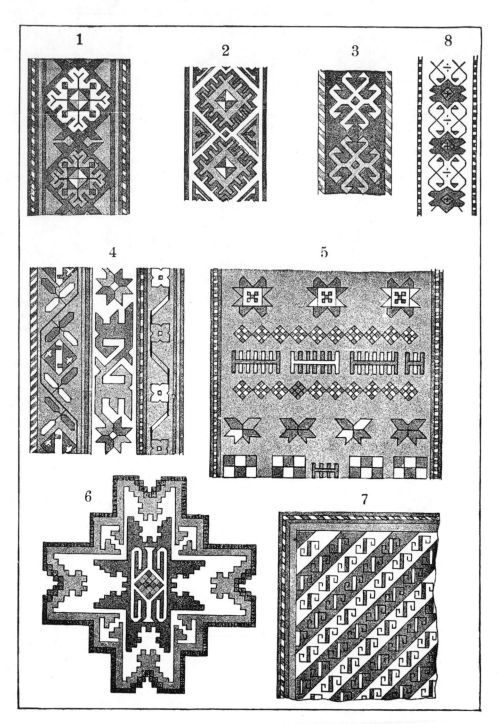

Plate 197. Motives found in Caucasian carpets. (See page 162.)

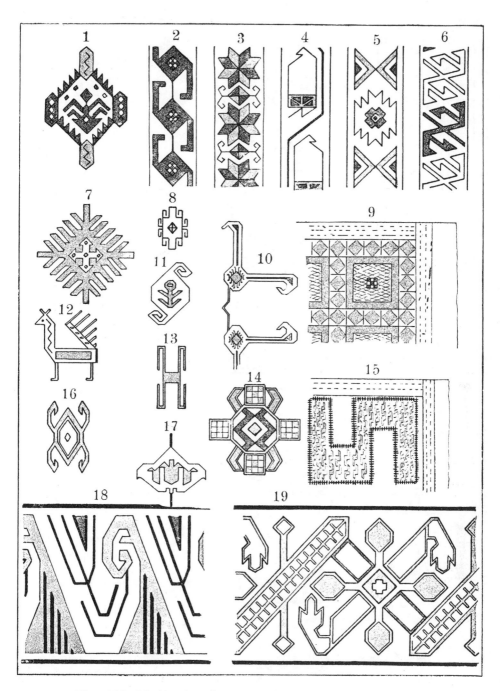

Plate 198. Motives found in Caucasian carpets. (See page 162.)

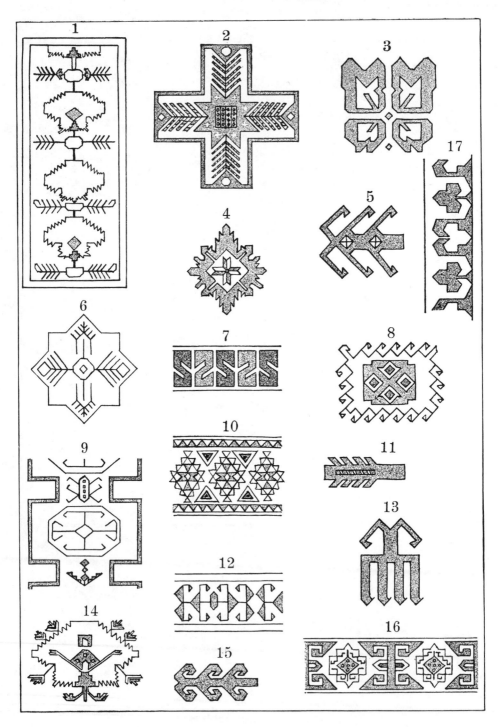

Plate 199. Motives found in Caucasian carpets. (See page 162.)

Plate 200. Motives found in Central Asiatic carpets. (See page 187.)

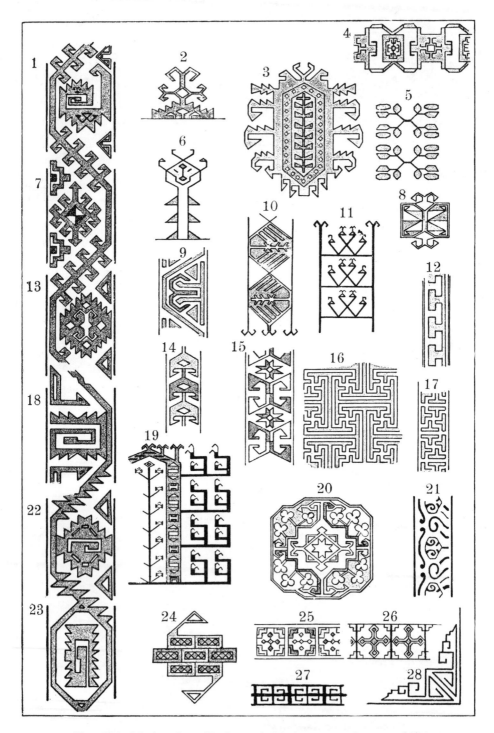

Plate 201.   Motives found in Central Asiatic carpets. (See page 187.)

Plate 202. Motives found in Persian carpets. (See page 174.)

Plate 203. Motives found in Old Persian carpets. (See page 132.)

Plate 204. Motives found in Old Persian carpets. (See page 132.)

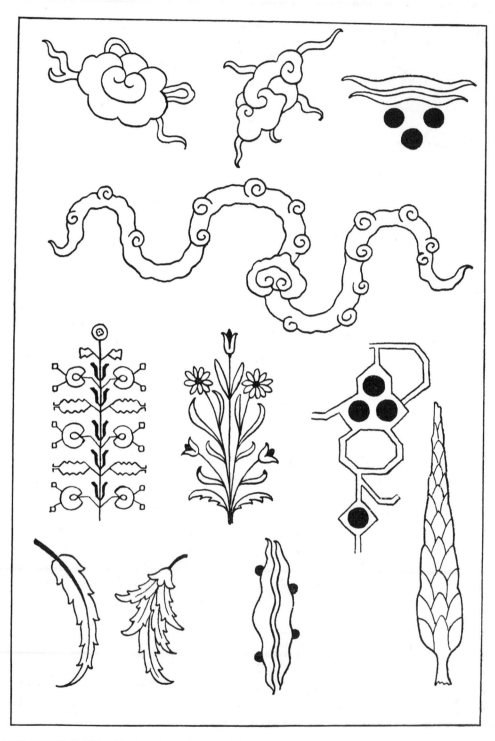

Plate 205. Motives found in Old Persian or Old Turkish carpets. (See page 132.)

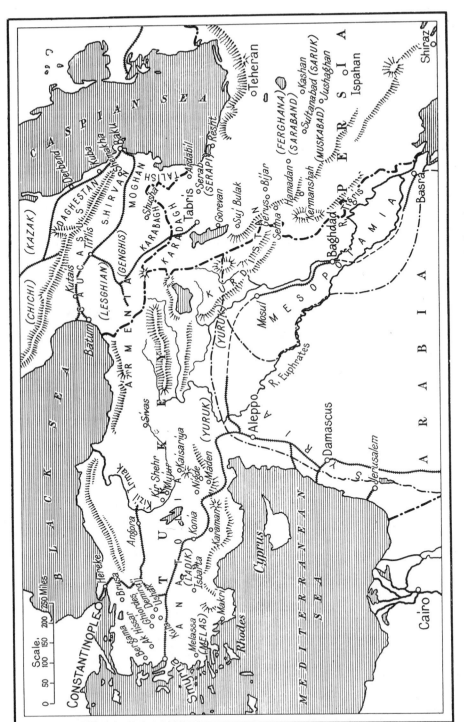

Turkey, the Caucasus, and part of Persia. (The names in brackets are those of tribes or indefinite localities after which rugs are called.)

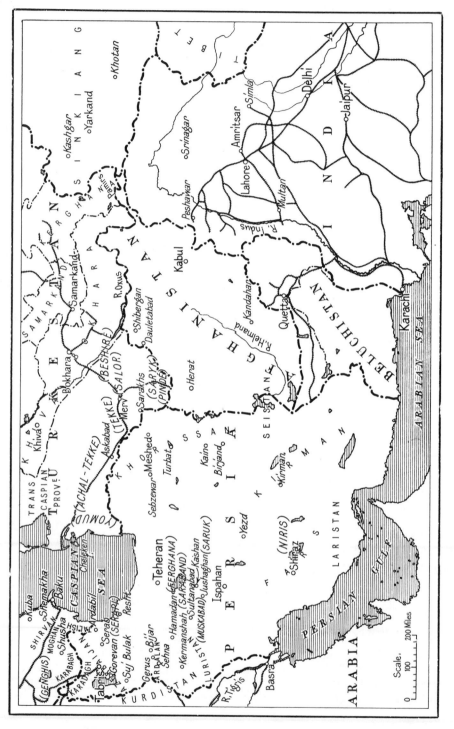

Persia and Central Asia. (The names in brackets are those of tribes or indefinite localities after which rugs are called.)

INDEX

INDEX

INDEX

Dover Books on Art

200 DECORATIVE TITLE-PAGES, edited by A. Nesbitt. Fascinating and informative from a historical point of view, this beautiful collection of decorated titles will be a great inspiration to students of design, commercial artists, advertising designers, etc. A complete survey of the genre from the first known decorated title to work in the first decades of this century. Bibliography and sources of the plates. 222pp. 8⅜ x 11¼.

21264-5 Paperbound $3.50

ON THE LAWS OF JAPANESE PAINTING, H. P. Bowie. This classic work on the philosophy and technique of Japanese art is based on the author's first-hand experiences studying art in Japan. Every aspect of Japanese painting is described: the use of the brush and other materials; laws governing conception and execution; subjects for Japanese paintings, etc. The best possible substitute for a series of lessons from a great Oriental master. Index. xv + 117pp. + 66 plates. 6⅛ x 9¼.

20030-2 Paperbound $2.50

PAINTING IN THE FAR EAST, L. Binyon. A study of over 1500 years of Oriental art by one of the world's outstanding authorities. The author chooses the most important masters in each period—Wu Tao-tzu, Toba Sojo, Kanaoka, Li Lung-mien, Masanobu, Okio, etc.—and examines the works, schools, and influence of each within their cultural context. 42 photographs. Sources of original works and selected bibliography. Notes including list of principal painters by periods. xx + 297pp. 6⅛ x 9¼.

20520-7 Paperbound $3.00

THE ALPHABET AND ELEMENTS OF LETTERING, F. W. Goudy. A beautifully illustrated volume on the aesthetics of letters and type faces and their history and development. Each plate consists of 15 forms of a single letter with the last plate devoted to the ampersand and the numerals. "A sound guide for all persons engaged in printing or drawing," Saturday Review. 27 full-page plates. 48 additional figures. xii + 131pp. 7⅞ x 10¾.

20792-7 Paperbound $2.25

PAINTING IN ISLAM, Sir Thomas W. Arnold. This scholarly study puts Islamic painting in its social and religious context and examines its relation to Islamic civilization in general. 65 full-page plates illustrate the text and give outstanding examples of Islamic art. 4 appendices. Index of mss. referred to. General Index. xxiv + 159pp. 6⅝ x 9¼.

21310-2 Paperbound $2.75

Dover Books on Art

THE STYLES OF ORNAMENT, A. Speltz. The largest collection of line ornament in print, with 3750 numbered illustrations arranged chronologically from Egypt, Assyria, Greeks, Romans, Etruscans, through Medieval, Renaissance, 18th century, and Victorian. No permissions, no fees needed to use or reproduce illustrations. 400 plates with 3750 illustrations. Bibliography. Index. 640pp. 6 x 9.   20577-6 Paperbound $3.75

THE ART OF ETCHING, E. S. Lumsden. Every step of the etching process from essential materials to completed proof is carefully and clearly explained, with 24 annotated plates exemplifying every technique and approach discussed. The book also features a rich survey of the art, with 105 annotated plates by masters. Invaluable for beginner to advanced etcher. 374pp. 5⅜ x 8.   20049-3 Paperbound $3.00

EPOCHS OF CHINESE AND JAPANESE ART, E. Fenollosa. Classic study of pre-20th century Oriental art, revealing, as does no other book, the important interrelationships between the art of China and Japan and their history and sociology. Illustrations include ancient bronzes, Buddhist paintings by Kobo Daishi, scroll paintings by Toba Sojo, prints by Nobusane, screens by Korin, woodcuts by Hokusai, Koryusai, Utamaro, Hiroshige and scores of other pieces by Chinese and Japanese masters. Biographical preface. Notes. Index. 242 illustrations. Total of lii + 439pp. plus 174 plates. 5⅝ x 8¼.

Two-volume set, 20364-6, 20365-4 Paperbound $5.90

OF THE JUST SHAPING OF LETTERS, Albrecht Dürer. This remarkable volume reveals Albrecht Dürer's rules for the geometric construction of Roman capitals and the formation of Gothic lower case and capital letters, complete with construction diagrams and directions. Of considerable practical interest to the contemporary illustrator, artist, and designer. Translated from the Latin text of the edition of 1535 by R. T. Nichol. Numerous letterform designs, construction diagrams, illustrations. iv + 43pp. 7⅞ x 10¾.   21306-4 Paperbound $2.00

DESIGN MOTIFS OF ANCIENT MEXICO, J. Enciso. Nearly 90% of these 766 superb designs from Aztec, Olmec, Totonac, Maya, and Toltec origins are unobtainable elsewhere. Contains plumed serpents, wind gods, animals, demons, dancers, monsters, etc. Excellent applied design source. Originally $17.50. 766 illustrations, thousands of motifs. 192pp. 6⅛ x 9¼.

20084-1 Paperbound $2.50

DECORATIVE ART OF THE SOUTHWESTERN INDIANS,
D. S. Sides. 300 black and white reproductions from one of the
most beautiful art traditions of the primitive world, ranging
from the geometric art of the Great Pueblo period of the 13th
century to modern folk art. Motives from basketry, beadwork,
Zuni masks, Hopi kachina dolls, Navajo sand pictures and
blankets, and ceramic ware. Unusual and imaginative designs
will inspire craftsmen in all media, and commercial artists may
reproduce any of them without permission or payment. xviii +
101pp. 5⅝ x 8⅜. 20139-2 Paperbound $1.50

PENNSYLVANIA DUTCH AMERICAN FOLK ART, H. J.
Kauffman. The originality and charm of this early folk art give
it a special appeal even today, and surviving pieces are sought
by collectors all over the country. Here is a rewarding introduc-
tory guide to the Dutch country and its household art, concen-
trating on pictorial matter—hex signs, tulip ware, weather vanes,
interiors, paintings and folk sculpture, rocking horses and chil-
dren's toys, utensils, Stiegel-type glassware, etc. "A serious,
worthy and helpful volume," W. G. Dooley, N. Y. TIMES. Introduction. Bibliography. 279 halftone illustrations. 28 motifs
and other line drawings. 1 map. 146pp. 7⅞ x 10¾.
21205-X Paperbound $2.50

DESIGN AND EXPRESSION IN THE VISUAL ARTS, J. F. A.
Taylor. Here is a much needed discussion of art theory which
relates the new and sometimes bewildering directions of 20th
century art to the great traditions of the past. The first discussion of principle that addresses itself to the eye rather than to
the intellect, using illustrations from Rembrandt, Leonardo,
Mondrian, El Greco, etc. List of plates. Index. 59 reproductions.
5 color plates. 75 figures. x + 245pp. 5⅜ x 8½.
21195-9 Paperbound $2.50

GRAPHIC REPRODUCTION IN PRINTING, H. Curwen. A
behind-the-scenes account of the various processes of graphic
reproduction—relief, · intaglio, stenciling, lithography, line
methods, continuous tone methods, photogravure, collotype—
and the advantages and limitations of each. Invaluable for all
artists, advertising art directors, commercial designers, adver-
tisers, publishers, and all art lovers who buy prints as a hobby.
137 illustrations, including 13 full-page plates, 10 in color. xvi +
171pp. 5¼ x 8½. 20512-6 Clothbound $7.50

Dover Books on Art

PRINCIPLES OF ART HISTORY, H. Wölfflin. This remarkably instructive work demonstrates the tremendous change in artistic conception from the 14th to the 18th centuries, by analyzing 164 works by Botticelli, Dürer, Hobbema, Holbein, Hals, Titian, Rembrandt, Vermeer, etc., and pointing out exactly what is meant by "baroque," "classic," "primitive," "picturesque," and other basic terms of art history and criticism. "A remarkable lesson in the art of seeing," SAT. REV. OF LITERATURE. Translated from the 7th German edition. 150 illus. 254pp. 6⅛ x 9¼.   20276-3 Paperbound $2.50

FOUNDATIONS OF MODERN ART, A. Ozenfant. Stimulating discussion of human creativity from paleolithic cave painting to modern painting, architecture, decorative arts. Fully illustrated with works of Gris, Lipchitz, Léger, Picasso, primitive, modern artifacts, architecture, industrial art, much more. 226 illustrations. 368pp. 6⅛ x 9¼.   20215-1 Paperbound $3.00

METALWORK AND ENAMELLING, H. Maryon. Probably the best book ever written on the subject. Tells everything necessary for the home manufacture of jewelry, rings, ear pendants, bowls, etc. Covers materials, tools, soldering, filigree, setting stones, raising patterns, repoussé work, damascening, niello, cloisonné, polishing, assaying, casting, and dozens of other techniques. The best substitute for apprenticeship to a master metalworker. 363 photos and figures. 374pp. 5½ x 8½.
                    22702-2 Paperbound $3.50

SHAKER FURNITURE, E. D. and F. Andrews. The most illuminating study of Shaker furniture ever written. Covers chronology, craftsmanship, houses, shops, etc. Includes over 200 photographs of chairs, tables, clocks, beds, benches, etc. "Mr. & Mrs. Andrews know all there is to know about Shaker furniture," Mark Van Doren, NATION. 48 full-page plates. 192pp. 7⅞ x 10¾.   20679-3 Paperbound $2.75

ANIMAL DRAWING: ANATOMY AND ACTION FOR ARTISTS, C. R. Knight. 158 studies, with full accompanying text, of such animals as the gorilla, bear, bison, dromedary, camel, vulture, pelican, iguana, shark, etc., by one of the greatest modern masters of animal drawing. Innumerable tips on how to get life expression into your work. "An excellent reference work," SAN FRANCISCO CHRONICLE. 158 illustrations. 156pp. 10½ x 8½.   20426-X Paperbound $3.00

HANDBOOK OF DESIGNS AND DEVICES, C. P. Hornung. A remarkable working collection of 1836 basic designs and variations, all copyright-free. Variations of circle, line, cross, diamond, swastika, star, scroll, shield, many more. Notes on symbolism. "A necessity to every designer who would be original without having to labor heavily," ARTIST AND ADVERTISER. 204 plates. 240pp. 5⅜ x 8.   20125-2 Paperbound $2.00

THE UNIVERSAL PENMAN, George Bickham. Exact reproduction of beautiful 18th-century book of handwriting. 22 complete alphabets in finest English roundhand, other scripts, over 2000 elaborate flourishes, 122 calligraphic illustrations, etc. Material is copyright-free. "An essential part of any art library, and a book of permanent value," AMERICAN ARTIST. 212 plates. 224pp. 9 x 13¾.   20020-5 Clothbound $12.50

AN ATLAS OF ANATOMY FOR ARTISTS, F. Schider. This standard work contains 189 full-page plates, more than 647 illustrations of all aspects of the human skeleton, musculature, cutaway portions of the body, each part of the anatomy, hand forms, eyelids, breasts, location of muscles under the flesh, etc. 59 plates illustrate how Michelangelo, da Vinci, Goya, 15 others, drew human anatomy. New 3rd edition enlarged by 52 new illustrations by Cloquet, Barcsay. "The standard reference tool," AMERICAN LIBRARY ASSOCIATION. "Excellent," AMERICAN ARTIST. 189 plates, 647 illustrations. xxvi + 192pp. 7⅞ x 10⅝.   20241-0 Clothbound $6.50

AN ATLAS OF ANIMAL ANATOMY FOR ARTISTS, W. Ellenberger, H. Baum, H. Dittrich. The largest, richest animal anatomy for artists in English. Form, musculature, tendons, bone structure, expression, detailed cross sections of head, other features, of the horse, lion, dog, cat, deer, seal, kangaroo, cow, bull, goat, monkey, hare, many other animals. "Highly recommended," DESIGN. Second, revised, enlarged edition with new plates from Cuvier, Stubbs, etc. 288 illustrations. 153pp. 11⅜ x 9.
20082-5 Paperbound $3.00

VASARI ON TECHNIQUE, G. Vasari. Pupil of Michelangelo, outstanding biographer of Renaissance artists reveals technical methods of his day. Marble, bronze, fresco painting, mosaics, engraving, stained glass, rustic ware, etc. Only English translation, extensively annotated by G. Baldwin Brown. 18 plates. 342pp. 5⅜ x 8.   20717-X Paperbound $3.50

Dover Books on Art

THE COMPLETE BOOK OF SILK SCREEN PRINTING PRO-DUCTION, J. I. Biegeleisen. Here is a clear and complete picture of every aspect of silk screen technique and press operation—from individually operated manual presses to modern automatic ones. Unsurpassed as a guidebook for setting up shop, making shop operation more efficient, finding out about latest methods and equipment; or as a textbook for use in teaching, studying, or learning all aspects of the profession. 124 figures. Index. Bibliography. List of Supply Sources. xi + 253pp. 5⅜ x 8½.

21100-2 Paperbound $2.75

A HISTORY OF COSTUME, Carl Köhler. The most reliable and authentic account of the development of dress from ancient times through the 19th century. Based on actual pieces of clothing that have survived, using paintings, statues and other reproductions only where originals no longer exist. Hundreds of illustrations, including detailed patterns for many articles. Highly useful for theatre and movie directors, fashion designers, illustrators, teachers. Edited and augmented by Emma von Sichart. Translated by Alexander K. Dallas. 594 illustrations. 464pp. 5⅛ x 7⅛.

21030-8 Paperbound $3.50

CHINESE HOUSEHOLD FURNITURE, G. N. Kates. A summary of virtually everything that is known about authentic Chinese furniture before it was contaminated by the influence of the West. The text covers history of styles, materials used, principles of design and craftsmanship, and furniture arrangement—all fully illustrated. xiii + 190pp. 5⅝ x 8½.

20958-X Paperbound $2.00

THE COMPLETE WOODCUTS OF ALBRECHT DURER, edited by Dr. Willi Kurth. Albrecht Dürer was a master in various media, but it was in woodcut design that his creative genius reached its highest expression. Here are all of his extant woodcuts, a collection of over 300 great works, many of which are not available elsewhere. An indispensable work for the art historian and critic and all art lovers. 346 plates. Index. 285pp. 8½ x 12¼.

21097-9 Paperbound $4.00

Dover publishes books on commercial art, art history, crafts, design, art classics; also books on music, literature, science, mathematics, puzzles and entertainments, chess, engineering, biology, philosophy, psychology, languages, history, and other fields. For free circulars write to Dept. DA, Dover Publications, Inc., 180 Varick St., New York, N.Y. 10014.